# TEST PREPARATION

# GACE
## Media Specialist
## Secrets Study Guide

MW00806129

# DEAR FUTURE EXAM SUCCESS STORY

First of all, **THANK YOU** for purchasing Mometrix study materials!

Second, congratulations! You are one of the few determined test-takers who are committed to doing whatever it takes to excel on your exam. **You have come to the right place.** We developed these study materials with one goal in mind: to deliver you the information you need in a format that's concise and easy to use.

In addition to optimizing your guide for the content of the test, we've outlined our recommended steps for breaking down the preparation process into small, attainable goals so you can make sure you stay on track.

We've also analyzed the entire test-taking process, identifying the most common pitfalls and showing how you can overcome them and be ready for any curveball the test throws you.

Standardized testing is one of the biggest obstacles on your road to success, which only increases the importance of doing well in the high-pressure, high-stakes environment of test day. Your results on this test could have a significant impact on your future, and this guide provides the information and practical advice to help you achieve your full potential on test day.

### Your success is our success

**We would love to hear from you!** If you would like to share the story of your exam success or if you have any questions or comments in regard to our products, please contact us at **800-673-8175** or **support@mometrix.com**.

Thanks again for your business and we wish you continued success!

Sincerely,
The Mometrix Test Preparation Team

---

**Need more help? Check out our flashcards at:**
**http://MometrixFlashcards.com/GACE**

---

Copyright © 2023 by Mometrix Media LLC. All rights reserved.
Written and edited by the Mometrix Exam Secrets Test Prep Team
Printed in the United States of America

# TABLE OF CONTENTS

# Introduction

**Thank you for purchasing this resource**! You have made the choice to prepare yourself for a test that could have a huge impact on your future, and this guide is designed to help you be fully ready for test day. Obviously, it's important to have a solid understanding of the test material, but you also need to be prepared for the unique environment and stressors of the test, so that you can perform to the best of your abilities.

For this purpose, the first section that appears in this guide is the **Secret Keys**. We've devoted countless hours to meticulously researching what works and what doesn't, and we've boiled down our findings to the five most impactful steps you can take to improve your performance on the test. We start at the beginning with study planning and move through the preparation process, all the way to the testing strategies that will help you get the most out of what you know when you're finally sitting in front of the test.

We recommend that you start preparing for your test as far in advance as possible. However, if you've bought this guide as a last-minute study resource and only have a few days before your test, we recommend that you skip over the first two Secret Keys since they address a long-term study plan.

If you struggle with **test anxiety**, we strongly encourage you to check out our recommendations for how you can overcome it. Test anxiety is a formidable foe, but it can be beaten, and we want to make sure you have the tools you need to defeat it.

1

Copyright © Mometrix Media. You have been licensed one copy of this document for personal use only. Any other reproduction or redistribution is strictly prohibited. All rights reserved. This content is provided for test preparation purposes only and does not imply an endorsement by Mometrix of any particular political, scientific, or religious point of view.

# Secret Key #1 – Plan Big, Study Small

There's a lot riding on your performance. If you want to ace this test, you're going to need to keep your skills sharp and the material fresh in your mind. You need a plan that lets you review everything you need to know while still fitting in your schedule. We'll break this strategy down into three categories.

## Information Organization

Start with the information you already have: the official test outline. From this, you can make a complete list of all the concepts you need to cover before the test. Organize these concepts into groups that can be studied together, and create a list of any related vocabulary you need to learn so you can brush up on any difficult terms. You'll want to keep this vocabulary list handy once you actually start studying since you may need to add to it along the way.

## Time Management

Once you have your set of study concepts, decide how to spread them out over the time you have left before the test. Break your study plan into small, clear goals so you have a manageable task for each day and know exactly what you're doing. Then just focus on one small step at a time. When you manage your time this way, you don't need to spend hours at a time studying. Studying a small block of content for a short period each day helps you retain information better and avoid stressing over how much you have left to do. You can relax knowing that you have a plan to cover everything in time. In order for this strategy to be effective though, you have to start studying early and stick to your schedule. Avoid the exhaustion and futility that comes from last-minute cramming!

## Study Environment

The environment you study in has a big impact on your learning. Studying in a coffee shop, while probably more enjoyable, is not likely to be as fruitful as studying in a quiet room. It's important to keep distractions to a minimum. You're only planning to study for a short block of time, so make the most of it. Don't pause to check your phone or get up to find a snack. It's also important to **avoid multitasking**. Research has consistently shown that multitasking will make your studying dramatically less effective. Your study area should also be comfortable and well-lit so you don't have the distraction of straining your eyes or sitting on an uncomfortable chair.

 The time of day you study is also important. You want to be rested and alert. Don't wait until just before bedtime. Study when you'll be most likely to comprehend and remember. Even better, if you know what time of day your test will be, set that time aside for study. That way your brain will be used to working on that subject at that specific time and you'll have a better chance of recalling information.

Finally, it can be helpful to team up with others who are studying for the same test. Your actual studying should be done in as isolated an environment as possible, but the work of organizing the information and setting up the study plan can be divided up. In between study sessions, you can discuss with your teammates the concepts that you're all studying and quiz each other on the details. Just be sure that your teammates are as serious about the test as you are. If you find that your study time is being replaced with social time, you might need to find a new team.

Copyright © Mometrix Media. You have been licensed one copy of this document for personal use only. Any other reproduction or redistribution is strictly prohibited. All rights reserved. This content is provided for test preparation purposes only and does not imply an endorsement by Mometrix of any particular political, scientific, or religious point of view.

# Secret Key #2 – Make Your Studying Count

You're devoting a lot of time and effort to preparing for this test, so you want to be absolutely certain it will pay off. This means doing more than just reading the content and hoping you can remember it on test day. It's important to make every minute of study count. There are two main areas you can focus on to make your studying count.

## Retention

It doesn't matter how much time you study if you can't remember the material. You need to make sure you are retaining the concepts. To check your retention of the information you're learning, try recalling it at later times with minimal prompting. Try carrying around flashcards and glance at one or two from time to time or ask a friend who's also studying for the test to quiz you.

To enhance your retention, look for ways to put the information into practice so that you can apply it rather than simply recalling it. If you're using the information in practical ways, it will be much easier to remember. Similarly, it helps to solidify a concept in your mind if you're not only reading it to yourself but also explaining it to someone else. Ask a friend to let you teach them about a concept you're a little shaky on (or speak aloud to an imaginary audience if necessary). As you try to summarize, define, give examples, and answer your friend's questions, you'll understand the concepts better and they will stay with you longer. Finally, step back for a big picture view and ask yourself how each piece of information fits with the whole subject. When you link the different concepts together and see them working together as a whole, it's easier to remember the individual components.

Finally, practice showing your work on any multi-step problems, even if you're just studying. Writing out each step you take to solve a problem will help solidify the process in your mind, and you'll be more likely to remember it during the test.

## Modality

*Modality* simply refers to the means or method by which you study. Choosing a study modality that fits your own individual learning style is crucial. No two people learn best in exactly the same way, so it's important to know your strengths and use them to your advantage.

For example, if you learn best by visualization, focus on visualizing a concept in your mind and draw an image or a diagram. Try color-coding your notes, illustrating them, or creating symbols that will trigger your mind to recall a learned concept. If you learn best by hearing or discussing information, find a study partner who learns the same way or read aloud to yourself. Think about how to put the information in your own words. Imagine that you are giving a lecture on the topic and record yourself so you can listen to it later.

For any learning style, flashcards can be helpful. Organize the information so you can take advantage of spare moments to review. Underline key words or phrases. Use different colors for different categories. Mnemonic devices (such as creating a short list in which every item starts with the same letter) can also help with retention. Find what works best for you and use it to store the information in your mind most effectively and easily.

3

Copyright © Mometrix Media. You have been licensed one copy of this document for personal use only. Any other reproduction or redistribution is strictly prohibited. All rights reserved.
This content is provided for test preparation purposes only and does not imply an endorsement by Mometrix of any particular political, scientific, or religious point of view.

# Secret Key #3 – Practice the Right Way

Your success on test day depends not only on how many hours you put into preparing, but also on whether you prepared the right way. It's good to check along the way to see if your studying is paying off. One of the most effective ways to do this is by taking practice tests to evaluate your progress. Practice tests are useful because they show exactly where you need to improve. Every time you take a practice test, pay special attention to these three groups of questions:

- The questions you got wrong
- The questions you had to guess on, even if you guessed right
- The questions you found difficult or slow to work through

This will show you exactly what your weak areas are, and where you need to devote more study time. Ask yourself why each of these questions gave you trouble. Was it because you didn't understand the material? Was it because you didn't remember the vocabulary? Do you need more repetitions on this type of question to build speed and confidence? Dig into those questions and figure out how you can strengthen your weak areas as you go back to review the material.

Additionally, many practice tests have a section explaining the answer choices. It can be tempting to read the explanation and think that you now have a good understanding of the concept. However, an explanation likely only covers part of the question's broader context. Even if the explanation makes perfect sense, **go back and investigate** every concept related to the question until you're positive you have a thorough understanding.

As you go along, keep in mind that the practice test is just that: practice. Memorizing these questions and answers will not be very helpful on the actual test because it is unlikely to have any of the same exact questions. If you only know the right answers to the sample questions, you won't be prepared for the real thing. **Study the concepts** until you understand them fully, and then you'll be able to answer any question that shows up on the test.

It's important to wait on the practice tests until you're ready. If you take a test on your first day of study, you may be overwhelmed by the amount of material covered and how much you need to learn. Work up to it gradually.

On test day, you'll need to be prepared for answering questions, managing your time, and using the test-taking strategies you've learned. It's a lot to balance, like a mental marathon that will have a big impact on your future. Like training for a marathon, you'll need to start slowly and work your way up. When test day arrives, you'll be ready.

Start with the strategies you've read in the first two Secret Keys—plan your course and study in the way that works best for you. If you have time, consider using multiple study resources to get different approaches to the same concepts. It can be helpful to see difficult concepts from more than one angle. Then find a good source for practice tests. Many times, the test website will suggest potential study resources or provide sample tests.

Copyright © Mometrix Media. You have been licensed one copy of this document for personal use only. Any other reproduction or redistribution is strictly prohibited. All rights reserved.
This content is provided for test preparation purposes only and does not imply an endorsement by Mometrix of any particular political, scientific, or religious point of view.

# Practice Test Strategy

If you're able to find at least three practice tests, we recommend this strategy:

## UNTIMED AND OPEN-BOOK PRACTICE

Take the first test with no time constraints and with your notes and study guide handy. Take your time and focus on applying the strategies you've learned.

## TIMED AND OPEN-BOOK PRACTICE

Take the second practice test open-book as well, but set a timer and practice pacing yourself to finish in time.

## TIMED AND CLOSED-BOOK PRACTICE

Take any other practice tests as if it were test day. Set a timer and put away your study materials. Sit at a table or desk in a quiet room, imagine yourself at the testing center, and answer questions as quickly and accurately as possible.

Keep repeating timed and closed-book tests on a regular basis until you run out of practice tests or it's time for the actual test. Your mind will be ready for the schedule and stress of test day, and you'll be able to focus on recalling the material you've learned.

Copyright © Mometrix Media. You have been licensed one copy of this document for personal use only. Any other reproduction or redistribution is strictly prohibited. All rights reserved.
This content is provided for test preparation purposes only and does not imply an endorsement by Mometrix of any particular political, scientific, or religious point of view.

# Secret Key #4 – Pace Yourself

Once you're fully prepared for the material on the test, your biggest challenge on test day will be managing your time. Just knowing that the clock is ticking can make you panic even if you have plenty of time left. Work on pacing yourself so you can build confidence against the time constraints of the exam. Pacing is a difficult skill to master, especially in a high-pressure environment, so **practice is vital**.

Set time expectations for your pace based on how much time is available. For example, if a section has 60 questions and the time limit is 30 minutes, you know you have to average 30 seconds or less per question in order to answer them all. Although 30 seconds is the hard limit, set 25 seconds per question as your goal, so you reserve extra time to spend on harder questions. When you budget extra time for the harder questions, you no longer have any reason to stress when those questions take longer to answer.

Don't let this time expectation distract you from working through the test at a calm, steady pace, but keep it in mind so you don't spend too much time on any one question. Recognize that taking extra time on one question you don't understand may keep you from answering two that you do understand later in the test. If your time limit for a question is up and you're still not sure of the answer, mark it and move on, and come back to it later if the time and the test format allow. If the testing format doesn't allow you to return to earlier questions, just make an educated guess; then put it out of your mind and move on.

On the easier questions, be careful not to rush. It may seem wise to hurry through them so you have more time for the challenging ones, but it's not worth missing one if you know the concept and just didn't take the time to read the question fully. Work efficiently but make sure you understand the question and have looked at all of the answer choices, since more than one may seem right at first.

Even if you're paying attention to the time, you may find yourself a little behind at some point. You should speed up to get back on track, but do so wisely. Don't panic; just take a few seconds less on each question until you're caught up. Don't guess without thinking, but do look through the answer choices and eliminate any you know are wrong. If you can get down to two choices, it is often worthwhile to guess from those. Once you've chosen an answer, move on and don't dwell on any that you skipped or had to hurry through. If a question was taking too long, chances are it was one of the harder ones, so you weren't as likely to get it right anyway.

On the other hand, if you find yourself getting ahead of schedule, it may be beneficial to slow down a little. The more quickly you work, the more likely you are to make a careless mistake that will affect your score. You've budgeted time for each question, so don't be afraid to spend that time. Practice an efficient but careful pace to get the most out of the time you have.

Copyright © Mometrix Media. You have been licensed one copy of this document for personal use only. Any other reproduction or redistribution is strictly prohibited. All rights reserved.
This content is provided for test preparation purposes only and does not imply an endorsement by Mometrix of any particular political, scientific, or religious point of view.

# Secret Key #5 – Have a Plan for Guessing

When you're taking the test, you may find yourself stuck on a question. Some of the answer choices seem better than others, but you don't see the one answer choice that is obviously correct. What do you do?

The scenario described above is very common, yet most test takers have not effectively prepared for it. Developing and practicing a plan for guessing may be one of the single most effective uses of your time as you get ready for the exam.

In developing your plan for guessing, there are three questions to address:

- When should you start the guessing process?
- How should you narrow down the choices?
- Which answer should you choose?

## When to Start the Guessing Process

Unless your plan for guessing is to select C every time (which, despite its merits, is not what we recommend), you need to leave yourself enough time to apply your answer elimination strategies. Since you have a limited amount of time for each question, that means that if you're going to give yourself the best shot at guessing correctly, you have to decide quickly whether or not you will guess.

Of course, the best-case scenario is that you don't have to guess at all, so first, see if you can answer the question based on your knowledge of the subject and basic reasoning skills. Focus on the key words in the question and try to jog your memory of related topics. Give yourself a chance to bring the knowledge to mind, but once you realize that you don't have (or you can't access) the knowledge you need to answer the question, it's time to start the guessing process.

It's almost always better to start the guessing process too early than too late. It only takes a few seconds to remember something and answer the question from knowledge. Carefully eliminating wrong answer choices takes longer. Plus, going through the process of eliminating answer choices can actually help jog your memory.

**Summary**: Start the guessing process as soon as you decide that you can't answer the question based on your knowledge.

Copyright © Mometrix Media. You have been licensed one copy of this document for personal use only. Any other reproduction or redistribution is strictly prohibited. All rights reserved.
This content is provided for test preparation purposes only and does not imply an endorsement by Mometrix of any particular political, scientific, or religious point of view.

# How to Narrow Down the Choices

The next chapter in this book (**Test-Taking Strategies**) includes a wide range of strategies for how to approach questions and how to look for answer choices to eliminate. You will definitely want to read those carefully, practice them, and figure out which ones work best for you. Here though, we're going to address a mindset rather than a particular strategy.

Your odds of guessing an answer correctly depend on how many options you are choosing from.

| Number of options left | 5 | 4 | 3 | 2 | 1 |
|---|---|---|---|---|---|
| Odds of guessing correctly | 20% | 25% | 33% | 50% | 100% |

You can see from this chart just how valuable it is to be able to eliminate incorrect answers and make an educated guess, but there are two things that many test takers do that cause them to miss out on the benefits of guessing:

- Accidentally eliminating the correct answer
- Selecting an answer based on an impression

We'll look at the first one here, and the second one in the next section.

To avoid accidentally eliminating the correct answer, we recommend a thought exercise called **the $5 challenge**. In this challenge, you only eliminate an answer choice from contention if you are willing to bet $5 on it being wrong. Why $5? Five dollars is a small but not insignificant amount of money. It's an amount you could afford to lose but wouldn't want to throw away. And while losing

$5 once might not hurt too much, doing it twenty times will set you back $100. In the same way, each small decision you make—eliminating a choice here, guessing on a question there—won't by itself impact your score very much, but when you put them all together, they can make a big difference. By holding each answer choice elimination decision to a higher standard, you can reduce the risk of accidentally eliminating the correct answer.

The $5 challenge can also be applied in a positive sense: If you are willing to bet $5 that an answer choice *is* correct, go ahead and mark it as correct.

**Summary**: Only eliminate an answer choice if you are willing to bet $5 that it is wrong.

Copyright © Mometrix Media. You have been licensed one copy of this document for personal use only. Any other reproduction or redistribution is strictly prohibited. All rights reserved.
This content is provided for test preparation purposes only and does not imply an endorsement by Mometrix of any particular political, scientific, or religious point of view.

# Which Answer to Choose

You're taking the test. You've run into a hard question and decided you'll have to guess. You've eliminated all the answer choices you're willing to bet $5 on. Now you have to pick an answer. Why do we even need to talk about this? Why can't you just pick whichever one you feel like when the time comes?

The answer to these questions is that if you don't come into the test with a plan, you'll rely on your impression to select an answer choice, and if you do that, you risk falling into a trap. The test writers know that everyone who takes their test will be guessing on some of the questions, so they intentionally write wrong answer choices to seem plausible. You still have to pick an answer though, and if the wrong answer choices are designed to look right, how can you ever be sure that you're not falling for their trap? The best solution we've found to this dilemma is to take the decision out of your hands entirely. Here is the process we recommend:

**Once you've eliminated any choices that you are confident (willing to bet $5) are wrong, select the first remaining choice as your answer.**

Whether you choose to select the first remaining choice, the second, or the last, the important thing is that you use some preselected standard. Using this approach guarantees that you will not be enticed into selecting an answer choice that looks right, because you are not basing your decision on how the answer choices look.

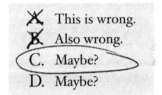

This is not meant to make you question your knowledge. Instead, it is to help you recognize the difference between your knowledge and your impressions. There's a huge difference between thinking an answer is right because of what you know, and thinking an answer is right because it looks or sounds like it should be right.

**Summary**: To ensure that your selection is appropriately random, make a predetermined selection from among all answer choices you have not eliminated.

Copyright © Mometrix Media. You have been licensed one copy of this document for personal use only. Any other reproduction or redistribution is strictly prohibited. All rights reserved.
This content is provided for test preparation purposes only and does not imply an endorsement by Mometrix of any particular political, scientific, or religious point of view.

# Test-Taking Strategies

This section contains a list of test-taking strategies that you may find helpful as you work through the test. By taking what you know and applying logical thought, you can maximize your chances of answering any question correctly!

It is very important to realize that every question is different and every person is different: no single strategy will work on every question, and no single strategy will work for every person. That's why we've included all of them here, so you can try them out and determine which ones work best for different types of questions and which ones work best for you.

## Question Strategies

### ⊘ READ CAREFULLY

Read the question and the answer choices carefully. Don't miss the question because you misread the terms. You have plenty of time to read each question thoroughly and make sure you understand what is being asked. Yet a happy medium must be attained, so don't waste too much time. You must read carefully and efficiently.

### ⊘ CONTEXTUAL CLUES

Look for contextual clues. If the question includes a word you are not familiar with, look at the immediate context for some indication of what the word might mean. Contextual clues can often give you all the information you need to decipher the meaning of an unfamiliar word. Even if you can't determine the meaning, you may be able to narrow down the possibilities enough to make a solid guess at the answer to the question.

### ⊘ PREFIXES

If you're having trouble with a word in the question or answer choices, try dissecting it. Take advantage of every clue that the word might include. Prefixes can be a huge help. Usually, they allow you to determine a basic meaning. *Pre-* means before, *post-* means after, *pro-* is positive, *de-* is negative. From prefixes, you can get an idea of the general meaning of the word and try to put it into context.

### ⊘ HEDGE WORDS

Watch out for critical hedge words, such as *likely, may, can, sometimes, often, almost, mostly, usually, generally, rarely,* and *sometimes*. Question writers insert these hedge phrases to cover every possibility. Often an answer choice will be wrong simply because it leaves no room for exception. Be on guard for answer choices that have definitive words such as *exactly* and *always*.

### ⊘ SWITCHBACK WORDS

Stay alert for *switchbacks*. These are the words and phrases frequently used to alert you to shifts in thought. The most common switchback words are *but, although,* and *however*. Others include *nevertheless, on the other hand, even though, while, in spite of, despite,* and *regardless of.* Switchback words are important to catch because they can change the direction of the question or an answer choice.

10

Copyright © Mometrix Media. You have been licensed one copy of this document for personal use only. Any other reproduction or redistribution is strictly prohibited. All rights reserved. This content is provided for test preparation purposes only and does not imply an endorsement by Mometrix of any particular political, scientific, or religious point of view.

## ⊘ FACE VALUE

When in doubt, use common sense. Accept the situation in the problem at face value. Don't read too much into it. These problems will not require you to make wild assumptions. If you have to go beyond creativity and warp time or space in order to have an answer choice fit the question, then you should move on and consider the other answer choices. These are normal problems rooted in reality. The applicable relationship or explanation may not be readily apparent, but it is there for you to figure out. Use your common sense to interpret anything that isn't clear.

# Answer Choice Strategies

## ⊘ ANSWER SELECTION

The most thorough way to pick an answer choice is to identify and eliminate wrong answers until only one is left, then confirm it is the correct answer. Sometimes an answer choice may immediately seem right, but be careful. The test writers will usually put more than one reasonable answer choice on each question, so take a second to read all of them and make sure that the other choices are not equally obvious. As long as you have time left, it is better to read every answer choice than to pick the first one that looks right without checking the others.

## ⊘ ANSWER CHOICE FAMILIES

An answer choice family consists of two (in rare cases, three) answer choices that are very similar in construction and cannot all be true at the same time. If you see two answer choices that are direct opposites or parallels, one of them is usually the correct answer. For instance, if one answer choice says that quantity $x$ increases and another either says that quantity $x$ decreases (opposite) or says that quantity $y$ increases (parallel), then those answer choices would fall into the same family. An answer choice that doesn't match the construction of the answer choice family is more likely to be incorrect. Most questions will not have answer choice families, but when they do appear, you should be prepared to recognize them.

## ⊘ ELIMINATE ANSWERS

Eliminate answer choices as soon as you realize they are wrong, but make sure you consider all possibilities. If you are eliminating answer choices and realize that the last one you are left with is also wrong, don't panic. Start over and consider each choice again. There may be something you missed the first time that you will realize on the second pass.

## ⊘ AVOID FACT TRAPS

Don't be distracted by an answer choice that is factually true but doesn't answer the question. You are looking for the choice that answers the question. Stay focused on what the question is asking for so you don't accidentally pick an answer that is true but incorrect. Always go back to the question and make sure the answer choice you've selected actually answers the question and is not merely a true statement.

## ⊘ EXTREME STATEMENTS

In general, you should avoid answers that put forth extreme actions as standard practice or proclaim controversial ideas as established fact. An answer choice that states the "process should be used in certain situations, if..." is much more likely to be correct than one that states the "process should be discontinued completely." The first is a calm rational statement and doesn't even make a definitive, uncompromising stance, using a hedge word *if* to provide wiggle room, whereas the second choice is far more extreme.

11

Copyright © Mometrix Media. You have been licensed one copy of this document for personal use only. Any other reproduction or redistribution is strictly prohibited. All rights reserved.
This content is provided for test preparation purposes only and does not imply an endorsement by Mometrix of any particular political, scientific, or religious point of view.

### ⊘ Benchmark

As you read through the answer choices and you come across one that seems to answer the question well, mentally select that answer choice. This is not your final answer, but it's the one that will help you evaluate the other answer choices. The one that you selected is your benchmark or standard for judging each of the other answer choices. Every other answer choice must be compared to your benchmark. That choice is correct until proven otherwise by another answer choice beating it. If you find a better answer, then that one becomes your new benchmark. Once you've decided that no other choice answers the question as well as your benchmark, you have your final answer.

### ⊘ Predict the Answer

Before you even start looking at the answer choices, it is often best to try to predict the answer. When you come up with the answer on your own, it is easier to avoid distractions and traps because you will know exactly what to look for. The right answer choice is unlikely to be word-for-word what you came up with, but it should be a close match. Even if you are confident that you have the right answer, you should still take the time to read each option before moving on.

## General Strategies

### ⊘ Tough Questions

If you are stumped on a problem or it appears too hard or too difficult, don't waste time. Move on! Remember though, if you can quickly check for obviously incorrect answer choices, your chances of guessing correctly are greatly improved. Before you completely give up, at least try to knock out a couple of possible answers. Eliminate what you can and then guess at the remaining answer choices before moving on.

### ⊘ Check Your Work

Since you will probably not know every term listed and the answer to every question, it is important that you get credit for the ones that you do know. Don't miss any questions through careless mistakes. If at all possible, try to take a second to look back over your answer selection and make sure you've selected the correct answer choice and haven't made a costly careless mistake (such as marking an answer choice that you didn't mean to mark). This quick double check should more than pay for itself in caught mistakes for the time it costs.

### ⊘ Pace Yourself

It's easy to be overwhelmed when you're looking at a page full of questions; your mind is confused and full of random thoughts, and the clock is ticking down faster than you would like. Calm down and maintain the pace that you have set for yourself. Especially as you get down to the last few minutes of the test, don't let the small numbers on the clock make you panic. As long as you are on track by monitoring your pace, you are guaranteed to have time for each question.

### ⊘ Don't Rush

It is very easy to make errors when you are in a hurry. Maintaining a fast pace in answering questions is pointless if it makes you miss questions that you would have gotten right otherwise. Test writers like to include distracting information and wrong answers that seem right. Taking a little extra time to avoid careless mistakes can make all the difference in your test score. Find a pace that allows you to be confident in the answers that you select.

Copyright © Mometrix Media. You have been licensed one copy of this document for personal use only. Any other reproduction or redistribution is strictly prohibited. All rights reserved.
This content is provided for test preparation purposes only and does not imply an endorsement by Mometrix of any particular political, scientific, or religious point of view.

## ⊘ KEEP MOVING

Panicking will not help you pass the test, so do your best to stay calm and keep moving. Taking deep breaths and going through the answer elimination steps you practiced can help to break through a stress barrier and keep your pace.

# Final Notes

The combination of a solid foundation of content knowledge and the confidence that comes from practicing your plan for applying that knowledge is the key to maximizing your performance on test day. As your foundation of content knowledge is built up and strengthened, you'll find that the strategies included in this chapter become more and more effective in helping you quickly sift through the distractions and traps of the test to isolate the correct answer.

Now that you're preparing to move forward into the test content chapters of this book, be sure to keep your goal in mind. As you read, think about how you will be able to apply this information on the test. If you've already seen sample questions for the test and you have an idea of the question format and style, try to come up with questions of your own that you can answer based on what you're reading. This will give you valuable practice applying your knowledge in the same ways you can expect to on test day.

**Good luck and good studying!**

Copyright © Mometrix Media. You have been licensed one copy of this document for personal use only. Any other reproduction or redistribution is strictly prohibited. All rights reserved.
This content is provided for test preparation purposes only and does not imply an endorsement by Mometrix of any particular political, scientific, or religious point of view.

Copyright © Mometrix Media. You have been licensed one copy of this document for personal use only. Any other reproduction or redistribution is strictly prohibited. All rights reserved.
This content is provided for test preparation purposes only and does not imply an endorsement by Mometrix of any particular political, scientific, or religious point of view.

# Learning and Teaching

## Classroom Management

### CLASSROOM MANAGEMENT

Classroom management is a necessary skill for all types of instruction, because students cannot learn and teachers cannot instruct when the classroom is constantly being disrupted. Current approaches to classroom management are **proactive** rather than reactive, meaning that teachers organize their classrooms to be physically and emotionally **positive and supportive**, with the hope that this will prevent problem behaviors, rather than merely punitively reacting to misbehavior. Unlike military discipline, which focuses on obtaining total obedience to orders, positive classroom management teaches students **responsibility** for their behavior. This student self-discipline means they do not require constant supervision to behave appropriately. Proactive teachers design routines, lesson structures, activities, interactions, and discipline strategies to facilitate student development of self-control. According to the Association for Supervision and Curriculum Development (ASCD), classroom management is a *gestalt*—a whole beyond the sum of its parts. Proactive teachers organize classrooms so that all students are **integral** to a productive classroom community, regardless of skill. Less time for discipline equals more time for learning.

> **Review Video: Classroom Management - Rhythms of Teaching**
> Visit mometrix.com/academy and enter code: 809399

### PROACTIVE CLASSROOM MANAGEMENT

Teachers with proactive approaches do not seek quick ways to fix classroom behavior problems. Instead, they commit themselves to achieving long-term student **behavior changes**. Three main **principles** (cf. Brophy, 1983) that govern the classroom management approaches of proactive teachers are:

- Proactive teachers take the **responsibility** for control of their classrooms. They do not blame their students or the students' families for student problem behaviors.
- Proactive teachers do not place excessive importance on strategies of punishments and rewards. Instead, they look for **long-term solutions** to behavioral problems.
- Proactive teachers analyze disruptive classroom behaviors to determine potential **sources**, such as family, emotional, and developmental variables.

Three primary **characteristics of proactive teachers** are:

- They have resilient, positive attitudes.
- They enable at-risk students to experience growth.
- They do not accept any excuses for behavioral and other classroom and school problems. Instead, they find or create solutions.

> **Review Video: Student Behavior Management Approaches**
> Visit mometrix.com/academy and enter code: 843846

### FREUD'S MODEL OF EMOTIONAL STABILITY

Sigmund Freud proposed that emotional stability requires balance among the personality's three basic structures: the id, ego, and superego. The **id**, or pleasure principle, urges us to gratify impulses immediately. The **superego**, or conscience, tells us what is right and wrong. The **ego**, or

Copyright © Mometrix Media. You have been licensed one copy of this document for personal use only. Any other reproduction or redistribution is strictly prohibited. All rights reserved. This content is provided for test preparation purposes only and does not imply an endorsement by Mometrix of any particular political, scientific, or religious point of view.

reality principle, mediates between the id and superego. For example, when we see something we want, the id tells us to take it, the superego tells us it is wrong to steal, and the ego tells us we will get arrested if we are caught stealing. Freud found that **neurosis** was the result of imbalance among these components. People might be overly impulsive, overly repress all of their urges, or ignore the consequences of their actions in reality. While Freudian psychotherapy historically focused on exploring the unconscious to help patients discover insights into their motivations for their behaviors, in time his theory was applied practically through various **psycho-educational interventions** in the classroom. These include group dynamics, crisis management, and social skills curricula.

## BEHAVIOR MODIFICATION

**Behaviorist theory** finds that feelings, thoughts, and other inner states are hypothetical and cannot be outwardly observed, recorded, or analyzed. **Behaviorism** maintains that only externally observable, measurable behaviors can be studied scientifically, and hence changed. **Behavior modification** manipulates the antecedents and consequences of observable behaviors to change them. **Positive reinforcement** increases the probability of repeating a behavior with a desirable consequence. **Negative reinforcement** does the same by removing an undesirable consequence. **Punishment** decreases probable repetition of a behavior with an undesirable consequence. **Extinction** of a behavior decreases probable behavior repetition by removing any reinforcing consequences, such as attention. Some examples of common school applications of behavior modification include prizes for good schoolwork or behavior in elementary school, detention as punishment for incomplete schoolwork or misbehavior in high school, or being excused from weekend homework as negative reinforcement for doing all weekday homework in middle school. Some criticize behavior modification, stating that students may learn to value rewards above learning or that instructors use consequences but do not collect data to assess their effectiveness.

## PROBLEM BEHAVIORS

Students with **dysfunctional family backgrounds** are more likely to display problem classroom behaviors, learned from their home models. Students with **neurological or emotional problems** are also more likely to act out in classrooms. Some **hereditary factors** contribute to behavioral problems, and students exposed to toxins and/or drug abuse are more likely to exhibit problem behaviors. In addition, students with deficits in **social skills** often lack knowledge of appropriate classroom behaviors, or may behave inappropriately to compensate for lacking more proactive skills to meet their needs and wants. **Teacher behaviors** such as boring or disorganized lessons also significantly contribute to classroom misbehavior. Additionally, when teachers **overreact** to disruptive behaviors, stereotype students, or exhibit burnout, this exacerbates the problem behaviors. Finally, teachers who overuse **punishment** as a response to unacceptable behaviors increase more than decrease misbehavior in their classrooms.

> **Review Video: Promoting Appropriate Behavior**
> Visit mometrix.com/academy and enter code: 321015

## PEER INTERACTIONS AND BEHAVIOR

**Peer approval** is a powerful student motivation, particularly at certain ages. Students may engage in disruptive behaviors to gain classmates' acceptance or admiration. Students with **dysfunctional group identities or roles** are more likely to misbehave in group settings. Students involved in **cliques** may reinforce undesirable class behaviors as desirable within their group. **Bullying** promotes various classroom behavior problems, by both bullies and their victims. Students with **hostile or apathetic attitudes** are likely to engage in disruptive or distracting classroom behaviors. In classroom organization, **inconsistent teacher routines** promote classroom

16

Copyright © Mometrix Media. You have been licensed one copy of this document for personal use only. Any other reproduction or redistribution is strictly prohibited. All rights reserved. This content is provided for test preparation purposes only and does not imply an endorsement by Mometrix of any particular political, scientific, or religious point of view.

misbehavior because students need consistency and predictability to feel secure and know what to expect and what is expected of them. Student misbehavior is also stimulated by **physically uncomfortable class environments** or **curriculum that is irrelevant** to their needs and interests. Classrooms lacking adequate **learning materials** encourage misbehavior as students become frustrated and disengaged. Teachers who are unaware or in denial of **student cultural differences** also promote classroom behavior problems by allowing students to feel ignored, misunderstood, or not accepted.

## TEACHER ATTITUDES THAT PROMOTE POSITIVE STUDENT BEHAVIORS

Multiple surveys of students (Henley, 2000; Stanford, 2000; Corbett & Wilson, 2002) have found that teachers with **resilient, positive attitudes** are most liked and respected by students. Students report that these teachers were enthusiastic, challenged them, believed in them, and cared about them as people. Researchers found that students consistently reported a teacher's positive personal qualities as reasons for their **effectiveness** rather than any particular instructional methods. Research finds that teachers and administrators who personally take responsibility for school conditions, and reciprocally expect their students to take responsibility for their own learning, are associated with successful school outcomes. Educators who combine high standards for students, belief in student abilities, and supportive relationships with students are most successful. At less successful schools, research has found that teachers often had **negative attitudes** toward students with **learning problems**: They blamed students, saw diverse student cultures and languages as impossible barriers to learning, and stereotyped students. These teachers adhered to a "deficit model," using things "wrong" with students as excuses for failure.

## DEVELOPMENTAL THEORY

Developmental theory focuses on the changes in children's behavior, thinking, and feeling due to maturation and learning as they grow and develop. Development is viewed as progressing through predictable **stages** as children first learn simple skills and then increasingly complex skills. Physical and environmental factors that disrupt normal development can cause problems, some life-long. The major **developmental domains** are motor, cognitive, language, and social-emotional development. Some prominent **developmental theorists** include Jean Piaget, Alfred Adler, Erik Erikson, Abraham Maslow, and William Glasser. **Piaget** focused on cognitive development, while the others focused more on emotional and social needs, including the need for belonging and acceptance. **Adler** stressed human needs for community and connection. **Maslow** emphasized needs for self-actualization and fulfilling one's potential, with physical, safety, belonging, and esteem needs as prerequisites. **Erikson** posited stages of psychosocial development, each with a nuclear conflict to resolve. For example, the conflict of industry versus inferiority accompanies beginning school ages. Positive resolution of this conflict results in a sense of industry and competence, while negative outcome is a sense of inferiority and inertia.

## BIOPHYSICAL THEORY PRINCIPLES

Biophysical theory analyzes genetic, metabolic, and neurological variables to explain human behavior. Research advances in brain function and brain chemistry have revealed evidence of **genetic factors** involved in such disorders as Asperger's syndrome and schizophrenia. Also, recent neuroimaging discoveries show not only differential brain activity associated with various cognitive and emotional states, but also **neuroplasticity**, or the brain's malleability. The brain can often be retrained through **cognitive exercises** to change attitudes and even improve skills impaired by some conditions. Several **biophysical explanations** have been suggested for various problem behaviors. These include neurological deficits; allergies; lead poisoning; nutritional and sleep deficiencies, infections, and visual impairments for child attention deficit and hyperactivity disorders; and preservatives and sugars in foods. Treating this with prescription drugs, such as

Copyright © Mometrix Media. You have been licensed one copy of this document for personal use only. Any other reproduction or redistribution is strictly prohibited. All rights reserved. This content is provided for test preparation purposes only and does not imply an endorsement by Mometrix of any particular political, scientific, or religious point of view.

stimulants for ADHD, lithium for bipolar disorder, and other medications for schizophrenia, anxiety, and depression, is based on biophysical theory. Neurological research supports the theory's explanation that **emotional status** affects learning, and biophysical principles can help educators understand emotional impacts on learning.

## DIFFERENTIAL APPROACHES TO A STUDENT'S CLASSROOM PROBLEM BEHAVIOR

Suppose Leo, a middle-school student, often disrupts classes with attention-getting behaviors like inappropriate jokes and snide comments. **Developmental theory** might explain that this behavior stems from a psychosocial conflict common in adolescence: Leo feels insecure and has trouble making friends, so he is attempting to gain peer acceptance through his behavior. **Behaviorist theory** would say that Leo's behaviors are positively reinforced every time his classmates laugh at them, so he repeats them. **Biophysical theory** might point to the fact that Leo lives in a public housing development underneath an interstate bridge and suggest that his nervous system has suffered from a gradual accumulation of lead; his impulsive behavior is attributable to lead toxicity. **Psychodynamic theory** might suggest that Leo exhibits most inappropriate behaviors when reading is expected of him because he feels insecure about his poor reading skills. His self-control difficulties are triggered by circumstances reactivating memories of past failure experiences, his insecurity about reading escalates his anxiety, and his impulsive behavior acts out this anxiety.

## STRUCTURE, INSTRUCTION, AND DISCIPLINE

Research studies have found that in the area of structure, teachers who manage their classrooms effectively create regular **routines** for all daily needs and tasks. They strive for continuity throughout the day and smooth transitions between activities. They also display good **multitasking** abilities. Effective classroom managers find a good balance between **challenge and variety** in student activities. They also make use of every "teachable moment" and consistently enhance their students' interest and engagement in learning. Teachers who are effective at classroom management use **proactive disciplinary practices** and apply them consistently. They are always keenly aware of what is going on in their classrooms. They **move** about the classroom to get students' attention and stay close to problem and potential problem areas. To prevent or limit disruption, they **anticipate** possible problems and resolve minor disruptions or inattention before they can escalate into major problems.

## PROACTIVE CLASSROOM MANAGEMENT

- **Community**: The foundation for proactive classroom management is **teacher-student rapport and respect**. Proactive teachers create classroom atmospheres that invite students in and offer security. They address **student diversity** by connecting interpersonally, providing a nurturing environment, empowering students, listening to them, and applying group process principles. Rapport supports class cohesion, dialogue overcomes disagreements, and enthusiasm supersedes apathy.
- **Prevention**: Students are less disruptive when they are **engaged** in learning. Unenthusiastic instruction and disorganized lessons invite disruptions. Teachers can prevent many disturbances by focusing on quality of instruction, motivation, and group dynamics. When they understand group dynamics' influences on individual behavior, they can foster **group cohesion** through disciplinary practices and class structures. They identify and modify class routines and events that contribute to discipline issues. They also analyze reasons or functions of problem behaviors for preventive discipline.
- **Positive behavioral supports**: Teachers respond to student behavior challenges with confidence and flexibility. They design **proactive interventions** to prevent classroom events that trigger problem behaviors, teach constructive behaviors, and apply strategies to de-escalate potential increases in misbehavior.

Copyright © Mometrix Media. You have been licensed one copy of this document for personal use only. Any other reproduction or redistribution is strictly prohibited. All rights reserved. This content is provided for test preparation purposes only and does not imply an endorsement by Mometrix of any particular political, scientific, or religious point of view.

## FEEDBACK GIVEN ABOUT THE ENVIRONMENT OF THE LIBRARY MEDIA CENTERS

Researchers surveying schools to evaluate and identify the best practices in library media centers and best library media specialists have found that in schools with the best library media programs, students want to visit the library **more frequently**. Their teachers recognize this interest and strive to bring their classes to the media center often. Some of these schools have waiting lists for class visits. Some teachers go to the library media center daily before school starts to see if there are openings for visits. Students have responded very positively to **surveys** about their media centers, commenting that the variety of media is so diverse that anybody could find something interesting. They appreciate the help they get with schoolwork and they find the atmosphere relaxing, an environment that invites them to visit.

## MODEL ENVIRONMENT

In the 21st century, school library media centers are becoming learning hubs for school learning communities. They empower students to engage with **diverse formats and types of information** beyond traditional print media. Experts also believe that school library media programs humanize and enrich school educational programs. Students access resources and technology efficiently and effectively, learning information literacy, independent learning skills, and personal social responsibility. One proposed model (Xu) aligned with AASL standards for 21st-century information literacy and the learner-in-action is a "4C model," with C standing for "center."

The library media center is a center for:

- **Resources**: providing information, collection development, censorship, administration, organization, professionalism, availability, access, and service in all formats;
- **Technology**: providing access to technology, information, media, creation, products, interaction, and social networking;
- **Learning**: enabling inquiry, critical thinking, construction of knowledge, analysis, and decision-making; and
- **Collaboration**: for student-student, student-teacher, and teacher-teacher collaboration; teamwork; shared knowledge; creation; democracy; ethics; and personal growth. This model aims for students to become information-literate, independent, socially responsible, ethical, and democratic lifelong learners who efficiently, effectively, critically, and creatively access, evaluate, and use technology and resources to generate and share knowledge.

## ENVIRONMENTAL PSYCHOLOGY RELATIVE TO THE HUMAN ENVIRONMENT

- **Personal space**: This is an extension of a person and his personality. In proxemics (Hall, 1963), these distances include:
    o *intimate distance* (up to a one-and-a-half feet)
    o *personal distance* (one-and-a-half feet to four feet)
    o *social distance* (four to 12 feet)
    o *public distance* (12 to 25 feet or more)
  Social distance enables individuals to work among others yet ignore them, without rudeness. Library tables and chairs should be a minimum of four to five inches apart. To establish mutual respect and prevent behavior proglems, teachers and library media specialists should not invade students' personal spaces.
- **Territoriality**: Research finds that students prefer empty chairs and spaces around them at tables. To meet this need but avoid wasting seats and space, librarians can provide smaller tables, not larger ones.

Copyright © Mometrix Media. You have been licensed one copy of this document for personal use only. Any other reproduction or redistribution is strictly prohibited. All rights reserved. This content is provided for test preparation purposes only and does not imply an endorsement by Mometrix of any particular political, scientific, or religious point of view.

- **Privacy**: Children in particular need secluded, private spaces. Researchers have observed elementary-age children who need to concentrate working happily inside school library closets. Carrels, portable partitions, and alcoves that do not interfere with visibility or traffic flow are recommended.
- **Variety**: Ideally, library media centers should combine public, private, and semi-private study areas to accommodate all needs:
  o quiet areas for concentration
  o areas with background music for light reading and quiet conversation
  o break, snack, socializing, and walking-around areas for respite from tedious work

## COLOR, CARPETING, SEATING, AND PRIVACY AND VARIETY IN SPACES

- **Color**: Bright, warm colors—red, orange, and yellow—are good library accents, but overstimulating to young children, who become too active for interest in books. Softer peaches, pinks, and yellows are recommended for young children, while teens and young adults respond best to cool blues and greens. Color can be used to:
  o visually alter perceived room size, shape, scale, and proportion
  o disguise design flaws
  o emphasize physical features
  o eliminate need for extensive remodeling
  o create a more welcoming atmosphere
- **Carpeting**: This is valuable for reducing noise and appealing to children, and can even be used as inexpensive child seating. While wall-to-wall carpeting is recommended, large carpet remnants or area rugs can work well with prohibitive budgets.
- **Seating**: Experts recommend non-intimidating circulation desks, student-sized chairs and tables for younger children, cushions, beanbag chairs, rockers, stuffed armchairs, and stools for an inviting atmosphere.
- **Private spaces**: Children seek private nooks, crannies, and corners for quiet reading. Library media specialists can create these using large boxes covered with contact paper, lofts, antique bathtubs, and so on.
- **Variety in spaces**: Researchers recommend varied atmospheres for quiet, group work, and relaxation including carrels, conference rooms, different table sizes, casual furniture, and back-to-back chairs for privacy.

## OWNERSHIP AND CONTROL

Students appreciate some ownership of school library media centers. Whereas teachers frequently dominate classrooms, media centers are successful when students have more **freedom** to interact there. They should be permitted (within reason) to move tables, chairs, and cushions to facilitate group work or reading. Research finds that students find or make **private spaces**. Some students vary their space according to activities, such as sitting at a table for quiet work or conversation some days, and sitting on a stool behind the circulation desk for silent reading on other days. Library media specialists extend flexibility and freedom by encouraging student initiative with space whenever they can. While students need some solitude and control, media specialists still must visually supervise their areas. They should consider what **physical features** communicate: Lofts and tree houses invite active play, confusing children when staff enforces quiet. Graffiti artists are tempted by hidden corners. Tables shoved together closely invite interaction. Research finds that both elementary and secondary students want quiet environments. Secondary students prefer open spaces over clustered furniture. Generally, students want varied spaces for both **private and group activities**.

Copyright © Mometrix Media. You have been licensed one copy of this document for personal use only. Any other reproduction or redistribution is strictly prohibited. All rights reserved. This content is provided for test preparation purposes only and does not imply an endorsement by Mometrix of any particular political, scientific, or religious point of view.

# Collaboration for Information Literacy

## COLLABORATION BETWEEN K–12 AND HIGHER-EDUCATION LIBRARIES

The joint task force of the American Association of School Libraries (AASL) and Association of College and Research Libraries (ACRL) gave recommendations for K–12 and higher education libraries to work together more closely.

These **recommendations** included:

- Advocating that the move from *Information Literacy Standards for Student Learning* developed by the AASL to the *Information Literacy Competencies for Higher Education* developed by the ACRL be conducted seamlessly to support **transitions** from secondary to post-secondary education
- Sharing the information from both the *Standards* and *Competencies* to applicable groups in order to **generate discussion**
- Developing specific, measurable **results and performance indicators** of information literacy for education students
- Including academic librarians on the instructional team in **undergraduate and graduate teacher education programs**
- Including academic librarians on the instructional team in **continuing education and professional development programs** for teachers

## IMPLEMENTING COLLABORATIVE PRACTICES

The American Association of School Libraries (AASL) and Association of College and Research Libraries (ACRL) formed a joint task force to study how libraries for K–12 schools and higher education libraries could implement better **collaborative practices**.

With input from open forums and round tables, they produced a series of recommendations:

- To encourage the members of education faculty, academic librarians, school library media specialists, and library school faculty members to **collaborate on research**
- To make **joint presentations** at professional conferences
- To publish **research reports** together
- To engage in other activities involving **professional collaboration**

They recommended that K–12 and post-secondary library professionals collaborate with ALISE (Association for Library and Information Science Education) to include **instruction** in the education of library school media specialists and librarians. They also recommended that K–12 and higher education library professionals develop relationships with their local **school boards** to establish and further continuing education programs in information literacy for school librarians.

## RECOMMENDATIONS OF THE JOINT TASK FORCE
### PROMOTING COLLABORATIVE EFFORTS

The Joint Task Force of the American Association of School Libraries (AASL) and Association of College and Research Libraries (ACRL) developed a number of recommendations to encourage increased collaboration between K–12 and post-secondary library programs and professionals. These recommendations include joint association activities to promote information literacy. Additionally, library professionals are encouraged to **identify** organizations engaged with information literacy, make a comprehensive **list** of such organizations, and provide **links** for this list on the AASL and ACRL websites.

21

Copyright © Mometrix Media. You have been licensed one copy of this document for personal use only. Any other reproduction or redistribution is strictly prohibited. All rights reserved.
This content is provided for test preparation purposes only and does not imply an endorsement by Mometrix of any particular political, scientific, or religious point of view.

The responsibility for monitoring and managing opportunities in information literacy should be jointly adopted by the AASL and ACRL, and this joint responsibility includes the following functions:

- Setting up an **information literacy website** with shared ownership
- Serving as "watch dogs" for **national opportunities** where librarians and non-librarians could make collaborative presentations
- Establishing a centralized process to identify **grant opportunities** and **publish collaboratively** on the subject of information literacy

## GENERAL RECOMMENDATIONS OF THE JOINT TASK FORCE

The Joint Task force from the AASL and ACRL recommended the following for increasing information literacy in secondary and post-secondary students:

- **Promoting standards for information literacy**
  - Library professionals should compile lists of **standards for information literacy** and provide access to this list on the websites of the American Library Association (ALA), AASL, and ACRL.

- **Partnering library associations with colleges**
  - Library professionals should explore opportunities for collaborating with **information power implementation (IP2)** and **affiliate regions coordinators** from the AASL. In addition, library professionals at both educational levels are encouraged to identify staff members of the American Library Association (ALA) who had job responsibilities related to instruction and therefore would be good **contacts for outreach efforts** to increase collaboration.

- **Incentivizing attendance of conferences**
  - Library professionals can create awards for collaboration among libraries, colleges, and school districts on information literacy projects. The task force recommended encouraging the recipients to attend conferences that will promote collaboration methods and models by offering **stipends and paid travel expenses**.

- **Regional networking**
  - Library professionals should promote **regional networks** so that librarians, teachers, administrators, and students and faculty of education colleges and programs would have a regular forum for sharing practical information and ideas on information literacy issues.

- **Modeling collaborative efforts**
  - Library professionals should model collaborative efforts with professional organizations to reach out to local school districts. This may include building a speaker circuit to promote literacy in a larger region.

- **Planning for updates**
  - Literacy standards change periodically, so it should be considered a funamental element of collaborative efforts to ensure that changes are reviewed and discussed among collaborators.

Copyright © Mometrix Media. You have been licensed one copy of this document for personal use only. Any other reproduction or redistribution is strictly prohibited. All rights reserved.
This content is provided for test preparation purposes only and does not imply an endorsement by Mometrix of any particular political, scientific, or religious point of view.

- **Planning events to promote information literacy**
  - Library professionals should hold events, such as think tanks to brainstorm new methods for promoting information literacy. Much of modern information literacy comes through the medium of computers and the internet, which are constantly changing. Methods for promoting information literacy must be recursive, so that they can keep up with modern technology and events.

## PAST INITIATIVE THAT EXPLORED THE ROLE OF LIBRARIES IN EDUCATION

The presidents of the American Association of School Librarians (AASL) and Association of College and Research Libraries (ACRL) established a joint task force in 1998 to study libraries' educational functions and recommended methods for encouraging collaboration between K–12 libraries and post-secondary education libraries via AASL and ACRL organizational structures. One factor demonstrating the benefits of joint work was that both associations were writing **information literacy standards** for their respective educational levels. At an open forum of this joint task force during the ALA's Midwinter 2000 meeting, participants reviewed task force draft recommendations and suggested further recommendations. Two collaborative recommendations were proposed: Co-sponsoring **model collaboration programming** for information literacy at national, state, and local levels to encourage community partnerships, and promoting **information literacy competency standards** for higher education through a formal relationship with the National Council for Accreditation of Teacher Education (NCATE) Standards Steering Committee.

## FUNCTIONS AND ROLES OF LIBRARY MEDIA CENTERS AND LIBRARY MEDIA SPECIALISTS

Studies report that in most school library media centers, the librarians spend only a small portion of their time on teaching, and then only on basic instruction. Researchers recommend that as the prevalence of technology in schools and media centers increases, the majority of librarians should transition from teaching computer and research basics to **higher-level instruction** of students in using **technology as a research and learning tool**. For instance, they could teach students how to filter information, how to synthesize information rather than simply copying it, how to interpret and integrate information, and how to evaluate Internet sources for credibility. Research also finds most librarians spend little time collaborating with teachers, and mainly in identifying documents and information sources for the teachers. The best media specialists spend more time **collaborating**—they help teachers expand, enrich, enhance, and enliven curriculum. Additionally, they increase its relevance and help teachers improve instructional quality.

## UNIQUE POTENTIAL OF LIBRARY MEDIA SPECIALISTS

Library media specialists have the unique potential to influence students by teaching them **skills** they do not normally learn from classroom teachers in typical curriculum units. For example, librarians can teach students how to locate and access information, review it, select from among information sources, synthesize information, and present the information to others. Also, librarians can be influential regarding their schools' curricula, helping teachers identify new **information sources**. They can also help teachers improve the **relevance** of the curriculum. They can impact the content being taught in their schools and the quality of instruction. Experts view school librarians as **change agents**, crucial to integrating **technology** into curriculum. Fulfilling these roles requires administrative support, so it is necessary to **redefine** librarian and library support staff responsibilities, teachers' perceptions of librarians, and teachers' use of librarians' services.

Copyright © Mometrix Media. You have been licensed one copy of this document for personal use only. Any other reproduction or redistribution is strictly prohibited. All rights reserved. This content is provided for test preparation purposes only and does not imply an endorsement by Mometrix of any particular political, scientific, or religious point of view.

## CHARACTERISTICS OF PROBLEMS SOLVABLE BY BUILDING CONSENSUS

Some general characteristics of problems that may be solved through **consensus-building approaches** include:

- The problem is poorly defined, or people disagree on the definition.
- Several interdependent stakeholders have vested interests in the problems and their solutions.
- The interested stakeholders are not necessarily members of a cohesive organization or group.
- Stakeholders have different access to information about the problem and different levels of expertise related to it. Their resources and/or power for dealing with the problem are disparate.
- The problem is both scientifically ambiguous and technically complex.
- Because their viewpoints or perspectives about the problem are variable, stakeholders develop adversarial relationships through disagreements over it.
- Attempts to solve the problem unilaterally, or in increments, generally tend not to bring satisfactory results.
- When people tried to solve the problem using processes already in place, they either found these methods inadequate or that they made the problem worse.

## STAGES OF CONSENSUS SEEKING AND PROCESS CRITERIA

### EIGHT CONSENSUS-SEEKING PROCESS STAGES:

1. Identify the problem.
2. Identify and recruit participants.
3. Convene: acquire funding, find a meeting location, and appoint a facilitator.
4. Design the process.
5. Define and analyze the problem.
6. Identify and evaluate solution alternatives.
7. Make decisions.
8. Approve the agreement.
9. Implement the solution.

### PROCESS CRITERIA:

- All significantly differing and relevant interests are represented.
- A group-shared, practice purpose drives the process.
- Participants self-organize the process.
- The process adheres to respectful, civil, face-to-face conversational principles.
- High-quality data, facts, and personal experiences are incorporated and adapted.
- Process participants are encouraged to be creative, explore alternatives, and challenge assumptions.
- The process keeps participants involved, at the table, and learning new things.
- Only after thoroughly exploring all interests and issues, and making sufficient efforts to discover creative solutions to participant disagreements, does the process seek consensus.

Copyright © Mometrix Media. You have been licensed one copy of this document for personal use only. Any other reproduction or redistribution is strictly prohibited. All rights reserved. This content is provided for test preparation purposes only and does not imply an endorsement by Mometrix of any particular political, scientific, or religious point of view.

# Information Literacy

## AUTHENTIC ASSESSMENT OF INFORMATION LITERACY

Research has found that for information literacy to be assessed realistically, teachers must learn to stop viewing information literacy as simply the ability to locate information in the library. Information literacy must also go beyond the physical space of the school library. Greater teacher support for **assessing information literacy** must be enlisted. Also, pressure on teachers and their focus on meeting core content standards must be balanced with an equal focus on meeting **school district information literacy standards**. Assessment instruments should increase emphasis on the role of the library media specialist as a teacher and assessor. Assessment design needs to establish **reliability** across core content areas and classrooms and to address the **time-consuming nature** of authentic assessments. The **locations** of media centers in schools can interfere with collaboration and library use, so assessment design must address location, as well as opening up the closed assessment systems of libraries.

## DESIGNING AUTHENTIC INFORMATION LITERACY ASSESSMENTS

Some researchers have studied school library media centers as closed systems. They have concluded that the design of **innovative alternative assessment instruments** requires maintaining a focus on authentic assessment, asking students to demonstrate their information literacy skills in **real-world contexts**. They have also found that authentic information literacy projects involve only **some students**, like those who were active members of a book club, who researched various real-life topics and then informed the rest of the students about those topics as reflected in real-world contexts. Researchers therefore recommended that such authentic projects be expanded to include **all students**. To facilitate this, it is important to address logistical problems of getting students out of classrooms to work on projects.

Additionally, the following issues should be addressed:

- time issues, like the time required by the authentic activities of alternative assessments
- lack of library media specialist time, particularly for part-time media specialists
- time for completing other responsibilities

## VIRTUAL REALITY

Investigators have identified challenges to library participation and media specialist teaching and assessment partnership based on temporal and spatial constraints, as well as on authentic and real-life learning and assessment. **Virtual reality (VR)** is one solution to these limitations. As a meta-medium, VR can support **all other available media** including HTML, multimedia, hypermedia, video games, desktop presentations, and more. VR includes three-dimensional simulations and full-immersion experiences. VR navigation via keyboard and mouse is a relatively inexpensive way of affording first-person experiences, a great value in classroom and library environments. Students can process information more easily with VR, they access information in an immediate and dynamic way, and they have a setting for problem-solving activities.

VR has **educational potential** in several areas:

- as an instrument to evaluate student performance
- as an experimental learning instrument
- as an instrument for gathering data and feedback
- as a tool to aid non-traditional learners

Copyright © Mometrix Media. You have been licensed one copy of this document for personal use only. Any other reproduction or redistribution is strictly prohibited. All rights reserved. This content is provided for test preparation purposes only and does not imply an endorsement by Mometrix of any particular political, scientific, or religious point of view.

## USING TECHNOLOGY FOR INNOVATIVE INFORMATION LITERACY ASSESSMENT SYSTEM DESIGN

Some researchers (Newell, 2004) have developed innovative designs that combine multiple technologies for the **virtual assessment of information literacy learning**. Such designs are based on the concept of **authentic assessment** that involves student problem-solving in real-life contexts through the practical demonstration and/or application of information literacy knowledge and skills. Via virtual reality (VR) technology, designers can give students realistic, three-dimensional, interactive information environments such as libraries, books, museums, homes, TVs, computers, and people. Via **avatars** they create, using movements, gestures, and chat features, students can move about, interact, and collaborate with one another. Such realistic settings **engage** students more in problems, and they better enable educators to **assess** the way students' reason, think, and utilize information for problem-solving across various contexts. School district **information literacy standards** are addressed during realistic, authentic tasks.

Students are required not only to locate and differentiate information but also to:

- identify problems
- collect, organize, integrate, evaluate, and utilize information
- make observations
- collect and analyze data
- use various equipment types

## INFORMATION LITERACY GOALS OF ASSESSMENT SYSTEMS

Researchers have found that even though school district information literacy standards clearly state goals for students to achieve competencies to seek, access, evaluate, utilize, and communicate information, teachers consistently limit their information literacy instruction to **physically** locating information sources in the library. Another conflict between information literacy goals and teacher perceptions is that teachers are primarily concerned with ensuring that students meet **core content area standards** rather than attain information literacy. Teachers express that covering curriculum-based material and related class projects requires too much of their time to allow for doing research or developing information literacy. Also, although school districts present their information literacy standards in research studies, teachers are often unsure of how to **assess student attainment** of these standards.

## EDUCATIONAL ROLES RELATIVE TO INFORMATION LITERACY

Researchers have received responses from library media specialists indicating that they know how to **teach**, and that they believe there should be a **partnership** between teachers and librarians for curriculum planning and development, instruction, and assessment, but that teachers often do not realize this. Some media specialists have suggested that colleges of education should **collaborate** more closely with colleges of library science, and that a lack of such collaboration results in teachers' not comprehending what librarians do. While librarians believe they share the teacher's role in helping students to **learn**, teachers may see them as responsible only for collecting and providing resources, organization, scheduling, and simple tutorials in how and where to locate information sources and basic research skills. In contrast, media specialists feel they are or should be equal partners with teachers in planning, implementing, and assessing learning activities to promote information literacy as well as maintaining and managing the library.

## OBSTACLES TO HELPING STUDENTS ATTAIN INFORMATION LITERACY

In the more recent, less traditional paradigm of alternative assessment, tools for assessing student information literacy are **authentic**, such as **portfolio assessments**. While these give more realistic

Copyright © Mometrix Media. You have been licensed one copy of this document for personal use only. Any other reproduction or redistribution is strictly prohibited. All rights reserved. This content is provided for test preparation purposes only and does not imply an endorsement by Mometrix of any particular political, scientific, or religious point of view.

representations of student learning, progress, and achievement than traditional tests, they also consume more time. As a result, teachers have reported that they do not have time to do extensive research, collect student work products, or lead learning exercises enabling student demonstration of skills and knowledge they have attained in authentic contexts. At the same time, a significant consideration for school library media specialists is their **job and school conditions**. For example, in some school systems media specialists may work only part-time at the school due to budget constraints. In such conditions, they are too busy in the library to go to classrooms as well. They report they would like more teachers to come to the library to plan information literacy instruction and assessment collaboratively, but they realize that time constraints make this difficult.

## PHYSICAL CONSTRAINTS ON TEACHER AND STUDENT PARTICIPATION IN THE SCHOOL LIBRARY MEDIA CENTER

Researchers have found that **physical proximity** affects library accessibility for teachers and students. In multiple-story school buildings, teachers cannot easily come to the library, so they send students with notes to the library media specialist. At the same time, the media specialist cannot leave the library to go to classrooms on other floors. Libraries **not centrally located** are visited more by students and teachers in classrooms closest to them. **Space and time** also interfere with middle and high school projects: the logistics of getting all students to the library across all periods of the school day are difficult.

Authentic **assessment of information literacy**, such as through library personal contact, is difficult due to several factors:

- the media specialist usually does not know teacher goals and objectives for class projects
- the media specialist is not seen as a teaching or learning partner in information literacy
- many teachers do not value the library content domain
- the media specialist does not see all of the students throughout the school year

Lastly, authentic project assessments are time-consuming and often do not involve or assess all students.

## STANDARDS OF INFORMATION LITERACY

According to the American Library Association and the Association for Educational Communications and Technology (cf. *Information Power: Building Partnerships for Learning,* 1998), there are **nine information literacy standards** for student learning, three in each of three areas: Information Literacy, Independent Learning, and Social Responsibility. **Information Literacy** includes three standards. First, when a student has developed information literacy, that student is more effective and efficient in **accessing** the information that he or she needs. Second, when a student has developed information literacy, that student is able to **evaluate** accessed information with more competence and critical thinking. Third, when a student has developed good information literacy, that student makes use of the information that s/he accesses with more **accuracy and creativity**.

### INDEPENDENT LEARNING AND INFORMATION LITERACY STANDARDS

The American Library Association and the Association for Educational Communications and Technology, in their 1998 publication *Information Power: Building Partnerships for Learning,* have set nine information literacy standards for student learning, addressing the areas of Information Literacy, Independent Learning, and Social Responsibility. **Independent Learning** includes three standards. The first of these, or Standard 4 in the complete list, states that when a student is an independent learner, that student possesses information literacy and will seek out information of

Copyright © Mometrix Media. You have been licensed one copy of this document for personal use only. Any other reproduction or redistribution is strictly prohibited. All rights reserved. This content is provided for test preparation purposes only and does not imply an endorsement by Mometrix of any particular political, scientific, or religious point of view.

**personal interest** to him or her. Standard 5 explains that because a student who is identified as an independent learner also has information literacy, that student has an **appreciation** of literature and of other channels of creatively communicating information. Standard 6 states that because an independent learner is information literate, s/he seeks to **achieve excellence** in attaining the skills of **looking for information** and **generating knowledge**.

### INFORMATION LITERACY STANDARDS AND SOCIAL RESPONSIBILITY

The book *Information Power: Building Partnerships for Learning* (1998), published jointly by the American Library Association (ALA) and the Association for Educational Communications and Technology (AECT), defines nine standards of information literacy for student learning. These are grouped into three categories: Information Literacy, Independent Learning, and Social Responsibility, with three standards in each category. The first standard of **Social Responsibility** (Standard 7 in the full list) states that a student who has attained information literacy, and realizes the significance of information in a democratic society, makes **positive contributions** to the learning community and to the larger society. Standard 8 states that a student who has achieved information literacy not only makes positive contributions to the learning community and to society, but also practices **ethical behaviors** regarding information and information technology. Standard 9 states that the student with information literacy, in addition to positively contributing to the learning community and society, effectively **participates in groups** for the purposes of seeking and generating information.

### THE BIG6™ MODEL

The Big6™ (Eisenberg and Berkowitz, 2000) is the best-known, most-used model for teaching **information and technology skills** worldwide, not only in K–12 and post-secondary education, but also adult and corporate training programs as a problem-solving approach. It integrates skills for finding and using information with technology tools for systematically locating, utilizing, applying, and evaluating information for specified tasks and needs. It focuses on both content and process.

Its stages are:

1. **Task Definition**: Define the problem and necessary information.
2. **Information-Seeking Strategies**: Ascertain all potential sources and select the best.
3. **Location and Access**: Physically and intellectually find sources and information within sources.
4. **Use of Information**: Engage by reading, viewing, listening, touching, then extract pertinent information.
5. **Synthesis**: Organize information from multiple sources and present it.
6. **Evaluation**: Judge product effectiveness and process efficiency.

Stages need not be time-consuming or sequential. Library media specialists and teachers can apply Big6 immediately by:

- using its terminology in assignments and tasks
- talking students through its process for specific assignments
- directing attention to particular Big6 actions to complete
- asking key questions

Copyright © Mometrix Media. You have been licensed one copy of this document for personal use only. Any other reproduction or redistribution is strictly prohibited. All rights reserved. This content is provided for test preparation purposes only and does not imply an endorsement by Mometrix of any particular political, scientific, or religious point of view.

## RESEARCH CYCLE

The Research Cycle (McKenzie, 2000) information literacy model contains seven steps for **student research teams** to follow:

1. **Questioning**: Formulate and "map out" or diagram research questions requiring decision-making, problem-solving, and construct their own answers.
2. **Planning**: Think strategically how to find the most reliable, relevant information for answering the questions, getting information mediation from library media specialists and considering selection, storage, and retrieval.
3. **Gathering**: Informed by stage 2, collect only pertinent and useful information.
4. **Sorting and Sifting**: According to a question's complexity, do even more systematic organization than was done in the gathering step to isolate and organize pieces of information most likely to provide insights.
5. **Synthesizing**: Arrange and rearrange pieces of information, as with jigsaw puzzles, until patterns and a picture are revealed.
6. **Evaluating**: Ask if more research is necessary. With demanding and complex questions, students typically repeat these first six steps of the cycle several times until the "information harvest" is of sufficient quality to report.
7. **Reporting**: Find and create solutions and make decisions. Report or present findings and recommendations to real or simulated decision-maker audiences.

## ALBERTA MODEL

Alberta Education's *Focus on Learning* (1990) instructional model is a five-stage **process approach** to information literacy. Reviewing the process throughout all stages is crucial.

1. **Planning**: Select the topic. Identify information sources, audience, and presentation format. Establish criteria for evaluation. Review the process.
2. **Information Retrieval**: Find and gather resources, review the process.
3. **Information Processing**: Select pertinent information. Evaluate, organize, record, make associations and connections and inferences. Synthesize it. Make a product. Revise and edit the product. Review the process.
4. **Information Sharing**: Present findings meaningfully to the specified audience, demonstrate suitable audience behaviors, and review the process.
5. **Evaluation**: Assess the product, evaluate the research skills and procedures used, and review the process again.

Reviewing the process is important for developing **student metacognition** ("thinking about thinking") and an understanding of **research as a learning process**. Major themes are developing emotional literacy, time to explore, supporting students as they work, librarian as teacher, and understanding the process approach. (Note: Due to governmental and political changes, this model has lost official support and component job positions in Alberta. However, that does not negate the value of the model itself.)

## SAUCE

The SAUCE model (Bond, revised 2009) for research, inquiry learning, and problem-solving stands for:

- Set the scene
- Acquire (information)
- Use (information)

Copyright © Mometrix Media. You have been licensed one copy of this document for personal use only. Any other reproduction or redistribution is strictly prohibited. All rights reserved. This content is provided for test preparation purposes only and does not imply an endorsement by Mometrix of any particular political, scientific, or religious point of view.

- Celebrate understanding
- Evaluate

In a summary of this model, students go through **stages** of:

- listing **contextual vocabulary**, which are key words and phrases essential to the subject they are researching
- writing important **research questions** using those key words and phrases, plus statements of need
- selecting which information they found to be **relevant** to their subject
- **validating** the information
- **reviewing** the selected information

Review is essential. If students find that any of the information they collected is inappropriate to their subject or purpose, or inadequate to their needs, they must repeat the previous stages to find better information. Bond visualizes this model in a circular diagram, showing the nature of the process. Within the circle are a figure labeled "**task or problem overview**," supported by pillars of "**subtasks**," which rest on a foundation of "**needed information**" and "**prior knowledge**." Below this structure are the stages listed above, radiating from a central "**Review**" hub.

## MISPERCEPTIONS ABOUT THE ROLE OF THE LIBRARY MEDIA SPECIALIST

According to research findings, school administrators and teachers commonly believe that school library media specialists have **roles** different from those expected by the profession itself. They tend to classify librarians according to their earlier traditional roles, which restricts the potential for which roles they can play and what results they can accomplish in schools. For example, some researchers have found that school administrators and teachers see librarians only as book stewards, and that only expect them to provide resources to the "real" educators. Researchers have concluded that media specialists who could participate more actively in instruction are **impeded** from doing so because principals and teachers do not perceive them as teachers and do not expect them to teach. The idea that school librarians only check out books rather than contributing to well-rounded, strong curriculum development, as well as ignorance of the library media center's importance to such curriculum development, interfere with fulfillment of their abilities for curriculum leadership, instruction, and assessment.

Research on the roles of librarians in school systems have found that, as reflected by educational practices, teachers and school administrators typically do not view them in the roles of curriculum development, instruction, and assessment. Because many public school personnel persist in viewing school librarians from outdated traditional perspectives, teachers often do not see them as **fellow teachers**. This perspective results in teachers' reluctance to **collaborate** with librarians, to realize that they need to assign library projects to their students, or to change their habits and cooperate with librarians. Researchers find that when teachers and administrators misperceive them this way, it **marginalizes** media specialists in terms of teaching, learning, and assessment. This prevents them from participating in **assessment**. Additionally, a media specialist serves a great many more students than each teacher does. This, combined with **understaffing**, interferes with his or her instruction and assessment.

## CHALLENGES OF TIME

National guidelines and professional research literature on library media programs have identified **time** as a factor interfering with complete development and implementation of curricular, instructional, and assessment roles of library media specialists. For example, in publications such as

Copyright © Mometrix Media. You have been licensed one copy of this document for personal use only. Any other reproduction or redistribution is strictly prohibited. All rights reserved. This content is provided for test preparation purposes only and does not imply an endorsement by Mometrix of any particular political, scientific, or religious point of view.

*Information Power* (1998), the **number of roles** theoretically defined for media specialists has met with responses by actual media specialists of feeling overwhelmed, and not believing that anyone would have the time to accomplish all of the identified roles and activities. Multiple researchers (Van Deusen and Tallman 1994, Giorgis and Peterson 1996, McCracken 2001) have found, in support of earlier study results (Ervin 1989, Stoddard 1991, Fedora 1993, McCarthy 1997), that time is consistently a factor that has impeded them from developing and implementing their roles as instructors and assessors.

## THEORY VERSUS PRACTICE

Some researchers study information literacy assessment systems through a perspective based on **activity theory (AT)**. They find this theory to facilitate analysis on multiple levels, going beyond conflicts and dualities between assessment theory and practice. AT focuses on analyzing the total object-oriented, artifact-mediated **activity system**. It emphasizes neither the wider system nor its individual subjects.

Basic system elements are:

- object and subject
- signs and tools (mediating artifacts)
- community, rules, and division of labor

The **object** is the collective, socially distributed purposes of within-system activity. This may be concrete or abstract, such as a shared idea or plan. For example, activity participants may collectively share manipulating and changing a plan into results. This is object-oriented activity's **materialization**. Participants are subjects, and collectively they form a **community**. Information literacy assessment is a **collective activity**. Community transformation of objects into results is mediated by **artifacts**. These are tools, both non-physical (as in methods, procedures, and language) and physical (technological instruments, etc.). AT can investigate **conflicts** among system elements and create new, transformative artifacts.

## ALTERNATIVE ASSESSMENT

In the Information Age, the concept of "information use" reflects a shift from emphasis on **library skills**, which are skills for locating information, to emphasis on **information skills**, which are skills for processing information. This has brought more focus on developing student cognitive skills that they can transfer and generalize, not only for using particular libraries and resources, but also for generally using information more effectively. Another influence on the movement toward **alternative assessment** is that its **philosophy** is similar to the philosophy of school library media centers. Both focus on a characteristic of continuity, complex thinking abilities, and information use. Both find the most significant part of intellectual pursuits to be using information instead of simply having it. In alternative assessments, students are required to show and utilize their knowledge and information skills through implementing some kind of activity. Media programs have missions of supporting **lifelong learning** through activities and resources. This is consistent with the alternative assessment philosophy of natural, continuous evaluation.

### NECESSITY OF ALTERNATIVE ASSESSMENTS FOR INFORMATION LITERACY

To school library media specialists, skills for **locating and utilizing information** are essential to the process of lifelong learning. So they are committed to establishing foundations for students to develop these skills and pursue such learning throughout their lives. In addition, they hold that student performance should be assessed on a **direct and continual basis**. This concept of ongoing assessment is central to the media specialist goal of constant improvement of student information

Copyright © Mometrix Media. You have been licensed one copy of this document for personal use only. Any other reproduction or redistribution is strictly prohibited. All rights reserved. This content is provided for test preparation purposes only and does not imply an endorsement by Mometrix of any particular political, scientific, or religious point of view.

literacy skills. This is consistent with the **alternative assessment philosophy** that student progress is evaluated by educators along a continuum of **performance and comprehension**. This continuum moves from elementary skills, knowledge, and understanding levels to gradually more advanced levels through qualitative differentiations of performance. Also, students are encouraged to develop and apply **higher-order cognitive skills** by both alternative assessments (which demand using skills, knowledge, and judgment in complex projects and settings) and school library media centers (which offer ways to find, analyze, interpret, evaluate, and communicate ideas and information).

## TRENDS IN ASSESSING INFORMATION LITERACY

Traditionally, school libraries emphasized developing student library skills for **locating** information. More recently, they have moved to developing student information skills for **applying** information. Library media centers agree with alternative assessments in valuing **authentic application of knowledge and higher-level cognitive processes**, such as application, analysis, synthesis, and evaluation, rather than simply knowledge and comprehension as in Bloom's taxonomy. In contrast to traditional objective tests, alternative assessments are open-ended, continuing, and use real-life contexts for more comprehensive pictures of student achievement, progress, and information use. **Portfolio assessments** give more complete, complex views of in-context student performance by collecting student products over time. They are naturally compatible with media specialist understanding because documenting activities relative to library collections and school curricula are increasingly becoming media specialist practices. **Performance assessments**, in having students complete real-world projects as professionals, show their skills in real life and let teachers assess both process and product effectiveness. Benefits include positive teaching and learning motivations, authentic incentives, and developing complex cognitive abilities.

## OBSTACLES IN IMPLEMENTING ALTERNATIVE ASSESSMENT

According to experts, to implement alternative assessments in school library media centers, media specialists must build an appropriate **learning environment**. The roles of **instruction** and **assessment** must also be correctly delimited within the assessment system. School librarians must create learning environments that:

- cultivate student reflection and complex cognitive processes
- value not only student achievement but also student progress (formative as well as summative assessment)
- establish continuity in both learning and assessment
- view and construct assessment as a learning experience
- encourage time flexibility, ownership, utilizing multiple resources, and collaboration

However, experts also caution against concentrating only on librarian-built environments in implementing alternative assessment, as this overlooks **obstacles to assessment**, which include:

- insufficient interest, time, staffing, and classroom teacher support
- excessive numbers of students or schools for adequate service
- misapprehensions of the media specialist's role

Copyright © Mometrix Media. You have been licensed one copy of this document for personal use only. Any other reproduction or redistribution is strictly prohibited. All rights reserved. This content is provided for test preparation purposes only and does not imply an endorsement by Mometrix of any particular political, scientific, or religious point of view.

# Instructional Design

## ADULT LEARNERS VERSUS YOUNGER LEARNERS

To design instruction for adult students, teachers must consider some differences between **adult learners** and **younger students**. Young students are **subject-oriented**, wanting to succeed in each course regardless of or in the absence of life goals. Adult students are **problem-centered**, wanting to find educational resources to further their life or professional goals. Young learners are **future-oriented**, as their education is. Adult learners are **result-oriented**, seeking specific educational outcomes. Young students' educations are usually **mandatory**, while adult educations are usually **voluntary**. Because young students' futures are frequently undefined, they may not **apply** knowledge immediately. Adult students frequently have **defined future plans**, seeking knowledge they can apply directly and immediately to their current lives and near-future needs. Young learners typically depend on others for **direction**; adult learners are typically **self-directed**. Young students often **accept** new information without testing or questioning. Adult students tend to **question** or test new information, skeptical about accepting it until proven. Children rely on adults to design their instruction and may not take **responsibility** for their learning. Adults are willing to be **responsible** for appropriate learning.

## PRIOR KNOWLEDGE AND EXPERIENCE

Adult learners have more knowledge and more years of experience than children. Teachers should take advantage of this, using adult students as **resources** for both their classmates and the teachers themselves. They should elicit adults' experience and knowledge through open-ended questions and design class opportunities for students to engage in **dialogues**. Adults have established opinions, beliefs, and values.

Teachers should:

- elicit adult expectations for a class or course
- invite them to challenge ideas and to engage in debate
- be protective of minority opinions within the group

Teachers should show respect for adults' comments and questions, acknowledge their contributions to classes, and not expect students to always accept or even agree with their instructional plans. Since adults require **self-direction**, teachers should:

- adapt starting and stopping times and learning paces flexibly for student needs
- expect adults to seek varied learning activities and media
- engage and include them in designing the learning process

## DIFFERENT APPROACHES TO LEARNING

Adult learners frequently take **problem-centered approaches** to learning, not merely acquiring knowledge for its own sake. Therefore, teachers should employ problem-solving groups, case studies, and other participatory strategies in their classes. Additionally, they should introduce new skills and knowledge by pointing to their practical application. Rather than academic, survey courses, adult students are usually more interested in **straightforward** instruction that tells them how to accomplish things. Therefore, when teachers present concepts and theories, they should explain their use in solving specific problems relevant to their adult students. They should also orient their course content more toward **direct applications** than to theoretical principles and orientations. Because individual differences are magnified with age, adult classes vary even more in learning styles than younger classes. Therefore, teachers should draw on a **variety of instructional**

Copyright © Mometrix Media. You have been licensed one copy of this document for personal use only. Any other reproduction or redistribution is strictly prohibited. All rights reserved. This content is provided for test preparation purposes only and does not imply an endorsement by Mometrix of any particular political, scientific, or religious point of view.

methods and materials to make connections with adults' differing styles, modalities, paces, and times of learning.

## FACTORS THAT TEACHERS OF ADULT LEARNERS SHOULD CONSIDER IN DESIGNING THEIR INSTRUCTION

Teachers should realize that adults are more **self-guided** than children in learning. Because they have greater and broader **experience**, they can bring more to a class and also take more away from it. Adults need instruction to be **logical**. Therefore, they may not engage in a learning activity simply because the teacher orders it. Although some gifted or mature young students are also known to question some learning tasks or materials ("How will I use this in my life?"), adults view themselves as **age peers** with teachers, even if not knowledge peers in some subjects. Thus they are more likely than minors to refuse certain tasks. Teachers will find **student-centered instructional design** more effective with adults than instructor-centered design. They must carefully balance the elements of the academic calendar, presentation of new material and applications, and student participation and discussion. Paradoxically, through willingness to relinquish control, teachers will achieve control, as **learner-centered approaches** are most successful with adults.

## BLOOM'S TAXONOMY

Bloom et al (1956) developed a taxonomy to classify **learning behaviors**. The domains of learning they identified were cognitive, affective or attitudinal, and psychomotor. **Bloom's Taxonomy** moves from simpler to more advanced levels in learning behaviors:

1. **Knowledge**—acquiring and retaining information.
2. **Comprehension**—understanding the information.
3. **Application**—taking information and applying it to different circumstances.
4. **Analysis**—breaking down information into its component parts and understanding their relationships.
5. **Synthesis**—putting separate pieces of information together and seeing or showing how they are related.
6. **Evaluation**—the highest level, examining or testing information and making judgments about its value and significance.

**Gagne's Taxonomy of learning** (1972) has five categories:

- Verbal information
- Intellectual skill
- Cognitive strategies
- Attitudes
- Motor skills

**Morrison** developed his formula for **mastery learning** in the 1930s: "Pretest, teach, test the result, adapt procedures, teach and test again to the point of actual learning." Bloom elaborated on this. However, mastery learning works with Bloom's lower learning levels, but not higher levels.

## INSTRUCTIONAL DESIGN

In the 1950s and 1960s, **language laboratories** became popular as automated learning tools for students to study foreign languages independently as a supplement to classes, giving them many more hours of practice time without instructors. Emerging technology led to multimedia presentations, instructional computer use, and the programmed instruction movement. B. F. Skinner and other behaviorists advocated using **teaching machines** to free teachers for more interactive, personal, higher-level relationships with students, less bound by accountability

Copyright © Mometrix Media. You have been licensed one copy of this document for personal use only. Any other reproduction or redistribution is strictly prohibited. All rights reserved. This content is provided for test preparation purposes only and does not imply an endorsement by Mometrix of any particular political, scientific, or religious point of view.

standards and requirements that machines could address. The **systems approach**, influenced by military and business applications, emphasized:

- resource analysis
- goal- and objective-setting
- action plans
- ongoing program evaluation and modification

## STANDARD SYSTEMS PERSPECTIVE

The standard systems perspective of instruction design follows a flowchart model using the following progression:

1. Conduct a needs assessment
2. Establish an overall goal
3. Conduct a task analysis
4. Specify the objectives
5. Develop the assessment methods
6. Select the media
7. Produce the materials
8. Conduct a formative assessment
9. Conduct a summative assessment
10. Revise the program as needed

## BEHAVIORIST LEARNING THEORY

Behaviorist theory proposes that all individuals learn by receiving an **environmental stimulus**, responding with an **outward behavior**, and receiving an **environmental response**, which affects future behavior by increasing or decreasing the probability of repeating the same behavior. Behaviorism disregards internal states and focuses only on **outwardly observable and measurable behaviors**. **Behavior modification** changes or shapes behavior by manipulating the antecedents that elicit behavioral responses and the consequences that increase or decrease probable repetition. Behaviorism influenced instructional design, resulting in required **behavioral learning objectives**, which are specified, measurable end results. For example, educators might specify that after finishing a learning unit, a student will answer 90 percent of post-test questions correctly.

The mnemonic ABCD represents:

- **Audience** (in this case, the student)
- **Behavior** (to answer correctly)
- **Condition(s)** (after finishing the unit; on the post-test)
- **Degree** (90 percent)

Via **task analysis**, learning tasks are broken down into smaller, measurable steps. These are connected and build on previous steps via chaining, or they reach end results through successive approximations via shaping.

### STRENGTHS AND WEAKNESSES OF BEHAVIORISTIC INSTRUCTIONAL DESIGN

A strength of **instructional design based on behaviorism** is that learners have **clear goals** and can be conditioned to **respond** automatically to cues toward those goals. Weaknesses of behaviorist instructional designs include that learners may not be able to respond when the

Copyright © Mometrix Media. You have been licensed one copy of this document for personal use only. Any other reproduction or redistribution is strictly prohibited. All rights reserved. This content is provided for test preparation purposes only and does not imply an endorsement by Mometrix of any particular political, scientific, or religious point of view.

**stimulus** required for a correct response is not presented. Also, when anomalies occur, learners or workers conditioned to respond to specific cues can fail to respond because they lack **comprehension** of the system. A strength of **cognitivist instructional designs** is that learners are trained to perform the same tasks in the same way, producing **consistency**. This can prevent problems when all workers or learners conduct exacting routines in the same manner. Weaknesses of cognitivist instructional designs include that the one way everybody learns to perform a task may not be the **optimal** way, or that it may not be the best way for certain individuals or situations.

## COGNITIVE PSYCHOLOGY

Cognitive psychology offered alternatives when behaviorism could not explain certain socially-based behaviors. For example, children demonstrate new behaviors they observed weeks before without having received reinforcement for them. And children do not imitate all behaviors receiving reinforcement. **Albert Bandura's Social-Cognitive and Social Learning Theory** addressed behaviorism's limitations, proposing that people could learn **vicariously**: rather than always needing demonstrated behaviors and reinforcement, they could observe others demonstrating behaviors and receiving reinforcement and then imitate what they observed to obtain similar reinforcements. Without discarding behaviorist models, **cognitive instructional design models** also broke learning tasks into smaller steps. They elaborated on behaviorist task analysis and added **learner analysis**, additionally developing instruction from simpler to more complex by building on **schemata** (mental constructs) developed earlier. They also set **behavioral objectives** and measured performance accordingly. The use of mnemonic devices, "chunking" of information into meaningful units, metaphors, and advance organizers, and organizing learning materials into sequences of increasing complexity all reflect cognitivist influences on instructional design.

### COGNITIVE THEORY AND INSTRUCTIONAL DESIGN

Cognitive theory has dominated instructional design and strategies. Also, cognitivists have applied many teaching strategies practiced and recommended by behaviorists, albeit for different purposes. Behaviorists determine a beginning point for instruction through learner assessments; cognitivists determine predispositions for learning through examining learners. Thus, **instructional design practices** seem more **behaviorist and cognitivist** than constructivist in orientation. The system for designing instruction used in behaviorist and cognitive approaches is more closed than in constructivist approaches, which demand more open systems. **Objective design** is more prescriptive, while constructive design is more facilitative. Objective approaches are **convergent**, with instructors predetermining content and direction. Constructive approaches are more subjective and divergent, with students determining content and direction. Hence with constructivism, **assessment** is also more subjective: rather than using specified quantitative criteria, assessment methods and tools rely on qualitative learner processes and self-evaluations. Objective instruction is considered not better, but **easier** than constructive design. Some have characterized constructivism as less of a teaching approach and more of a learning theory. Still, instructional properties ultimately determine assessment properties.

## OBJECTIVIST PSYCHOLOGY

**Behavioral and cognitive approaches** are both considered **objectivist**. They determine learning outcomes in advance. They seek to instill predetermined concepts of reality into learners' thinking via interventions in the learning process. In contrast, **constructivist approaches** view the learning process as **individualized** and hence somewhat unpredictable. They therefore believe that teaching should not control learning, but rather facilitate it. The design of learning environments to support learners' construction of their own knowledge is founded on the **internal negotiation process** of expressing mental models and using them for explaining, inferring, predicting, and

Copyright © Mometrix Media. You have been licensed one copy of this document for personal use only. Any other reproduction or redistribution is strictly prohibited. All rights reserved. This content is provided for test preparation purposes only and does not imply an endorsement by Mometrix of any particular political, scientific, or religious point of view.

reflecting on their usefulness. Another foundation is the **social negotiation process**, similar to that of internal negotiation, to the end of sharing individual realities with others. Processes of exploring real-life environments and the interventions of new environments governed by the needs, expectations, and intentions of each individual expedite constructing knowledge. Constructivist design provides **mental models** and affords authentic, relevant **context** for applying constructed knowledge. Authentic exercises should be used to support this.

## CONSTRUCTIVIST LEARNING THEORY

Whereas both behaviorist and cognitivist models of instructional design support dividing **learning tasks** into steps via task analysis, setting behavioral objectives, and measuring performance against those objectives, constructivist philosophy and psychology influenced instruction to encourage learning experiences that were more **open-ended**, depending on the individual learner. Learners are believed to construct their own knowledge. As this varies among individuals, learning methods and outcomes vary and are less readily measured. Constructivism and cognitivism share the **information-processing model's** analogy of **cognitive processes** to **computer processes**. These two approaches also commonly share schema theory, connectionism, hypermedia, and multimedia. However, while cognitivism's objective components were compatible with models used in the systems approach to instructional design, **constructivism** was not. Systems approaches design common learning outcomes for all learners, while constructivism views knowledge as constructed differently among individuals.

Constructivism implies that **learning environments**:

- offer multiple representations of reality's natural complexities
- present contextualized, authentic, real-life tasks (not predetermined teaching sequences)
- cultivate reflection
- facilitate content- and context-dependent construction of knowledge
- support collaboration versus competition

### INSTRUCTIONAL ENVIRONMENTS AND CONSTRUCTIVIST LEARNING THEORY

Instructional environments that are consistent with constructivist learning theories are based on **internal and social negotiation**—processes of creating schemata and mental models and using them to interact with the environment. Piaget called this "**accommodation**" and Norman and Rumelhart called it "**tuning and restructuring**." Creating these environments also involves sharing those constructed realities with others, as well as conducting real-life environmental exploration, individually regulated and supported by authentic learning tasks that reflect real-life experiences. Constructivist instructional design requires **learner metacognition**; i.e., analysis and understanding of one's own cognitive processes and problem-solving strategies. This is because constructivism finds that problems differ according to context. Constructivism implies that instructional design should **model** behaviors to be acquired by learners who perform at skilled, but not necessarily expert, levels. **Collaboration** among teachers and learners—with teachers as mentors and coaches, not knowledge dispensers—is another characteristic of constructivist instructional design. Constructivist design also gives learners an intellectual toolkit to enable the internal negotiations needed for constructing **mental models**.

### TECHNOLOGICAL ADVANCES AND CONSTRUCTIVISM

Technological progress in the late 20th and early 21st centuries has facilitated instructional design based on constructivist approaches. **Hypermedia** and **hypertext** permit **branching formats**, instead of limiting designers to linear modes. Also, learners have the control over instructional materials required by the active, individualized nature of constructivist learning. One drawback is

Copyright © Mometrix Media. You have been licensed one copy of this document for personal use only. Any other reproduction or redistribution is strictly prohibited. All rights reserved.
This content is provided for test preparation purposes only and does not imply an endorsement by Mometrix of any particular political, scientific, or religious point of view.

that beginning learners can get overwhelmed, disoriented, or "lost" in hypermedia. Some experts have suggested that **early learning** be accomplished via traditional, sequenced teaching and learning interactions, preset results, and criterion-referenced testing while saving constructivist learning environments for **higher learning levels**. Others recommend **prescriptive systems**, in which learners have acquired prior background knowledge and received some instruction to develop individual metacognitive techniques, so they have greater control and can retrace their steps if needed. Overall, most experts recommend **combinations** of both objectivist and constructivist instructional design. However, others reject objective and embrace constructive approaches, which they find comparable to the traditional analysis, synthesis, and evaluation of Bloom's taxonomy.

## STRENGTHS OF CONSTRUCTIONIST INSTRUCTIONAL DESIGN

One strength of instructional designs based on constructivist theory is that because learners have learned to conceive of multiple realities and have had authentic learning experiences in which both the stimuli and the students' responses vary, they are better equipped for responding to the circumstances of the **real world**, with its complexity and variance. This is in contrast to prescribed, objective learning exercises that are presented and practiced in a more uniform manner. In addition, the problem-solving skills that are nurtured in learners by constructivist instructional designs enable those learners to better **apply** their acquired knowledge to new situations. A weakness of instructional designs that are based on constructivist theory is that the divergent thinking they encourage can introduce problems into institutional systems that require all individuals to **conform** to certain standards in their behaviors.

## BEST APPLICATIONS OF LEARNING THEORIES

When learners need to master content within a field or discipline, **behavioral approaches** to instructional design are most effective. When learners need to develop problem-solving strategies and to apply acquired rules and facts to new, unfamiliar, or different circumstances than those in which they learned this information, **cognitive approaches** to instructional design are most effective. When learners need to respond to poorly-defined problems via reflection-in-action, **constructivist approaches** to instructional design are most effective. The behaviorist **stimulus-organism-response paradigm**, and its application of **reinforcement or feedback** in connection to learner responses, expedites learning rote memory tasks, stimulus discriminations, and basic paired associations—all of which require lower amounts of processing. Cognitivism lends itself to **learning strategies** like analogies, problem-solving via algorithms, and schematic structures requiring classification and executing procedures, all of which demand more processing and cognitive focus. Constructivism uses **social negotiation, cognitive apprenticeship**, and **situated learning strategies**. These help with personal choice and monitoring cognitive strategies and heuristic problem-solving—tasks again demanding high processing levels.

Copyright © Mometrix Media. You have been licensed one copy of this document for personal use only. Any other reproduction or redistribution is strictly prohibited. All rights reserved.
This content is provided for test preparation purposes only and does not imply an endorsement by Mometrix of any particular political, scientific, or religious point of view.

# Knowledge of Children's and Young Adult Literature

## GENRES OF CHILDREN'S LITERATURE

**Picture books** are one children's literature genre. Illustrations and text are interdependent in these, so they are especially suitable and engaging for younger children. Picture books are classified according to their format rather than their genre, and all genres of children's literature may be included in picture books. The **folklore** genre comes from the oral tradition, without identified authors. It comprises our literary heritage, including myths, legends, traditional stories, fairy tales, nursery rhymes, and songs from history. The **poetry and verse** genre features rhythmic language (sometimes rhyming), concentrated language and images, and imaginative perceptions and ideas. The **fantasy** genre has fantastical stories set in imaginary worlds, with creatures, characters, and events that could not exist in the real world. **Science fiction** extends the principles and physical laws of science to their logical ends, including stories about potential future events. **Realistic fiction** tells "what-if" stories presenting an illusion of reality about characters, settings, and events that could happen in reality. **Historical fiction** is set in past historical times, telling stories of real or imagined events. **Biographies and autobiographies** tell of someone's life, including memoirs, journals, diaries, and/or letters. **Nonfiction** is factual, giving information explaining concepts, subjects, or how-to instructions.

> **Review Video: Myths, Fables, Legends, and Fairy Tales**
> Visit mometrix.com/academy and enter code: 347199

## PICTURE BOOKS

Picture books (with or without text) include:

- alphabet books
- counting and number books
- books of nursery rhymes
- the Mother Goose books (considered a subcategory in themselves)
- concept books, each dedicated to a single concept, such as color, size, shape, etc.
- wordless picture books, like *Do You Want to Be My Friend?* by Eric Carle, which help children become oriented to **basic print elements** like:
  o top-to-bottom and left-to-right directionality
  o page-turning
  o story development
  o fostering imagination
  o sensory imagery
  o visual literacy
- picture books with minimal words
- toy books
- baby books
- interactive books
- predictable or patterned books, like *Brown Bear, Brown Bear, What Do You See?* by Bill Martin Jr. and Eric Carle
- picture books for older children, such as *Thank You, Mr. Falker* by Patricia Polacco, a best-selling, autobiographically-inspired story about learning disabilities, bullying, and an influential teacher

Copyright © Mometrix Media. You have been licensed one copy of this document for personal use only. Any other reproduction or redistribution is strictly prohibited. All rights reserved. This content is provided for test preparation purposes only and does not imply an endorsement by Mometrix of any particular political, scientific, or religious point of view.

**Picture story books** include pictures but do not have pictures on every single page, but only every several pages. Among picture story books are included the subgenres of nonfictional books, humorous books, and books of jokes and riddles.

### TRADITIONAL LITERATURE

Traditional literature includes **fairy tales**, such as the Brothers Grimm's collection and the English fairy tales. **Trickster tales** (stories about characters that trick others), a common theme in many cultures' folklore and oral traditions, include *Raven: A Trickster Tale from the Pacific Northwest* and *Zomo: The Rabbit,* both by Gerald McDermott. **Tall tales** also often derive from oral tradition and folklore, like *Pecos Bill and His Bouncing Bride* or Julian Lester's *John Henry.* Some examples of **religious stories** include the story of Noah and the Ark or of Jonah and the Whale, both taken from the Judeo-Christian Old Testament. **Epics** include the *Iliad* and the *Odyssey,* both long heroic poems originally sung orally by the ancient Greek poet Homer and later transcribed to print. John Steptoe's *Mufaro's Beautiful Daughters* is an example of a **folk tale**. **Fables** include Aesop's famous tales and the story of the Three Little Pigs. Gerald McDermott's *Arrow to the Sun* is an example of a **myth**. Terri Cohlene's *Dancing Drum: A Cherokee Legend* is an example of a **legend**.

### CONTEMPORARY REALISTIC FICTION IN CHILDREN'S LITERATURE

Faith Ringgold's books *Tar Beach* and *Walk Two Moons* are realistic fictional works dealing with **family** themes. Cynthia Rylant's *Missing May*, winner of the 1993 Newbery Medal, has themes of **physical, mental, and behavioral challenges**. Katherine Paterson's novel *Bridge to Terabithia,* which includes a magical forest world, involves fantasy yet still tells a realistic story on the theme of **peer relationships**. It won the 1978 Newbery Medal and has been adapted into film twice. Christopher Paul Curtis's *The Watsons Go to Birmingham – 1963* is a fictional historical novel with a **cultural diversity** theme. E. W. Hildick's *The Case of the Wiggling Wig* is a **realistic fictional mystery**. M. D. Bauer's *On My Honor* is realistic fiction on the theme of **moral decisions**. Bruce Brooks's *Moves Make the Man* is realistic fiction with a **sports** theme. Scottish-British author Sheila Burnford's famous *The Incredible Journey*, adapted into a Disney film, is a realistic story about **animals' adventures**. Beverly Cleary's (of Beezus and Ramona fame) *Dear Mr. Henshaw,* a realistic epistolary novel that won the 1984 Newbery Medal, has **rites of passage** as a theme.

### NON-FICTION AND INFORMATIONAL CHILDREN'S LITERATURE

Non-fictional and informational books in children's literature include books about foreign languages, sciences, and humanities. For example, in the **humanities**, an excellent book in the art category is Diane Stanley's *Leonardo da Vinci*, which won the 1997 Orbis Pictus Award for nonfictional children's literature. In the **music** category, a 2003 Orbis Pictus Award winner is *When Marian Sang: The True Recital of Marian Anderson: The Voice of the Century,* a biography of the legendary singer of folk and opera music who attracted integrated audiences before the Civil Rights era, by Pam Munoz Ryan and Brian Selznick. In the **social sciences** category, books about historical periods and events include Jerry Stanley's *Children of the Dust Bowl: The True Story of the School at Weedpatch Camp,* Shelley Tanaka's *Attack on Pearl Harbor: The True Story of the Day America Entered World War II,* and *The Bombing of Pearl Harbor* by Earle Rice, Jr. In the **physical sciences** category, Laurence Pringle's and Bob Marstall's book *An Extraordinary Life: The Story of a Monarch Butterfly,* for children around grades 3–4 or ages 7–8, is told in narrative style and features beautiful illustrations.

## PROMINENT AUTHORS OF HIGH-QUALITY CHILDREN'S LITERATURE
### EXAMPLES OF HIGH-QUALITY ILLUSTRATED WORKS

**Eric Carle** both writes and illustrates children's books and is well known for colorful illustrations and simple storylines for infants and preschoolers. He typically writes about animals and uses

Copyright © Mometrix Media. You have been licensed one copy of this document for personal use only. Any other reproduction or redistribution is strictly prohibited. All rights reserved.
This content is provided for test preparation purposes only and does not imply an endorsement by Mometrix of any particular political, scientific, or religious point of view.

unusual devices, like smaller pages opening to larger pages and holes in some pages. His best-known books include *The Very Hungry Caterpillar*, *The Very Quiet Cricket*, and *The Grouchy Ladybug*. Among contemporary authors, **Kevin Henkes** is prized for writing stories of animal and child characters that children find lovable, everyday circumstances to which children can relate, imaginary friends, and more. Some titles are *Jessica*, *Owen*, and *Wemberly Worried*. **Steven Kellogg** writes and illustrates children's books appealing to many different ages, using outlandish plots and creative illustrations. Some of his titles are *The Day Jimmy's Boa Ate the Wash*, *Pecos Bill*, and *The Mysterious Tadpole*. **Ruth Krauss** writes simple, direct stories full of charm, with excellent word choice and vocabulary. Many of her books feature illustrations by great children's artists like Maurice Sendak and Crockett Johnson. Her titles include *I'll Be You and You Be Me*, *The Carrot Seed*, and *A Hole Is to Dig*.

## Examples of Works with Effective Storylines and Effective Language Use

**Arnold Lobel** is an author and illustrator of children's literature. His characters are funny and their dialogue is witty. His illustrations are also known for their beauty. Some of his best-known and loved works include all of the *Frog and Toad* series, *Fables*, *Mouse Soup*, and *Owl at Home*. **Robert McCloskey** writes books with simple yet appealing story lines. He is known for using language that does not patronize children. He also provides his own detailed illustrations with old-fashioned style. Some favorite titles by McCloskey include *Make Way for Ducklings*, *One Morning in Maine*, and *Blueberries for Sal*. **Beatrix Potter**, famed for *The Tale of Peter Rabbit*, *The Tale of Benjamin Bunny*, and *The Tale of Jemima Puddle-Duck*, is the all-time best-selling children's book author. She includes wonderful characters, excellent vocabulary, a humorous and warm narrative style, and illustrations famous for their beauty.

## Other Examples of Bestselling Children's Books

**Margret and H. A. Rey** are best known for the seven original *Curious George* books (other authors later wrote books about this main character, but the Reys' original works are the most famous). As a married co-writer couple, the Reys wrote plots with universal appeal, expressed in simple, classic language. In addition to the beloved *Curious George* series, their other titles include *Billy's Picture*, *Katy No-Pocket*, and *Whiteblack the Penguin Sees the World*. **E. B. White** (also co-author with William Strunk of *The Elements of Style*) is famous for his memorable characters, brilliant writing style, excellent description, droll wit, exemplary word choice, and ability to make both his positive and negative characters appealing. His well-known titles include *Charlotte's Web*, *Stuart Little*—both illustrated by Garth Williams—and *The Trumpet of the Swan*, later illustrated by Fred Marcellino, winner of the Caldecott Award for his illustrations of Charles Perrault's *Puss in Boots*. **Margaret Wise Brown** is famous for read-aloud books for the youngest children, including *Goodnight Moon*, *Big Red Barn*, *The Runaway Bunny*, and *Seven Little Postmen*. She uses rhythmic, well-chosen language.

## Examples of Multi-Book Series in Children's Literature

Many fine children's literature authors have created **series** of books, all revolving around the same main character. For example, **Eric Hill** wrote a series about his main character, Spot. **Russell and Lillian Hoban** wrote multiple books about the main character Frances. Ian Falconer wrote a series about main character Olivia. And **Bernard Waber** published multiple stories about Lyle the Crocodile. Some great authors of literature for older children include **Madeleine L'Engle**, whose science-fiction novel *A Wrinkle in Time* (1962) won the 1963 Newbery Medal, Sequoyah Book Award, and Lewis Carroll Shelf Award, and was runner-up for the Hans Christian Andersen Award. Its sequels include *A Wind in the Door*, *A Swiftly Tilting Planet*, (which won the National Book Award), *Many Waters*, and *An Acceptable Time*. **C. S. Lewis** is best known for his *Chronicles of Narnia*, which include *The Magician's Nephew*; *The Lion, the Witch and the Wardrobe*; and five

Copyright © Mometrix Media. You have been licensed one copy of this document for personal use only. Any other reproduction or redistribution is strictly prohibited. All rights reserved. This content is provided for test preparation purposes only and does not imply an endorsement by Mometrix of any particular political, scientific, or religious point of view.

others. **Beverly Cleary** is known for her series about Beezus and Ramona. **Laura Ingalls Wilder** is famous for her *Little House on the Prairie* series. Young children can also enjoy these books via parent and teacher read-alouds and audio versions.

## AWARDS OR COMMENDATIONS GIVEN TO CHILDREN'S LITERATURE

The **Boston Globe-Horn Book Awards** are given to authors of children's literature for picture books, fiction, nonfiction, and poetry books. The **Caldecott Medal** is awarded to illustrators of children's literature by the Association of Library Service to Children. **The Charlotte Zolotow Award**, given to authors for outstanding writing in a children's picture book, is bestowed by the Cooperative Children's Book Center. The **Chickadee Award**, a part of the Maine Children's Choice Picture Book Project (a project sponsored by the Maine Association of School Libraries), is given to authors of picture books for children. The **Children's Choices Reading List**, co-sponsored by the International Reading Association (IRA) and the Children's Book Council, is a list of books evaluated and reviewed by children themselves. The **Geisel Award**, named after Theodor Geisel (more famously known as Dr. Seuss), is given by the Association of Library Service to Children to authors of books for beginning readers.

### GLOBAL AND MULTICULTURAL AWARDS

The **Golden Kite Award** is given to authors and illustrators by the Society of Children's Book Writers & Illustrators. The **Newbery Medal**, named after 18th-century British bookseller John Newbery, is awarded to authors by the Association of Library Service to Children. The **Orbis Pictus Award** is given to authors of children's nonfiction books by the National Council of Teachers of English (NCTE). The **Outstanding Science Trade Books for Students K–12 lists** are chosen by the National Science Teachers Association (NSTA) and the Children's Book Council. The **Sibert Award** is given to authors of children's nonfiction books by the Association of Library Service to Children. Global and multicultural awards include the **American Indian Youth Services Literature Award**, given to authors and illustrators by the American Indian Library Association. The **Asian/Pacific American Award for Literature** is given to authors and illustrators by the Asian American Library Association. The Association of Library Service to Children gives the **Batchelder Award** to publishers of translated books and the **Belpré Medal** to Latin-American authors and illustrators. The Ethnic & Multicultural Information Exchange Round Table gives the **Coretta Scott King Book Awards** to authors and illustrators.

### LITERARY AWARDS IN OTHER COUNTRIES

The Children's Book Council of Australia gives Australian authors and illustrators the **Children's Book of the Year Awards**. In Canada, the Canadian Library Association gives authors the **Book of the Year Award for Children**. The Canadian Library Association also gives the **Amelia Frances Howard-Gibbon Illustrator's Award** to children's book illustrators. Also in Canada, the **Governor General Literary Awards** include awards for children's literature authors and illustrators. In Great Britain, the **Carnegie Medal** is awarded to authors of children's literature by the Chartered Institute of Library and Information Professionals, which also awards the **Kate Greenaway Medal** to illustrators of children's literature.

Copyright © Mometrix Media. You have been licensed one copy of this document for personal use only. Any other reproduction or redistribution is strictly prohibited. All rights reserved. This content is provided for test preparation purposes only and does not imply an endorsement by Mometrix of any particular political, scientific, or religious point of view.

# School Library Media Center Program

**MISSION AND GOALS OF THE SCHOOL LIBRARY MEDIA CENTER PROGRAM**

The American Library Association and the Association for Educational Communications and Technology publication *Information Power: Guidelines for School Library Media Programs* (1988) describes the **mission** of the school library media center program. In their related publication, *Information Power: Building Partnerships for Learning* (1998), they define **information literacy standards** for student learning, including information literacy itself, independent learning, and social responsibility.

The mission of the media program is **ensuring effective use of information and ideas** by:

- affording physical and intellectual materials access in all formats
- instruction to further interest and competence in reading, viewing, and using ideas and information
- collaboration among educators in designing learning methods to fulfill individual student needs

The authors find this mission as relevant today as in 1988 despite social, educational, and technological changes. The way this mission is expressed in today's learning environments is in **providing services and programs** that focus on information literacy and are designed to bring about authentic, active student learning as represented in the information literacy standards.

**INFORMATION LITERACY STANDARDS AND ALIGNMENT WITH CURRICULUM**

According to the American Library Association and Association for Educational Communications and Technology, library media program goals aim to develop student-centered learning communities supported by active, creative library media programs. One goal is to design learning activities **integrated** into school curricula, giving all students intellectual access to information and assisting all students in attaining information literacy.

Educators design activities for these goals by developing **cognitive strategies** effective for student:

- selection
- retrieval
- analysis
- evaluation
- synthesis
- creation
- communication of information in all formats and all curriculum subject areas

Another goal is to give students **physical access** to information. This is achieved first by judiciously choosing and methodically organizing a local collection of **diversified learning resources** encompassing a broad range of formats, difficulty levels, and subject matter. Second, it can be gained by applying systematic procedures to acquire materials and information from **outside the library and school**, such as interlibrary loans, electronic networks, cooperative agreements with information agencies, and instruction in accessing local and remote data in all formats via various equipment.

Copyright © Mometrix Media. You have been licensed one copy of this document for personal use only. Any other reproduction or redistribution is strictly prohibited. All rights reserved.
This content is provided for test preparation purposes only and does not imply an endorsement by Mometrix of any particular political, scientific, or religious point of view.

## INTEGRATION OF TECHNOLOGY AND LIFELONG LEARNING

The goals of the school library media program include providing learning experiences to promote the development of students and others into both **discriminating information consumers** and **skillful information creators**. Such learning experiences are accomplished via the delivery of comprehensive instruction in the complete range of **communications technology and media**. The program also seeks to assist, collaborate with, and lead teachers and others to apply **instructional design principles** to the uses of information and instructional technology for student learning. An additional goal is to furnish students and educators with activities and resources that accommodate a broad range of **individual differences** in learning styles, teaching styles, interests, methods, and abilities, and that teach attitudes and behaviors that promote **lifelong learning**.

## PROVIDING PHYSICAL AND INTELLECTUAL ACCESS TO INFORMATION

**Goals** of the school library media center program include:

- providing physical and intellectual access to information
- teaching cognitive strategies to facilitate higher-order thinking skills, including discrimination and skill in working with, using, and creating information
- applying principles of instructional design to information use
- using available information technology for learning
- accommodating diverse needs, styles, abilities, and methods
- promoting attitudes and behaviors for lifelong learning

Another goal is to offer a program that serves as the school's **information center**—not only by being a center for interdisciplinary and integrated learning activities in the school, but also by providing access to comprehensive information for learning **beyond** this center. Additionally, the program seeks to furnish learning activities and resources representing **diverse** social and cultural perspectives, experiences, and opinions, and to reinforce the ideas of **information access** and **intellectual freedom** as prerequisites to responsible, effective democratic citizenship.

## LEARNING, TEACHING, AND INTEGRATING INFORMATION LITERACY INTO CURRICULUM

An example of a goal for a school library media program is that a program is necessary to teaching and learning, and therefore it must be **integrated** completely into the school's curriculum to facilitate the achievement of learning goals by the students.

Some examples of related objectives are that the library media specialist:

- must develop a comprehensive knowledge of the school's **curricula** at all grade levels and in all subject areas, and must further student skills in **information literacy** across the curriculum
- should participate actively in **school technology committees** at all levels where they are established
- should work together with the teachers and other members of the school's staff for the purpose of **integrating** the required competencies in information literacy throughout the entire process of learning and teaching

## KNOWLEDGE OF STATE STANDARDS AND SCHOOL CURRICULUM

The school library media specialist's knowledge of the school's curriculum and instruction is essential to how he or she contributes to teaching. Teachers regard media specialists as not only credible curriculum knowledge sources, but also as experts on curricula for **multiple grade levels and subject content areas**, as well as on the curricula for the teachers' own grade levels and the

Copyright © Mometrix Media. You have been licensed one copy of this document for personal use only. Any other reproduction or redistribution is strictly prohibited. All rights reserved. This content is provided for test preparation purposes only and does not imply an endorsement by Mometrix of any particular political, scientific, or religious point of view.

specific subjects they teach. Teachers realize that media specialists have the valuable, wider **perspective** afforded them by knowing what all of the teachers and classes in the school are doing. Teachers additionally regard them as **peers**: teachers as well as librarians. Furthermore, teachers respect their additional and unique **skills** that the teachers themselves do not have. For example, media specialists have higher levels of technological competency, broader knowledge of electronic and print resources, abilities for innovating, and fearlessness for trying out new things. They **motivate** teachers through their attitudes and beliefs of what teachers can accomplish.

## Change Agents for Teachers and Schools

According to research evaluating school library media centers and staff, the media specialists not only **enrich the curricula** for teachers by contributing many resources, but they also collaborate with teachers in **developing innovative new learning units** and **revising established units**. These contributions improve curriculum, raise student interest, revitalize the teachers, and enhance expectations. Thus media specialists are regarded as **agents of transformation and change** by teachers because they are not fearful of "pushing the envelope." They extend this courage to teachers in the form of **support**. As a result, the teachers become less afraid of trying new methods and processes as well. Teachers in schools with effective media programs have commented that the media specialists have **transformed their curricula** in ways such as changing from using only textbooks to incorporating research-based instruction and simulations.

## Collaborators, Resources, and Sources of Support

Because library media specialists spur teachers to experiment and progress, and function as change agents, one might think their tendency to disrupt the status quo would cause friction with teachers, but this is not the case. Instead, they have achieved **smooth collaborations** with teachers. Teachers continually seek out their expertise, finding them to be invaluable sources of support, assistance, and ideas. Their help in **identifying resources** saves countless hours of work for teachers. Even with time to search, teachers would lack **knowledge** that media specialists have to find such a variety of resources. Also, teachers realize that on their own they often cannot learn about **new technologies**, familiarize themselves with them, and incorporate them into the curriculum. Media specialists introduce these, so without their contributions, teachers recognize these innovations would not become part of their instructional programs. In schools with effective media programs, media specialists are indispensable learning community members.

## School Library Media Specialist as an Educator

In schools with superior library media programs, the school personnel regard these as **instructional programs**. They view their media specialists not simply as librarians, but as teachers and educators. In these schools, the principals arrange staff support to enable media specialists to spend most of their time working on **instructional activities** with the students and teachers.

These activities include:

- collaborative teaching
- teaching technology skills and information literacy
- planning instructional units with teachers
- helping students with school projects
- delivering professional development to other members of the school staff

Research surveying many schools has found that compared to most of their work hours in exemplary programs, media specialists with average programs spent only around one-quarter of their time on such activities. In the schools with exemplary programs, they acknowledge that to be

Copyright © Mometrix Media. You have been licensed one copy of this document for personal use only. Any other reproduction or redistribution is strictly prohibited. All rights reserved.
This content is provided for test preparation purposes only and does not imply an endorsement by Mometrix of any particular political, scientific, or religious point of view.

effective, they must be **teachers** as well as librarians, and that this role is essential to their media program because their primary goal is to help students learn.

## QUALITY LIBRARY MEDIA CENTERS

Studies find that the best library media centers are regarded as **central** to the life of the school by administrators, teachers, and students. They may be described as the "heart" of the school, and in these schools it is common for class demand for media center visits to exceed the capacity to accommodate them, due to limitations on staff and space. Some programs have books covering the entire school year, where teachers can **schedule class visits** far ahead of their instructional units because the demand is so great. In some schools, teachers check every morning for openings before the school day begins. Teachers want to bring their students to the media center because students want to be there, and because teachers recognize that working with media specialists benefits students. The best media centers provide safe, inviting, warm, and exciting **environments** for the students. Students appreciate the variety of resources, the relaxing atmosphere, and the help with schoolwork.

## EXCELLENT LIBRARY MEDIA CENTERS THAT ATTRACT STUDENTS

Students are attracted to library media centers partly because of the media program's ability to meet and accommodate the needs of all **individual students**, including those not interested in reading and those in special education. This is accomplished by the library media specialist. At schools with exemplary programs, teachers and principals alike observed that their media specialists could reach students initially uninterested in reading, encouraging them not only to read, but to read extensively, and even to compete in reading contests.

They use various techniques to achieve these results:

- enticing reluctant readers by including low-reading level, high-interest books and audiobooks in their collections
- finding jobs for these students in the media center, getting them engaged and excited about the program
- learning individual students' interests and finding books about these
- recruiting students to review books and publishing the reviews for student body access
- encouraging non-reading students by helping them create slide show presentations and demonstrate their technological competencies to express themselves

## RELATIONSHIPS BETWEEN SCHOOL ADMINISTRATORS AND EFFECTIVE LIBRARY MEDIA SPECIALISTS

In schools with the best library media programs and media specialists, principals have thorough knowledge of the program because media specialists have invited them to walk through the media center often and have initiated regular communications. Principals realize the impact of media programs on **teaching** and **student performance**. They trust, admire, and respect media specialists. They have high expectations for programs to fulfill the complete range of **roles** available. Media specialists have gained their principals' confidence for proposing good ideas and making a difference in their schools. Their abilities and contributions are noticed. Principals surveyed by researchers have responded that the media specialists have the best knowledge of **standards** among the school staff, initiates **planning and communication**, and knows the **curriculum**.

Copyright © Mometrix Media. You have been licensed one copy of this document for personal use only. Any other reproduction or redistribution is strictly prohibited. All rights reserved. This content is provided for test preparation purposes only and does not imply an endorsement by Mometrix of any particular political, scientific, or religious point of view.

Principals report that they are an essential asset to their instructional program and that their strengths include:

- teaching
- listening
- collaborating with teachers
- taking proactive positions
- finding better methods
- teaching students how to be active learners

Hence principals support and promote library media programs by holding **faculty and parent meetings** in the media center.

## COLLABORATIVE CURRICULUM PLANNING AND DEVELOPMENT FOR A SCHOOL LIBRARY MEDIA PROGRAM

One example of a goal for a library media center program is to provide both a **model** and the **promotion** of collaborative curriculum planning and development. Two objectives for the library media specialist related to this goal are:

- to use the school's essential curriculum in media as the foundation for planning the curriculum and instruction
- to work together with teachers and other members of the school staff to develop curriculum content that incorporates the requisite skills in library media and technology

The **library media and technology skills** for students to develop should be the ones identified in the goals and objectives found in the school system's essential curriculum in media, as well as those identified in the school system's description of the scope and sequence of library media skills.

## TEACHING AND LEARNING GOAL FOR A SCHOOL LIBRARY MEDIA PROGRAM

One example of a goal for a school library media center is that it should **model** and **further** collaborative, effective, and creative practices in teaching. Associated with this goal are two objectives for the library media specialist:

- to adhere to the school system's established guidelines or framework for excellence in teaching and learning
- to design and execute activities for teaching and learning, both on an individual basis and collaboratively with teachers and other members of the school staff, reflecting the best instances of the most current research and practice

Copyright © Mometrix Media. You have been licensed one copy of this document for personal use only. Any other reproduction or redistribution is strictly prohibited. All rights reserved.
This content is provided for test preparation purposes only and does not imply an endorsement by Mometrix of any particular political, scientific, or religious point of view.

# Collection Development

## Collection Development

### SELECTION POLICY AND CRITERIA

Many public-school systems dictate that each instruction department office form a committee for reviewing and selecting materials to set **criteria** that will further their essential curricula's knowledge and understanding. Philosophies and procedures established in national, state, and county documentation are expressed in school system **selection policies**. These policies in turn guide school library media specialists, who are responsible for reviewing, evaluating, and selecting their libraries' media collections. The media specialists collaborate with teachers and school administrators in **supplying resources** that promote development of thinking abilities, further the whole educational program of the system, and reflect diversity among points of view. They develop **collections** that can fulfill personal as well as curricular needs. To meet these needs, media specialists use recommended tools for selection and apply selection standards and approved selection criteria.

### PRINCIPLES OF INTELLECTUAL FREEDOM

The American Library Association's (ALA) *Library Bill of Rights* defines **principles of intellectual freedom** that are commonly reflected in the selection policies of most school systems' library media centers. The National Council of Teachers of English (NCTE) publication, *Students' Right to Read*, also expresses such principles. The ALA and the American Association of School Librarians publish additional position statements about intellectual freedom. An additional source is *Information Power: Guidelines for School Library Media Programs*, also from the American Association of School Librarians. In addition to reflecting these principles, school library media center selection policies also comply with federal laws governing **Internet protection and safety** by requiring that their wide-area networks (WANs) use proxy servers to filter information appropriately.

A few **selection criteria** for library media materials include:

- appropriateness for different ability levels, interests, and information needs among all students
- relevance to the school system's curriculum needs and instructional objectives
- content that is accurate, objectively presented, and from authoritative sources

### SUPPORTING DIVERSITY IN MATERIALS

In today's global environment, library media materials should share global perspectives, view and support diversity as a positive characteristic of society, and encompass materials from authors and illustrators representing all world cultures. Materials with political, social, and religious content should be of an **informing** rather than **indoctrinating** nature.

Media materials should represent all people's essential **humanity** and should not include:

- discrimination
- biases including racial, ethnic, sexual and other biases
- stereotypes, distortions, caricatures, or other offensive content

Copyright © Mometrix Media. You have been licensed one copy of this document for personal use only. Any other reproduction or redistribution is strictly prohibited. All rights reserved. This content is provided for test preparation purposes only and does not imply an endorsement by Mometrix of any particular political, scientific, or religious point of view.

Regarding controversial subject matter, library media should represent **diverse viewpoints**. Library media centers must afford equal student access to **all views and information** on a topic. Access to varied resources enables students to develop problem-solving and critical thinking skills. Media materials should be provided in print, non-print, multimedia, electronic, and other **varied formats** to address diverse student learning styles and needs, thus facilitating the most effective instruction in the school system's curricula.

## ONGOING ASSESSMENT OF MATERIALS

The materials in a school library's media center should be subjected to **ongoing assessment** regarding the currency of their information, relative to the purposes and content of the library items available. **Copyright dates** should be recent as these apply to the subject matter contained in the media items. When evaluating materials for selection, library media specialists should consider whether the literary style and quality, technical quality and merit, aesthetic properties, and physical arrangement of all media in all formats are acceptable. Media specialists should evaluate the **cost effectiveness** of their selections in terms of accessibility, expected frequency of use, and durability. In addition, library media specialists must consider whether materials will be appropriate for use by students with **special needs**, as well as by all other students.

## PRODUCTION AND EXPANSION OF INFORMATION IN THE INFORMATION AGE

The exponential increase in the speed and quantity of information produced in the Information Age poses challenges for library media specialists in their decision-making for current student and teacher resources. One expert, John Naisbitt, has commented that, "we have for the first time an economy based on a key resource (information) that is not only renewable, but self-generating. Running out of information is not a problem but drowning in it is." The selection policy's purpose is to raise **educator awareness** about multiple factors to consider when choosing information resources. Media specialists must communicate the **scope and purpose** of the selection policy, as well as coordinating **selection** of library media, with input from students, teachers, and parents. They should also use **reviews** of materials by professional review journals and other authoritative selection references, such as *Periodicals for Schools* from EBSCO Information Services (formerly *Periodicals Catalog*), *Public Library Core Collection* (formerly *H.W. Wilson's Standard Catalogs*), and *ICTS Instructional Materials Catalog*.

## SELECTING PRINT MATERIALS

Book materials are expensive, so library media specialists should consider these **criteria for selection**:

- durability of a book's bindings
- quality of paper
- density of printed text
- style of typeface
- layout
- illustrations (when applicable)
- readability
- the interest levels it appeals to and addresses
- indexing (where applicable)

Experts recommend **hardcover books** as first copies of picture books in library media centers. Another resource for saving money while adding to the collection is **paperback books**. These can support special student projects and in-depth studies, duplicate existing titles for multiple checkouts, and expand collection items for leisure reading.

Copyright © Mometrix Media. You have been licensed one copy of this document for personal use only. Any other reproduction or redistribution is strictly prohibited. All rights reserved. This content is provided for test preparation purposes only and does not imply an endorsement by Mometrix of any particular political, scientific, or religious point of view.

Media specialists can use the following considerations when choosing **hardbacks versus paperbacks**:

- cost and use of paperbacks versus hardback
- how books will be used (popular fiction, independent reading, duplication of classics, research)
- curriculum demands on the school's books

## PERIODICALS AND JOURNALS

Periodicals meet the needs of both school curriculum and student leisure reading. **Instructional library periodicals** and **professional review journals** are potential acquisitions. Library media specialists should also explore obtaining online access to **full-text periodical databases** for reference. They should also consider Internet access to both full-text databases and limited editions of **newspapers**, like the *New York Times* and local newspapers. They may also order hard copies of newspapers as needed. If library media specialists know of certain **pamphlets** that would support their schools' curricula, they may order these for their media collections. Experts recommend organizing pamphlets by subject in an information file rather than complete cataloging. General selection criteria apply to pamphlets. Schools need reference materials for access to **comprehensive information**, for both specific subject content areas and general application. Reference materials also function as tools for access to additional information from public, academic, school, and electronic collection sources.

Considerations for print and electronic reference materials include:

- projected use (and thus cost-effectiveness)
- authoritativeness
- indexing
- arrangement
- user-friendliness

## SELECTING NON-PRINT INSTRUCTIONAL MATERIALS

Many school systems include an **annual exhibit** in their process for reviewing instructional materials, where publishers and producers can showcase their **non-print instructional materials** and technologies. These are generally public for faculty, students, and other citizens to preview materials available to the schools. Library and Information Technology departments of school systems typically create committees to preview and evaluate non-print instructional materials under consideration for **acquisition**. Library media specialists can also request specific titles to preview and evaluate. Generally, when materials are included in a school system's library catalog of instructional media, their purchase is approved.

In addition to following selection criteria for print materials, non-print materials require other **criteria** to consider:

- audio and video presentation quality
- format appropriateness
- accuracy of information
- variety of media formats for meeting curricular needs
- technical quality
- text and graphics that are not overly dense
- whether non-print media support curriculum and further instructional objectives and goals

Copyright © Mometrix Media. You have been licensed one copy of this document for personal use only. Any other reproduction or redistribution is strictly prohibited. All rights reserved. This content is provided for test preparation purposes only and does not imply an endorsement by Mometrix of any particular political, scientific, or religious point of view.

## SELECTING ELECTRONIC RESOURCES

Software and online resources afford increased information access. Database services charging fees should provide 24-hour **remote access** from homes as well as schools. Website licensing agreements and available network versions should also be considered; state education departments often establish criteria for evaluating these. Print materials selection criteria also apply. Electronic resources should afford **control to students** via varied difficulty levels, optimized linking and branching, and flexibility in pace. Electronic information should be **maintained** reliably and accurately. Electronic resources should include navigation tools, search capability, and organization that facilitate the retrieval of information. When applicable, these resources should provide options for **management and record-keeping**. Electronic text should be readable, layouts should be visually appealing, and graphics should be attractive. The documentation provided in electronic resources should be comprehensive, yet easy for students to understand. Electronic resources should always be designed to be **user-friendly**.

## BUDGET

Experts have observed that one way of measuring the way a school values its library media program is by how robust and stable that program's **budget** is. Budgets have been impacted lately by the rise in cost of **printed materials**. Also, the **numbers of programs** required at the school level have multiplied in recent years. This larger number of total school programs causes more diversification, and hence division, of the school budget. As a result, the programs already existing within the school are left with even smaller budgets than before. Considering the impacts of these factors, the library media specialist must collect facts, figures, and other data; analyze these; understand them thoroughly; and then articulate them clearly to their school principals when they meet to discuss their budgets. They must have this **supporting information** at their fingertips in order to justify the needs for the library media program's budget.

## ASSESSING GAPS IN MEDIA CENTER COLLECTIONS

School library media specialists need to assess the status of their current media center collections to make a plan for remedying weaknesses and gaps. They also need to develop **collection development plans**. They need to know about local curricular initiatives and student performance to inform such planning. Additionally, they need to understand their district and school **budget processes**. They may have to do some detective work to discover this information, since the majority of media specialists are mostly uninvolved in the budget allocation process. To advocate for the budget they want, they need to know or find out what and who **influence** budget allocations. In the school library media center, the **constituents** include students, teachers, school administrators, parents of students, and other community members. The American Association of School Librarians (AASL) has published articles, such as the *School Library Program Health & Wellness Toolkit* (2008), which share ways to obtain budget support.

## ASSESSING AND PLANNING BUDGETS

Library media specialists must assess and plan their budgets to account for higher costs of materials. A budget that stays the same every year or is decreased is cause for concern. **Operations costs**, as well as **inflation**, have impacts on the library budget. Budget cuts are reflected in decreased library materials. Over time, this impact increases exponentially, damaging the enhancement or even maintenance of the collection. Reduced buying causes **gaps** in the collection. A substantial infusion of new money must be made within several years to fill these gaps and restore the collection to currency. By calculating average cost per book, plus inflation cost, the media specialist can deduce the collection's **deficit** and its actual **reduction** in the numbers of

Copyright © Mometrix Media. You have been licensed one copy of this document for personal use only. Any other reproduction or redistribution is strictly prohibited. All rights reserved. This content is provided for test preparation purposes only and does not imply an endorsement by Mometrix of any particular political, scientific, or religious point of view.

library books present. The Bureau of Labor Statistics website has an **inflation calculator** for determining inflation costs. They can add about a dollar a year per book for increased book costs.

## ADVOCATING FOR BUDGETARY CONSIDERATION

Library media specialists can refer to the **Bowker Annual** to determine the real costs of library materials and to find out the current increases in the costs for juvenile periodicals. In addition to these, they must account for higher numbers of student enrollments in their school, the expenses for adopting new school curricula and/or new initiatives, and also what impact such curricular adoptions will have on their collection development for the library media center. To **advocate** effectively for the media center budget, they must know their own influence in the process of budgetary education. When they present their budget to principals and others, they can argue for better student achievement by **correlating** media center needs with the school or district's academic content standards. They should relate any increased spending they request directly to **specific student performance** on academic achievement tests and to **specific curriculum requirements**. Traditional documentation of collection analysis gives a graphic representation of collection data, which can greatly help in preparing their budget reports to administrators.

## THE SCOPE OF SCHOOLWIDE BUDGETING

Experts advise library media specialists not to settle for seeing the budgeting process as entering purchase orders into the "black hole" of the system. Rather, they should fully understand the entire process of **budget allocation**. This will better prepare them to develop educational messages to district stakeholders to justify and advocate for library spending. They should also understand how the school district makes decisions about **district-wide spending**, not just library spending. They should additionally comprehend the school district's overall budget status. They should **meet** annually with either their administrators or the treasurer of the school district for the specific purpose of discussing the library budget. The first step for the media specialist to understand the budgeting process is to find out which school district personnel have **access** to the district budget and **influence** over it, and the role they play in the overall process of **budget allocation**.

## TRENDS IN DISTRICT-WIDE SPENDING

To identify trends in district-wide spending, school library media specialists should study:

- their school districts' expenditures
- their own libraries' past spending
- the logic used to justify that spending
- the timing of expenditures
- increases and decreases in spending over time

To educate and communicate effectively with **stakeholders** about the library media program budget, they should analyze **communication patterns** among the primary personnel who control the district budgeting process, and should make and implement a plan for disseminating information that stakeholders can easily grasp.

Media specialists should be able to:

- identify what kind of budgets they have
- know the categories of the budget and the "rules" that govern them
- set up a system for keeping records
- understand the terminology used relative to budgeting

Copyright © Mometrix Media. You have been licensed one copy of this document for personal use only. Any other reproduction or redistribution is strictly prohibited. All rights reserved.
This content is provided for test preparation purposes only and does not imply an endorsement by Mometrix of any particular political, scientific, or religious point of view.

## Long-Term Budgeting Plans

Library media specialists must work with a committee to prepare **long-term budget plans** to present to main stakeholders. First they must identify the library's **primary goal**. An excellent way of connecting library goals to school district goals is correlating library resources with academic content standards, which places focus on successful academic student performance. Supplemental resources enriching curriculum will assist teachers; this can be a library goal. To **correlate library and district goals**, media specialists should target the district or school "**bottom line**," such as student achievement or test scores and library services and expenses. They can then identify marketing evidence, and make an action plan for collecting, analyzing, and communicating documentation with administrators, teachers, parents, and community members. Stakeholders should not only witness such data, but also participate in evaluating them. Data should address both short-term and long-term planning.

**Budget plans** should cover:

- how to increase revenue and decrease spending (for instance, elimination and consolidation)
- collaborations for budget adjustments for library services affected
- publicizing budget information
- impacts of budget increases and reductions on curriculum support

## Factors that Affect Evaluating Budgets and Resources

As experts on research evaluating public school libraries have noted, evaluations made after funding, budgets, and staff have been cut will not yield findings as accurate or effective as those made during more **stable** times. For example, **student performance** may appear unchanged despite decreased library resources due to the time lag involved. Also, when **library staffing** that usually depends on the size and level of the school becomes flat because of resource reductions, evaluative studies may find correlations that are statistically significant but are very small; the amounts that library factors contribute to student performance will likewise be shown as very minor. Additionally, library studies in various states in the early 21st century did not examine how changes in student performance were related to **changes in library operations, resources, and staffing**. Considering trends toward decreasing library staffing, experts say that library evaluations need to research ways for libraries to continue their positive influences in spite of smaller staffs.

## Collection Development

Collection development is an integral part of the instructional process. **Collection development** is the continual process of finding library media collection **strengths and weaknesses** in meeting students' needs. This process shows that school funding is being used judiciously, and that the collection addresses both the demands of school curriculum and independent student needs in reading and viewing.

## Collection Development Process

There are three components of the collection development process:

- **School community analysis**: student needs at specific schools are analyzed for collection development to address their unique requirements, beyond the general library collection similarities nationally.
- **Library media collection assessment**: the current collection's quality is evaluated through systematically gathering data on the collection's number of titles, age, and ability to satisfy curriculum demands.

53

Copyright © Mometrix Media. You have been licensed one copy of this document for personal use only. Any other reproduction or redistribution is strictly prohibited. All rights reserved. This content is provided for test preparation purposes only and does not imply an endorsement by Mometrix of any particular political, scientific, or religious point of view.

- **Materials acquisition**: according to the school system's available funds, its selection policy, and the library media center's needs ascertained through collection assessment, library media center specialists select and acquire new materials.

## CORE COLLECTION TOOLS

Core collection tools are selection reference sources that are authoritative in nature. They differ from professional review journals mainly because they are updated on an **annual** basis, whereas review journals have new editions published on a bimonthly or monthly basis. **Core collection tools** can be useful to library media specialists because they can use them as references when evaluating the **quality** of their library media collections, and because they can consult them to determine whether specific resources are **available** from different producers and/or publishers.

Core collection tools that are recommended by experts include:

- Children's Catalog
- Elementary School Library Collection
- Junior High School Catalog
- Senior High School Catalog

Media specialists can obtain these core collection tools from the Library Administration and Management (LAMS) Professional Library. Alternatively, they can buy them in their local areas.

## ONLINE SOURCES USED AS REFERENCE TOOLS TO FIND REVIEWS OF MEDIA

In their collection development, school library media specialists can use a variety of online resources for reviews of library media materials to inform their selection of library media center materials.

Some of these **online review sources** include the following:

- the ALAN Review from Virginia Tech University Libraries
- the Barnes and Noble website
- The Book Reporter
- Booklist Online
- BookWire
- the Bulletin of the Center for Children's Books
- the Caldecott Medal Home Page
- Children's Book Reviews from the National Parenting Center
- the Children's Literature Web Guide
- the Education Review
- the Follett TITLEWAVE
- the Newbery Medal Home Page
- the Neverending Stories site
- the Teen Reading site from the YALSA (Young Adult Library Services Association)
- the Young Adult Books website

The *Periodicals for Schools* from EBSCO Information Services (formerly *Periodicals Catalog*) includes many of these online resources for library media specialists to purchase.

Copyright © Mometrix Media. You have been licensed one copy of this document for personal use only. Any other reproduction or redistribution is strictly prohibited. All rights reserved.
This content is provided for test preparation purposes only and does not imply an endorsement by Mometrix of any particular political, scientific, or religious point of view.

## USING APPROPRIATE RESOURCES FROM THE INTERNET

To aid in collection development, media center specialists working in school libraries can find many **Internet resources** for reviews of various books that are appropriate for media centers. These include both **professional review journals** and popular sources of **general reviews**.

Some of these online resources include:

- Amazon.com, under the headings of Children, Teens, and General
- the Book Links website
- BookReview.com
- BookPage
- the Boston Book Review site
- the website named Carol Hurst's Children's Literature
- the Children's Books website
- the Coretta Scott King Award Home website
- the Educational Software Review website
- the Multicultural Book Reviews site
- the website entitled Notes from the Windowsill
- World of Reading (a collection of children's book reviews written by actual children)

Media specialists can buy many of these online resources for book reviews from the *Periodicals for Schools* catalog from EBSCO Information Services (formerly *Periodicals Catalog*).

## ALIGNING COLLECTION DEVELOPMENT WITH SCHOOL CURRICULA

Collection development in school library media centers should focus on supplying media that satisfy the needs of the **school curriculum**. Library media specialists should be familiar with their school system's essential curriculum. They should also provide access to the school system's **curriculum guides**. Experts recommend that every school library media center keep a copy of each curriculum guide used in the school. Media specialists must also be aware of all current **additions and changes** made to school curricula, and understand what impacts these changes have on their collection development. A significant component of the selection process is **communicating with teachers** in evaluating curricular recommendations and needs. They can assure the value and strength of the media collection when teachers are actively engaged in the selection process, because this collection is a vital part of the learning and teaching processes. They should also invite **recommendations from students and parents** about subject areas and resources where they need more information for curricular and personal reasons.

## ASSESSMENT AND INVENTORY PROCESS

Collection development includes **assessing** curriculum and student body needs relative to the library's media resources. Library media specialists typically develop **long-range and annual plans** to guide continuing assessment. Assessing the library media collection includes taking inventory of its materials, assessing those materials relative to the needs generated by school units of curriculum and instruction, and weeding out inappropriate or outdated materials. During **inventory**, physical items are compared with automated cataloging system entries to discern whether resources are still present in the collection and whether they still meet current selection criteria. This is to assure that the automated cataloging system accurately reflects the collection so that students and teachers can find the information they need. **Barcode scanning** expedites this process without interrupting school library programs. Experts recommend performing inventories **annually**. This provides crucial data about collection quantity and quality to inform decision-making to meet student and staff needs.

Copyright © Mometrix Media. You have been licensed one copy of this document for personal use only. Any other reproduction or redistribution is strictly prohibited. All rights reserved.
This content is provided for test preparation purposes only and does not imply an endorsement by Mometrix of any particular political, scientific, or religious point of view.

## WEEDING

Weeding is essential to assessing a library's collection; for helping to maintain its utility, accuracy, and relevance; and for helping use space more efficiently. Materials should be **weeded** for several reasons:

- being in poor physical condition
- not having been circulated in the past five years
- being outdated in accuracy, content, or use

While **copyright dates** are considerations, they should not be the only criteria for weeding, as some materials are **historically valuable** and/or **classics** and should be preserved despite age.

Additional weeding criteria include:

- poor or mediocre material quality
- material content that includes stereotypes or biases
- materials with inappropriate reading levels
- materials duplicating information not in high demand
- materials with information now superseded by revised or newer information
- materials with unattractive and/or outdated design, format, illustrations, and graphics
- materials missing tables of contents, search capacity, and/or sufficient indexing, thereby making information inaccessible
- materials not aligned with selection criteria

## WITHDRAWING MEDIA MATERIALS AND KEEPING CONSIDERATION FILES

Ultimately, library media specialists decide whether to withdraw materials from the library's media collection. However, they may also invite grade-level teachers, subject area teachers, and other members of the school faculty to **review** the library items they have marked to be withdrawn before they remove them. Experts caution library staff and teachers not to send the withdrawn items to **classrooms** because all instructional materials in a school are subject to the same quality standards. Withdrawn materials are typically sent to **school system distributions centers** or **warehouses** to be recycled. For future acquisitions, the media specialist should keep a **consideration file**. Staff recommendations, materials reviews, and information on school needs should be kept in this file. Creating and maintaining consideration files is expedited by current technology: **databases** can be created for entering resource recommendations and ordering information, and for generating resource ordering lists.

## REBINDING

Books that library media specialists or others cannot repair locally are reordered or rebound. **Rebinding** is typically not cost-effective or good-looking, resulting in plain cloth covers lacking dust jackets, illustrations, or printed titles. Likely rebinding candidates include **expensive reference books** and **updated textbooks** that must be kept in the collection. Books with torn, brittle, or dirty pages should not be rebound, but reordered. The merit of out-of-print books must be carefully considered before making rebinding decisions. A local school library's **materials allotment** for the following year pay for book rebinding costs, which are estimated at an average of **25 percent** of the books' replacement costs. To prepare for rebinding, media specialists should ensure that each book has the minimum binding requirement of **three-quarters of an inch inside margins** to make it readable. They should remove circulation cards from the books, update their library automation program with records of books sent for rebinding, box books according to their school system's specifications for pickup, and deduct rebinding charges from their budgets.

Copyright © Mometrix Media. You have been licensed one copy of this document for personal use only. Any other reproduction or redistribution is strictly prohibited. All rights reserved. This content is provided for test preparation purposes only and does not imply an endorsement by Mometrix of any particular political, scientific, or religious point of view.

## VENDOR CATALOGS AND ONLINE ORDERING

When library media specialists need to know whether materials are available, and to prepare orders for acquiring new materials, they can use **catalogs** from publishers and jobbers. However, they should remember that these sources are not selection tools but marketing devices. Experts advise media specialists to create and maintain a file **of publishers and producers**, but to use their judgment and only include the most appropriate and useful catalogs for their media collections. Although some of these catalogs include sources of materials reviews, those listed do not necessarily contain only positive reviews. Other resources include certain **jobbers** who will, on request, produce **bibliographies** of specified materials, such as multicultural media, including references to reviews of the items. These bibliographies can help media specialists prepare **purchase requisitions**. Ordering online expedites faster delivery of materials, significantly decreases paperwork, and saves the school systems the expense of preparing purchase requisitions.

## RECONSIDERATION OF INSTRUCTIONAL MATERIALS OR OTHER LIBRARY MEDIA RESOURCES

Library media specialists must consider **intellectual freedom principles** and the rights of citizens to express their opinions whenever someone raises a concern about library media resources and instructional materials. They must support student and parent or guardian rights to deem some materials **inappropriate**. Public school systems usually have a procedure and form for submitting objections about resources to their curriculum and instruction departments.

Experts recommend several steps for school library media specialists to respond to **reconsideration requests**:

- Listening to requests objectively and calmly
- Briefly outlining school materials' selection procedures or criteria for the complainant
- Asking the complainant to complete the school system's designated reconsideration request form and submit it to the designated office
- Informing the appropriate office of the identified resource and complaint
- Discussing the complaint, the resource's purposes and use, its professional reviews, and the selection procedures or criteria with the school principal
- NOT removing the item before a committee decision regarding the reconsideration request

## LIBRARY CATALOGING

According to the Association for Library Collections and Technical Services (ALCTS) Cataloging and Classification Section, Cataloging of Children's Materials Committee (*Cataloging Correctly for Kids*, 5th ed., Fountain, 2010), children's different developmental needs indicate different **bibliographic practices** with printed and non-printed library materials. Teachers, parents, and other adults also realize benefits from **cataloging for children** as they seek age-appropriate content for younger readers in catalogs designed to give straightforward yet complete information. General-use catalogs differentiate children's content in libraries through different locations, as well as through subject headings subdivided into "**juvenile literature**" for nonfiction and "**juvenile fiction**." In 1966, the Library of Congress (LC) created the Annotated Card (AC) program, including cataloging practices and policies for special classification options, subject heading modifications, and annotations. Today, headings used with children's materials are called **Children's Subject Headings (CSH)**. Originally on catalog cards with LC annotations, the AC program is now accessible in MARC (Machine-Readable Cataloging) records and the LC Cataloging-in-Publication (CIP) program.

### STANDARDIZATION OF CATALOGING PROCEDURES

In the 1960s it became easier and/or less expensive for libraries to use centralized and/or commercial processing services, so it became necessary to **standardize cataloging procedures**.

Copyright © Mometrix Media. You have been licensed one copy of this document for personal use only. Any other reproduction or redistribution is strictly prohibited. All rights reserved. This content is provided for test preparation purposes only and does not imply an endorsement by Mometrix of any particular political, scientific, or religious point of view.

Later, the emergence of **shared databases** with records contributed by multiple libraries reinforced this need. Without a universal standard, many libraries received **nonstandard cataloging** from different sources and customized their cataloging to meet individual library needs according to research from American Library Association (ALA)'s Resources and Technical services Division (RTSD)'s Cataloging of Children's Materials Committee. Additionally, cataloging standard and style changed with cataloging source changes, while cataloging customization expenses detracted from spending on other services. Moreover, the Committee anticipated broader distribution of standardized cataloging through widespread bibliographic utility use via MARC standards development. Such wider standardization would necessitate **standardization guidelines**, which resulted in the 1969 Committee recommendation for national adoption of **Library of Congress (LC) standards** for children's materials cataloging. The Cataloging and Classification Section of the RTSD (renamed Association for Library Collections and Technical Services [ALCTS] in 1989) later adopted this recommendation.

## TECHNOLOGICAL ADVANCEMENTS IN CATALOGING

In the 1980s, the Association for Library Collections and Technical Services (ALCTS) adopted **Library of Congress (LC) practices** for cataloging children's resources as a national standard. Subsequently, commercial processors utilizing MARC (Machine-Readable Catalog) records and other bibliographic utilities have enabled more libraries to take advantage of **shared cataloging**. Technological progress makes data increasingly compatible, and increasingly cost-effective, for libraries to embrace standardization. Additionally, **globalization** has affected international production and exchanging of bibliographic data, with libraries as well as commercial processors accessing them. Consequently, ALA accepted the LC's cataloging practices for children's materials as its standard. The Cataloging of Children's Materials Committee developed "Guidelines for Standardized Cataloging of Children's Materials" with the cooperation of the LC's Children's Literature Team, History and Literature Cataloging Division (formerly Children's Literature Section). The board of directors of the ALCTS (then-Resources and Technical Services Division [RTSD] Cataloging and Classification Section) accepted these guidelines in 1982. Many smaller libraries were able to **automate** their catalogs from cards to online system via broad adoption of MARC records and acquire up-to-date records from materials vendors and LC. Globalizing content and MARC standards prompted renewed guideline updates in 2005.

## AGE APPROPRIATE MATERIALS

The Association for Library Collections and Technical Services (ALCTS), the American Library Association's (ALA) cataloging division, adopted Library of Congress (LC) practices as its standard for **children's literature cataloging**. Standardization guidelines were adopted in the 1980s and revised accordingly with advances in technology and globalization in 2005. Guidelines indicate **juvenile collections** apply to catalog users through roughly age 15, or 9th grade. However, high school libraries can benefit from the uniformity of applying the same guidelines optionally to grades 10 through 12. If library collections include materials for all levels of teenagers, ALA encourages catalogers to apply the **LC standard** for all ages and grade levels. MARC format dictates field 008 for Books, position 22 to show intended material level. General use through 9th grade, or age 15, is defined by code j.

Narrower target audience descriptors use the following codes:

- **a** = preschool
- **b** = K–3
- **c** = grades 4–8, or preadolescent
- **d** = grades 9–12, or adolescent

Copyright © Mometrix Media. You have been licensed one copy of this document for personal use only. Any other reproduction or redistribution is strictly prohibited. All rights reserved. This content is provided for test preparation purposes only and does not imply an endorsement by Mometrix of any particular political, scientific, or religious point of view.

- **g** = general, including adults
- **j** = grade 9, or age 15, also known as juvenile.

Items suited to multiple audiences take the code for the primary target audience.

## CATALOGING RESOURCES

***Anglo-American Cataloguing Rules,*** 2nd edition (AACR2, as of 2010) and its latest amendments and revisions is a national cataloging tool that can be used with the American Library Association (ALA) guidelines for cataloging children's library materials. When materials become available to each library, its final rules of **Resource Description and Access (RDA)** should be used instead of the amendments and revisions. Policies in ***Library of Congress Rule Interpretations* (LCRI)** are another tool to use with ALA guidelines. If a specific library applies AACR2, it should also apply Library of Congress interpretations of it. Another tool is ***Cataloger's Desktop***, a Web subscription product and CD-ROM with electronic versions of most often-used cataloging documentation resources. Some libraries use this instead of printed documents. Another tool is the ***Library of Congress Subject Headings* (LCSH)** and modifications to the Annotated Card (AC) program and Children's Subject Headings (CSH), with principles for application, issued yearly and published daily online at http://authorities.loc.gov whenever these deviate from *Subject Headings Manual* instructions for non-juvenile cataloging. Individual libraries using *Library of Congress Classification* or *Abridged Dewey Decimal Classification and Relative Index* schedules should use these with ALA guidelines.

## GUIDELINES AND RULES FOR CATEGORIZING JUVENILE CATALOGS

American Library Association (ALA) guidelines for cataloging library materials and resources for children, pertaining to **description and access**, cover these areas:

- description of print, electronic, and other non-print materials and resources
- names, titles, and series access points for different kinds of children's materials
- use of subject headings for juvenile catalogs
- how juvenile library collections are classified

**Rule 1.0D2** in the *Anglo-American Cataloguing Rules,* 2nd edition (AACR2), covering the **second level of description**, should be followed for descriptions of material to be **cataloged**. An exception is made for materials that require extremely detailed description; the **third level of description** is used in such instances. The **first level of description** is similar to the abbreviated cataloging that many libraries formerly used. However, because this level does not allow for components that many libraries find important, the guidelines require the second level.

Such significant components include:

- statements of responsibility
- subsequent responsibility statements, such as those about illustrators
- series information
- dimensions

## GENERAL MATERIAL DESIGNATION

American Library Association (ALA) guidelines strongly recommend rule 1.1C, subfield h of MARC field 245, or the **general material designation (GMD)** for all children's library materials that are in **non-book formats**. *Anglo-American Cataloguing Rules,* 2nd edition (AACR2) makes the GMD optional, and *Library of Congress Rule Interpretations* (LCRI) applies it only selectively; however,

Copyright © Mometrix Media. You have been licensed one copy of this document for personal use only. Any other reproduction or redistribution is strictly prohibited. All rights reserved. This content is provided for test preparation purposes only and does not imply an endorsement by Mometrix of any particular political, scientific, or religious point of view.

ALA guidelines urge its use. These guidelines dictate placing GMD in **[square brackets]** immediately after the title, because it is meant for identifying the wide category of materials in which the item belongs and differentiating among various forms of the same work at the beginning of the description. The GMD should come after the title proper, but before any other title information, including any subtitle. The GMD "text" for books is optional, and most libraries do not use it. The **International Standard Book Number (ISBN)**, whenever available, is required by ALA guidelines. It is MARC field 020. Multiple ISBNs should all be included in individual 020 fields. MARC records show ISBNs early in the record, preceding the rest of the description. In catalog cards, ISBN and price and availability are entered following the Notes area.

## SHARING LIBRARY RESOURCES

Federal copyright, copyright exemption and other laws enable and govern many **library resource-sharing activities**. From these laws, core guidelines for resource-sharing practices have developed. Resource-sharing librarians should know about **licenses and licensing agreements** between libraries, library consortia, and vendors, which supersede the laws. Librarians can offer **standardized services** that improve their libraries' lending and borrowing services, and that comply with current guidelines and laws for sharing resources when they know these rules and regulations. Best practices include the National Commission on New Technological Uses of Copyright Works (CONTU)'s **Rule of Five**—not requesting more than five articles from the same journal title from the last five years within one calendar year without paying copyright fees. Compliance with **U.S. Code, Title 17** copyright law and related guidelines, in providing local document scanning and borrowing copies, is another best practice. So are including **copyright restriction notices** on copies for patrons and other libraries, and on material request forms. Librarians should collaborate with consortium or library personnel to assure electronic resource licensing does not prevent **Interlibrary Loan**, and use databases, spreadsheets, and other mechanisms for tracking which subscriptions allow or disallow this.

### *TECHNOLOGY AND INTERLIBRARY LOAN*

Technology use saves library personnel time and money, reduces errors and user waiting time, and helps integrate **interlibrary loan (ILL) processes** into overall library functions. This streamlining can be accomplished through efficient, effective **technology use**, rather than necessarily buying the costliest, newest products.

**Best practices** include:

- familiarity with technology tools and offers
- possible ILL management software, either stand-alone or via the library media specialist or integrated library system
- using document transmission software
- using all ILL system features, such as custom Online Computer Library Center (OCLC) holdings
- taking advantage of tools colleagues have developed
- reviewing ILL automation yearly
- using ILLiad Odyssey trusted sender and DOCLINE routing tables
- implementing ILLiad, Relais, Clio or another ILL management system for statistical and tracking records management
- supplying staff with enough workstations for accessing bibliographic and electronic resources, and for electronic transmission and scanning
- networking workstations for sharing ILL forms, data, and other resources on group servers
- keeping software and hardware current

Copyright © Mometrix Media. You have been licensed one copy of this document for personal use only. Any other reproduction or redistribution is strictly prohibited. All rights reserved.
This content is provided for test preparation purposes only and does not imply an endorsement by Mometrix of any particular political, scientific, or religious point of view.

- requesting items via state-of-the-art electronic methods
- sending copies electronically whenever possible
- networking with colleagues
- maximizing overall technology use whenever possible

## RAPID CHANGES IN RESOURCE SHARING

The field of resource sharing is undergoing rapid changes and developments. This requires librarians to maintain current and continuing knowledge about a broad variety of subjects ranging from copyright law to software and hardware, like scanners. To keep up with technological changes and new and varying trends, and to learn new skills, librarians must pursue **continuing education**. They must also **network** with other resource-sharing librarians to learn about new products, trends, and changes in technology and practice. Additionally, librarians can develop personal relationships with colleagues through networking. This is important when they have a special request or need assistance locating an item.

**Best educational and networking practices** include:

- attending regional and national librarianship conferences
- joining pertinent discussion lists
- availing themselves of free or inexpensive webinars and other trainings
- visiting other libraries' ILL departments
- logging in to ALA Connect to volunteer for a RUSA STARS (Sharing and Transforming Access to Resources Section) Committee

## RESOURCE SHARING AND COPYRIGHT LAWS

RUSA recommends the following for **resource-sharing laws and guidelines**:

- Interlibrary Loan Code for the United States
- Circular 21: Reproductions of Copyrighted Works by Educators and Librarians (U.S. Copyright Office)
- updates on regulatory and legislative events affecting resource sharing and libraries from RUSA's STARS Legislative and Licensing Committee (available by logging into ALA Connect)
- U.S. Code Title 17, Section 109 – First Sale Doctrine, enabling libraries to lend physical resource materials they acquire under whatever conditions they decide
- the Rule of Five from the National Commission on New Technological Uses of Copyright Works, or CONTU, presented by the Coalition for Networked Information.

The **Library Copyright Alliance (LCA)** is highly recommended for exploring current topics regarding copyrights and libraries, including related U.S. court cases, like *Costco v. Omega* (2010) regarding copyright law's First Sale Doctrine and copyright infringement considerations. LCA is also recommended for international copyright and treaty information. The **Copyright Clearance Center** is a resource for content licensing clarifications; licensing solutions; and copyright verification, registration, and education.

Copyright © Mometrix Media. You have been licensed one copy of this document for personal use only. Any other reproduction or redistribution is strictly prohibited. All rights reserved. This content is provided for test preparation purposes only and does not imply an endorsement by Mometrix of any particular political, scientific, or religious point of view.

# Physical Arrangement of Resources

## CURRICULUM MATERIALS CENTER (CMC)

Curriculum materials centers are the physical locations of **curriculum materials collections**, serving the research and teaching needs of faculty and students in college and university programs that prepare P–12 school educators. These collections contain **educational resources** for curriculum and instructional development and lesson planning. Centers should be discrete facilities, located near the college or university library or within the Education Department building, accessible according to Americans with Disabilities Act (ADA) specifications. In the library, the center should keep library hours; in the education department, hours should accommodate user needs, including evenings and weekends as necessary.

**Size** should allow:

- collection growth
- materials
- equipment
- study areas
- workstations
- staff workspaces
- technical library functions

**Seating** should accommodate:

- average teacher education class sizes
- individual and collaborative work
- variety including carrels, tables, lounge seating
- child-sized seats if young children will use the center

Curriculum materials centers need their own classroom or formal teaching space, including technology enabling demonstration and hands-on practice with electronic and media resources. Sufficient computer ports and electrical connections are needed for users and staff, as well as maintenance to assure materials safety and security.

## GUIDELINES FOR PHYSICAL ACCESS TO CMCS

Curriculum materials center collections should be organized for easy user access. They should be arranged **systematically**, with some materials shelved as **discrete collections** and others **inter-shelved** when applicable. Collection materials should not be remotely stored, but rather **openly accessible**, except for historic or reserve collection resources. The collection's **organization** should enable ADA-compliant, easy physical access to all materials. The **shelving** should be adequate to accommodate all of the collection's items, and should be suitable for the different sizes, shapes, and types of collection materials present. The center should also have enough **signage**, and appropriate kinds of signs, posted clearly to direct users to the different areas included in its collection. Signs should be easily visible to all users of the curriculum materials center.

## PROCESSING CMC COLLECTIONS

Processing of any curriculum materials center collection should make access to materials easy. Processing of collection items should achieve a balance between **convenience** to ensure easy access and **reinforcement** to preserve items through multiple circulation transactions. The local **policies and procedures** relevant to collection materials should be documented in writing within

Copyright © Mometrix Media. You have been licensed one copy of this document for personal use only. Any other reproduction or redistribution is strictly prohibited. All rights reserved.
This content is provided for test preparation purposes only and does not imply an endorsement by Mometrix of any particular political, scientific, or religious point of view.

the center. Units with multiple pieces should be **packaged** sturdily, maintained to keep all pieces intact, and packaged with consideration of user access (labeling their containers with the numbers and types of items inside). When applicable, individual pieces within multiple-piece units should each be marked with the unit's **call number** to facilitate returning them to the right container if they are separated. All items should be consistently and clearly **labeled** to make it easier to retrieve collection items from the shelves. **Theft detection equipment** should be installed whenever possible.

## CMC CIRCULATION POLICY

In a curriculum materials center where future P–12 teachers preparing at colleges and universities research, study, and develop curriculum and instruction plans, the center should make its **circulation policy** available in writing. This policy should include identification of the different **user groups** that the center serves and of the privileges and restrictions for each of these groups. The policy should also identify **circulation periods** and any restrictions for each kind of collection material available in the center. Potential **penalties** should also be defined in the center's circulation policy.

Other policies to be defined include:

- recalls
- holds
- interlibrary loan policies and procedures
- policies with respect to distance-learning students

In addition, the circulation policy should include encouragement and/or support for the use of an **automated circulation system**.

## EQUIPMENT GUIDELINES IN CMCS

Equipment in a curriculum materials center should be **appropriate** and **current**, in numbers that meet user needs in accessing all electronic and other non-print materials contained in its collection. It should be located near the **non-print materials**. Equipment should be appropriate for accessing all kinds of non-print media in the CMC collection. It is important to maintain an amount sufficient for meeting usual levels of user demand. Equipment location should afford convenient user access to the non-print media collection. The CMC should have sufficient budget and technical support to assure regular maintenance, keeping equipment in good functioning condition. To address the demands introduced by new technologies, the equipment should be updated regularly. To enable CMC user access to hypermedia applications—the use and/or combination of plain text, graphics, video, audio, and hyperlinks for presenting information in non-linear formats—computer hardware and software should be supplied in the CMC.

## YOUNG ADULT LIBRARY SERVICES ASSOCIATION (YALSA) GUIDELINES

2012 YALSA guidelines include soliciting **community teen feedback** for designing and planning **teen library spaces** to meet their needs, develop policies promoting this space, and enable their sense of space ownership. The **environment** should promote teens' intellectual, emotional, and social development while being: age-appropriate, teen-friendly, current, vibrant, comfortable, open, inviting, fun, colorfully decorated and accessorized, and ADA-compliant.

It should also:

- enable extensive display of teen digital, print, and artistic products
- appeal to diverse interests, backgrounds, and groups

Copyright © Mometrix Media. You have been licensed one copy of this document for personal use only. Any other reproduction or redistribution is strictly prohibited. All rights reserved.
This content is provided for test preparation purposes only and does not imply an endorsement by Mometrix of any particular political, scientific, or religious point of view.

- include discrete areas for quiet, studying, entertainment, and socializing
- have digital and print collections
- foster teen senses of library appreciation, community engagement, and belonging
- reflect the communities served
- be sized proportionately to community teen population
- allow unobtrusive staff supervision via visibility
- provide teen librarian workspaces

Collection materials should support teen educational and leisure needs, including:

- diverse formats (like games, music, audiobooks, graphic novels, manga, and anime)
- timely evaluation, weeding, and maintenance
- durable, practical, and adaptive furnishings and technology
- teen-appropriate acceptable-use and age policies
- social networking and portable technology
- assistive hardware and software
- wireless capability and adequate network infrastructure

## USE OF SOCIAL MEDIA AND TECHNOLOGY IN TEEN LIBRARY SPACES

In teen library spaces, YALSA recommends:

- interaction
- supporting and utilizing social media and modeling their appropriate, safe use
- letting teens share work, exchange feedback, and develop community
- supporting peer and adult collaboration
- allowing content contributions and administrative rights to teens as well as staff
- library website use, networking, and support
- staff support of Skype, texting, and chat
- capabilities and support for virtual program participation
- virtual instruction, drop-in sessions, and/or classes in new technologies
- disability accessibility
- inclusion of teen-produced videos, photos, and other content adhering to library release policy

**Virtual spaces** should reflect:

- 21st-century learning standards
- complex information environments
- diverse perspectives
- ethical use of social tools and information

**Teen spaces** should:

- support multiple literacy development (textual, visual, digital, and technological information navigation)
- support global or diverse perspectives
- support virtual and physical sharing and learning
- support intellectual and social learning and information networks
- connect knowledge to community issues and real life
- teach teens to respect creator and/or producer intellectual property rights and copyrights

Copyright © Mometrix Media. You have been licensed one copy of this document for personal use only. Any other reproduction or redistribution is strictly prohibited. All rights reserved.
This content is provided for test preparation purposes only and does not imply an endorsement by Mometrix of any particular political, scientific, or religious point of view.

- express personal learning via artistic and creative formats
- use technology to organize and exhibit knowledge others can view, evaluate, and utilize

Copyright © Mometrix Media. You have been licensed one copy of this document for personal use only. Any other reproduction or redistribution is strictly prohibited. All rights reserved.
This content is provided for test preparation purposes only and does not imply an endorsement by Mometrix of any particular political, scientific, or religious point of view.

# Information Access

## DIFFERENT FORMATS OF LIBRARY RESOURCES

In libraries, information is found in several different **formats**. According to the individual format, it is stored, shelved, processed, and presented differently. For example, books are typically shelved in certain areas, while materials on microfilm or microfiche, magazine issues, and DVDs are all respectively shelved in separate areas.

When users come to the library to research, they should first check:

- what materials are available
- the format of the materials
- for which kinds of users the materials are designed
- where materials are located
- how to use various library tools to access these materials
- how to make effective use of the materials

Historically, libraries held mainly **print materials**, including books and periodicals. Today, they also include slides, audio, video, and other **multimedia materials**, as well as **electronic materials** like Internet databases and CD-ROMs. Regardless of the format, all information must always be **accessible** to researchers and other library users.

## ACCESS POINTS

Access points are methods for users to gain access to resources. The **four major access points** are by author, title, subject, and keyword. Historically, library resources could only be accessed via the first three of these, which all represent "group-concepts." With the advent of **digital library materials**, users could search for materials by **keywords** (meaningful words), in addition to or instead of looking only among author names, book or journal titles, or subjects. Keywords enable users to customize their searches and make them more **specific**, increasing the probabilities of finding what they want. They are not limited by knowing only certain author names, certain titles, or looking within only certain subject areas. Keywords include results across all of these fields, including ones the researcher did not know. Users of today's libraries may access print books and periodicals, multimedia, and electronic resources separately, as these differ in nature and intended use as well as format.

## FUNCTION AND FORMAT RELATIVE TO HOW USERS SEARCH FOR MATERIALS

Beginners at library research may sometimes confuse function with format with respect to library tools or resources. This interferes with searching efficiently. Library equipment and materials include **tools for accessing information resources** as well as the resources themselves. Library users are familiar with seeing newspapers, magazines, journals (periodicals) and books in print as the most common and visible library materials. However, books are also on tape, CD, and e-books. Periodicals may also be in electronic and/or microfiche formats. Likewise, tools for accessing library materials and information about them have various formats. The **library catalog** may be on traditional cards, in books, or in computer format. Regardless of its form, the catalog's function is to inform users of books available in that library and their locations. The **index** is a library tool that enables users to find periodicals on specific topics. It shows specifically which issues of each periodical include articles on given subjects, including dates and page numbers. Indexes may be in book or digital format.

Copyright © Mometrix Media. You have been licensed one copy of this document for personal use only. Any other reproduction or redistribution is strictly prohibited. All rights reserved. This content is provided for test preparation purposes only and does not imply an endorsement by Mometrix of any particular political, scientific, or religious point of view.

## MEETING DIVERSE STUDENT LEARNING NEEDS AND SUPPORTING SCHOOL CURRICULUM

A library media program should be developed and evaluated through collaborative efforts to meet diverse student learning needs and to support the school's curriculum.

Associated with this goal, the library media specialist has three objectives:

- to develop a **comprehensive knowledge**, and maintain the **currency**, of:
  o the school curriculum
  o its students' needs and characteristics
  o the informational and instructional resources available across the complete range of subject areas and formats
- to establish an ongoing **process** for collection development and evaluation, and to direct this process
- to keep and maintain a varied array of current and appropriate **techniques and tools** for locating and making selections among the available media materials

## CONNECTING SCHOOL TO THE WIDER LEARNING COMMUNITY

By providing the students, teachers, and other members of the school staff with access to information, a school library's media program has an important function of **connecting** the school to the **wider learning community**.

Two ways in which the library media specialist can help to fulfill this function of the library media program are:

- initiating, organizing, and directing the access to information resources, both inside of the school and out
- working to develop and advance relationships between the school and its library media center and external sources of information (for example, with government agencies, with public libraries, and with business organizations—both locally in the community and beyond—that will serve to support the process of learning)

## ESTABLISHING AN ATMOSPHERE THAT SUPPORTS LEARNING

Library media programs should afford atmospheres supportive of learning. Library media specialists can realize this goal by creating and maintaining an attractive, inviting **physical environment** in the library media center. They can also **organize** the media center's space, equipment, resources, and materials to promote learning.

To ensure the **conformation** of the program with legal, professional and ethical guidelines, media specialists can:

- develop and continue their understanding of current regulations and laws governing copyrights, access, and other legal concerns related to the library media program
- show their commitment to the intellectual freedom, confidentiality, users' rights, and other principles of the library profession related to intellectual property
- work together with school administrators, teachers, and others on developing and disseminating policies and procedures to advocate complying with copyright laws and similar pertinent regulations
- serve as models of responsible and ethical use of information and information technology

Copyright © Mometrix Media. You have been licensed one copy of this document for personal use only. Any other reproduction or redistribution is strictly prohibited. All rights reserved.
This content is provided for test preparation purposes only and does not imply an endorsement by Mometrix of any particular political, scientific, or religious point of view.

## INTELLECTUAL FREEDOM

An example of a goal for a school library media program is to have, as a part of its foundation, the commitment to ensuring the right to **intellectual freedom**. The library media specialist can have objectives that work to fulfill this goal:

- protecting against any obstacles that would interfere with such intellectual freedom
- serving as a model of the characteristics of freedom and vigor in debating, and of the attitude of being open to ideas, that are associated with a democratic society
- working to further the principles of intellectual freedom by offering resources and services that function to establish and maintain a climate of free and open inquiry, and by actively advocating for intellectual freedom within the school environment

## LIBRARY BILL OF RIGHTS

The American Library Association (ALA) Council adopted "Access to Electronic Information, Services, and Networks: An Interpretation of the Library Bill of Rights" in January 1996. Thereafter, the ALA Intellectual Freedom Committee generated a set of **sample questions and answers** to clarify the applications and implications of that interpretation. Facilitating **free access** to all information resources is the professional responsibility of librarians; however, ALA also acknowledges that with **digital information**, many questions cannot have single answers, and individual libraries must develop and implement their own policies consistent with their missions, goals, users, local laws and court rulings. Electronic media provide heretofore unknown **innovations** for sharing ideas and information, as the U.S. Constitution's Founding Fathers imagined. Free access to **digital networks, services, and information** is necessary for libraries to realize their vision. The nation's information infrastructure incorporates libraries as essential components. Libraries offer access to and participation with digital information, and are basic to the Constitution's requirement of **informed debate**, which includes all citizens.

### DIGITAL ACCESS TO INFORMATION AND MINORS

School and other libraries whose missions include services to **minors** are responsible for making information available to the fullest extent necessary for children to become members of the **informed electorate** conceived of in the U.S. Constitution. To develop the information literacy skills required today, students also need opportunities for **responsible participation** in the digital community. Minors have First Amendment rights as do adults. Though parents and guardians have rights to limit their children's access to digital information, librarians must also remember that federal and state laws and institutional policies affect **minors' access** to digital information resources, and must accordingly afford such access to the extent permitted by law. While parents have the responsibility to decide what digital information their children access, library personnel can help them understand their choices but should not enforce or police parental limits in libraries. The *Library Bill of Rights* and ALA guidelines espouse **children's rights** to library resource and information access as inalienable and integral to informed adulthood; this includes access to digital information resources.

### PROTECTING USER CONFIDENTIALITY RELATIVE TO DIGITAL INFORMATION ACCESS

Librarians must know their state and local user **confidentiality laws** regarding library records. Consistent with these laws and ethical and professional duties, librarians should routinely review and assure the policies and procedures to preserve **confidentiality** of personally identifiable information about use of library facilities, services, or materials. They must stringently protect electronic records of **individual usage patterns**. Protocols and software should be designed to delete **personal identifiers** from digital database tracking functions automatically and in a timely manner. **System computer terminal access** should also protect user privacy; for instance, users

Copyright © Mometrix Media. You have been licensed one copy of this document for personal use only. Any other reproduction or redistribution is strictly prohibited. All rights reserved. This content is provided for test preparation purposes only and does not imply an endorsement by Mometrix of any particular political, scientific, or religious point of view.

should not be able to see on a monitor, or readily retrieve from a cache or buffer, the previous user's access and use information. Libraries and their institutions' methods for monitoring the durations of using digital information, and amounts of computer time reserved by users, must also protect user confidentiality rights. Library-provided digital resources like databases, as well as third-party contractors, network providers, licensors, and vendors should permit **anonymous searches** without disclosing personally identifiable information, consistent with the American Library Association Code of Ethics and confidentiality laws.

## DIGITAL INFORMATION RELATIVE TO POLICIES, USER CATEGORIES, AND PATRONS WITH DISABILITIES

Librarians must consider several things when creating, distributing, archiving, retrieving, and accessing **digital information**. Thus the ALA firmly enjoins libraries to formally adopt, and periodically revisit, **policies** they develop out of their individual libraries' or institutions' missions and goals. Some libraries distinguish among **user categories**. For example, public libraries may differentiate between residents and non-residents. Accordingly with missions to espouse curriculum support, school library media centers may include parents and community members as groups that may access their collections. Academic libraries may classify users as students, faculty, or others. Depending on how they define their primary clients, special libraries may have policies of **variable access**. Such user classification should not automatically dictate differential access levels. The Americans with Disabilities Act (ADA), the Individuals with Disabilities Education Act (IDEA), and other federal and state laws prohibit **discrimination** against people with disabilities by public service providers, both publicly and privately regulated—including digital information access and all other library information services. Software, adaptive devices, and human help afford **universal digital information access**.

## FREE ACCESS VERSUS CHARGING FEES FOR DIGITAL INFORMATION

When librarians, facing economic challenges, consider charging fees versus providing more information, the ALA advises that **free services** take priority over charging fees, because charging patrons money constitutes an obstacle to their information access. ALA cautions that librarians should resist the temptation to institute **user fees** as a way to relieve economic constraints because it would not be worth the long-range costs of public loss of confidence in libraries and loss of institutional integrity. While ALA concedes that libraries without any public funding or other primary support may have greater needs to charge fees, it still recommends avoiding this whenever possible to prevent obstacles to accessing information and to attain equitable information access. According to the ALA, services without fees whenever possible means that digital information is free of charge on **monitor screens** (although some libraries may charge patrons for printouts). If interlibrary loan is free to all students, then special formats of interlibrary loan materials for students with disabilities must also be free.

## POLICIES CONCERNING DIGITAL INFORMATION ACCESS

The U.S. Constitution and the *Library Bill of Rights* are the foundations for policies related to access for all forms of media, including digital. Individual library missions and objectives as institutions also inform their access policies.

Specific **policies and guidelines** from the ALA include:

- "Economic Barriers to Information Access: An Interpretation of the Library Bill of Rights"
- "Guidelines for the Development and Implementation of Policies, Regulations and Procedures Affecting Access to Library Materials, Services and Facilities"

Copyright © Mometrix Media. You have been licensed one copy of this document for personal use only. Any other reproduction or redistribution is strictly prohibited. All rights reserved.
This content is provided for test preparation purposes only and does not imply an endorsement by Mometrix of any particular political, scientific, or religious point of view.

- "Services to Persons with Disabilities: An Interpretation of the Library Bill of Rights"
- "Minors and Internet Activity: An Interpretation of the Library Bill of Rights"

Any **restrictions** to place, time, and manner of library access should be reasonable—only when required for meeting important library management objectives and only in the least restrictive possible way. ALA advises libraries to establish policies assuring wide access to all types of information resources. Policies should never limit which patrons access information, how they access it, and information types accessed.

## INTELLECTUAL INFORMATION ACCESS

A goal for a school library media center program is to furnish **intellectual access** to ideas and information for the purpose of learning. Related to this goal, **objectives** for the library media specialist include:

- collaborating with teachers and others in developing and applying a **collection development policy** that enables access to appropriate and current information resources
- working together with teachers and others in developing **policies and procedures** that will give appropriate access to Internet and other external information resources
- helping students and school staff to identify **information resources** that are appropriate, and showing how to use them, via resource lists, bibliographies, and similar vehicles, and via providing comprehensive reference services
- participating in relevant **professional development activities** on a continuing basis

## PHYSICAL INFORMATION ACCESS

A goal for a school library media program is to give **physical access** to learning resources and information. Related to this goal, the library media specialist should:

- work together with teachers, administrators, and others in designing and renovating the **facilities** of the school library media center, as well as in identifying instructional and informational technology and all other physical elements for **acquisition**
- identify both the traditional and electronic **equipment and resources** that are the most advanced and appropriate to support the access and production of information associated with student learning needs.
- **organize** all of the school library media center's resources for their most efficient and effective application
- coordinate the **acquisition and circulation** of all library media center materials
- encourage **flexibility** in the access afforded to the services and programs that are available from the school library's media program

## EQUAL AND FLEXIBLE INFORMATION ACCESS

A goal for a school library media program is to provide equitable and flexible **access** to ideas, resources, and information in support of the purpose of learning. Associated with this goal, three objectives for the library media specialist are:

- working together with other members of the learning community in the development and implementation of **policies and practices** that will make available facilities, resources, and professional help at the same time that learning is taking place

Copyright © Mometrix Media. You have been licensed one copy of this document for personal use only. Any other reproduction or redistribution is strictly prohibited. All rights reserved.
This content is provided for test preparation purposes only and does not imply an endorsement by Mometrix of any particular political, scientific, or religious point of view.

- establishing and maintaining an **environment** in the library media center that fulfills the information needs of all of the students and teachers in the school
- encouraging all members of the learning community to **use** all of the library media program's services and resources as much as possible

## MARC

The acronym MARC stands for **Machine-Readable Cataloging**. "Machine-readable" means that this cataloging record can be read and interpreted by a computer. "Cataloging record" refers to the same bibliographic information that would appear on a paper card from a traditional card catalog.

The **cataloging record** includes the following contents:

- the main entry
- additional entries
- subject headings
- the call number or classification number
- a description of the item

These contents will not necessarily appear in the order listed here. MARC records frequently include a lot of additional information. The *Anglo-American Cataloguing Rules* (most recent edition revision) are used by librarians for composing **bibliographic descriptions** of an item in a library. The paragraph sections of a catalog card contain this description.

Included in the description are:

- title
- edition
- publication information
- physical description
- statement of responsibility
- details specific to materials
- standard numbers
- series
- notes

### ACCESS POINTS TO MARC

The AACR gives rules for people to look up library items in the library's catalog with "**access points**" to the MARC (Machine-Readable Cataloging) record. Access points are typically described as "**main entries**" and "**other added entries**." AACR rules tell how to determine these access points and what form they should be. Access points are catalog retrieval points where library users can look up specific items.

**AACR rules** are for determining:

- whether a book should have entries for multiple titles and/or authors
- whether a series title should be noted
- whether something is a "title main entry" item, meaning that no author is named
- how an author's name should be entered when present

Librarians use call numbers for shelving items about the same **subjects** together. Within subjects, items are usually alphabetized by author name. Librarians use the Dewey Decimal System or

Copyright © Mometrix Media. You have been licensed one copy of this document for personal use only. Any other reproduction or redistribution is strictly prohibited. All rights reserved.
This content is provided for test preparation purposes only and does not imply an endorsement by Mometrix of any particular political, scientific, or religious point of view.

Library of Congress classification schedule to determine **call numbers**. Author names are typically identified in the second part of a call number.

## STANDARDIZED SUBJECT HEADINGS

Librarians use lists of standardized subject headings to determine under which subjects to list items in the MARC (Machine-Readable Cataloging) record. Two examples are the *Library of Congress Subject Headings* (LCSH) and the *Sears List of Subject Headings* (Sears). It is important for librarians to use **approved listing sources** like these for ensuring consistency: all items about a certain subject should be listed under the same heading, which means they will also appear in the same location in the catalog. For example, if books on the subject of cats are assigned the heading "CATS," this means that all cat books will be listed under this heading. Some cannot then be listed under "FELINES." This includes even books with "Felines" in their titles—the subject heading for these would still be typed as "CATS." This makes it easier for library patrons to locate all books on this subject, rather than thinking of multiple synonyms for a specific subject.

## CONVERTING FROM ANALOG CATALOGS TO COMPUTERIZED CATALOGS

In converting card catalogs to computerized records, catalog information cannot just be typed into computers; computers must be able to **interpret** cataloging record information. MARC (Machine-Readable Cataloging) records include data "**signposts**," shorthand symbols, or content designators—guides to their data that label and explain bibliographical information. Each piece of information—title, author, call number, etc.—has a **field**. Although simpler digital files have limited numbers of fields, each with a limited number of characters, cataloging library items is best served by file structures with unlimited field lengths and numbers. This affords flexibility, because titles vary in length, some books or items are parts of a series, and audiovisual items have far longer physical descriptions than books. Also, parts of bibliographic records start and end in different places. Hence predefined standards determine miniature "tables of contents" in each MARC record. Correctly marking and saving bibliographic records in computer data files enable writing computer programs to search and retrieve specific information within certain fields, display item lists meeting search criteria, and format information to print catalog card sets.

## BENEFITS OF USING THE STANDARDIZED MARC SYSTEM

The main reason for using the MARC (Machine-Readable Cataloging) standard across the library industry is to catalog data reliably and predictably, which promotes communicating information. Uniformly applying the MARC standard enables libraries to **share** their resources and eliminates **work duplication**. Standards individualized by library would limit each library's choices, generate far more work for each librarian, and isolate libraries from one another. Applying the MARC standard also facilitates the **management** of library operations through automation systems that are available commercially. Many such systems are designed to be compatible with the MARC format, and can be found for libraries of different sizes. Libraries can enjoy the latest progress in technology because their vendors manage the maintenance and improvement of automation systems. In addition, a library can replace its current system with a new one and still preserve the compatibility of its data.

# MARC 21

The main source of U.S. and international cataloging records and the official depository of U.S. publications, the Library of Congress (LC), devised the **LC MARC** (Machine-Readable Cataloging) format in the 1960s for its initial adoption of computers. This format used short symbols, letters, and numbers within cataloging records for marking various kinds of information. Eventually, this LC MARC format developed into the current **MARC 21** format. MARC 21 has become the standard for the majority of computer programs in libraries. The Library of Congress maintains the

Copyright © Mometrix Media. You have been licensed one copy of this document for personal use only. Any other reproduction or redistribution is strictly prohibited. All rights reserved. This content is provided for test preparation purposes only and does not imply an endorsement by Mometrix of any particular political, scientific, or religious point of view.

bibliographical format and all official documentation of this system, published as *MARC 21 Format for Bibliographic Data.* The primary advantage of MARC tags is that they are much **shorter** and more **compact** than traditional textual information. For example, instead of "publication area," MARC 21 uses "260"; instead of "place of publication," it uses "$a"; instead of "name of publisher," "$b"; and instead of "date of publication," "$c." This saves storage space on computer hard drives.

### COMMONLY USED CONTENT DESIGNATORS

**Content designators**—shorthand symbols labeling and explaining bibliographic records used in the MARC 21 notation system—include fields, tags, indicators, and subfield codes. **Fields** are logical divisions of bibliographic records, such as title, author, and other pertinent details. Textual names are too long to copy into MARC (Machine-Readable Cataloging) records, so three-digit **tags** are used to identify fields. For example, tag 010 is for the Library of Congress Control Number (LCCN), 020 is for the ISBN (International Standard Book Number), 100 is for an author's personal name main entry, 245 is for title information, 250 is for the edition, and 260 is for publication information. Two-character **indicators** follow all tags from 010 on, usually two numerical values from 0–9. For example, if the first indicator in the title field has a value of 1, it means the catalog should have a separate title entry and a title card printed for that item, while a value of 0 means a title main entry is needed. **Subfield codes** identify numbers of pages, illustration and other physical information, dimensions, and so on.

Copyright © Mometrix Media. You have been licensed one copy of this document for personal use only. Any other reproduction or redistribution is strictly prohibited. All rights reserved. This content is provided for test preparation purposes only and does not imply an endorsement by Mometrix of any particular political, scientific, or religious point of view.

# Program Administration

## Assessing Program Needs

### EVALUATING PUBLIC SCHOOL LIBRARIES

One factor that greatly impacts the results of a study evaluating a public school library media center is the **timing**. The best time to evaluate a school library's operations, services, and resources, as well as their effects on student performance, is during a **"stable" period**: a time when library resources have not changed for some time. The literature review of previous studies revealed that states often conducted studies in reaction to reduced library resources. Such **reactive studies** on school libraries tend to obscure the relationship between library resources and student performance, as changes in student performance trends may take several years to develop. Thus, these studies may not be valid, since any data collected reactively is unlikely to capture a full picture of the effects of changing resources.

### FACTORS INFLUENCING THE SERVICE MODEL OF THE PUBLIC-SCHOOL LIBRARY MEDIA SPECIALIST

According to studies on public school library media centers, certain variables contribute to the instructional model of the librarian as a teacher. One factor is related to the research methodology itself: evaluations utilizing **case studies** and **surveys of students and teachers** established this instructional service model more clearly than those that did not. Another variable is the emergence of **technology**. Evaluations that were performed when technology was newer found that library media specialists often spent substantial time training teachers and students in basic technology use because they were the primary technical experts in their schools. However, as technology has become more widespread, teachers and students tend to already be technologically competent. This gives librarians more time to guide students in using technology for research. In other words, technology changed from being an end in itself to being a vehicle for improving research skills in students. Case studies also show that librarians significantly affect class content and teaching quality, transcending librarian-teacher boundaries. Librarians are also instrumental in teaching information and data analysis, synthesis, and interpretation; clear, convincing writing; and thinking skills.

### IDENTIFYING NEEDS FOR IMPROVEMENT

Ongoing assessment is necessary for a school library media program to be effective and relevant. This assessment should **identify needs for improvement** and **facilitate accomplishing those improvements**. To support this, the library media specialist should stay up to date on all methods, tools, and issues related to assessing media programs. The media specialist should work with other school personnel, developing and implementing a comprehensive plan to identify students' learning needs. To aid in assessment, he or she should schedule the systematic collection of data on a regular basis and should also gather information to analyze the data. These data analyses should guide decisions on policies and plans to ensure the library media program's continual improvement. Finally, the media specialist should share the results of annual reports with the school learning community.

### COMPREHENSIVE PLAN FOR BUDGETING

To prepare the school library media center budget, the library media specialist must make a thorough **needs assessment** of all areas that affect library services. **User needs** that impact school library services include student achievement (such as goals for student performance), achievement

74

Copyright © Mometrix Media. You have been licensed one copy of this document for personal use only. Any other reproduction or redistribution is strictly prohibited. All rights reserved.
This content is provided for test preparation purposes only and does not imply an endorsement by Mometrix of any particular political, scientific, or religious point of view.

and other test scores, and curriculum planning and development. In addition, the media center **collection**, including its strengths, weaknesses, and/or gaps, and existing resources, affects library user needs and resources. Media center **services**, such as the programs, classes, and other activities that support the school and district curriculum, also influence library resources and user needs. The media specialist and committee making the comprehensive library budget plan must assess all these needs to match library resources with user needs.

## LIBRARY MEDIA SPECIALISTS AS INSTRUCTIONAL EMPLOYEES

According to the National Center for Education Statistics (NCES), library media specialists are categorized as "non-instructional support personnel." In response, the American Association of School Librarians (AASL) issued a statement that certified media specialists should be classified as **instructional employees**. Another factor that can cause the public to think media centers do not offer essential instructional programs is the **"65 Percent Solution,"** a legislative act many states use to direct 65 percent of the educational budget into direct classroom resources, excluding media centers. Although many media specialists spend much of their time delivering instruction, this is often not apparent. Experts urge them to consider two factors: how their media center **supports student learning** and what convincing evidence they have that students have attained **their learning goals**. Addressing these considerations requires media specialists to change their evaluation and assessment approaches from object-oriented to student-oriented. **Object-orientation** focuses on "objects" or "things" like numbers of instructional sessions and planning meetings, circulation numbers, and new acquisitions. **Student-orientation** centers on student performance: not only what students learn, but also their demonstration of this learning.

## SUPPORTING CLASSROOM TEACHERS

Many library media specialists know they cannot conduct formal assessments of all the lessons they teach, so they have adopted strategic approaches to **assessment**. They first determine their students' most crucial **learning gaps** and then how their media center instruction supports the work of classroom teachers to eliminate these gaps. Media specialists must view the value of their own instructional content from a classroom perspective. Legislative origins of learning and teaching gaps include the requirements of the Elementary and Secondary Education (reauthorized in the NCLB and ESSA Acts) and the standards for content and performance in each state. Some media specialists, therefore, have been participating in state pilot projects (like in Hawaii) by collecting **evidence folders** to provide school community stakeholders with information on how their media centers contribute to academic performance. They select a lesson or two that highlight the learning gaps they have identified and then collaborate on improving their schools' curricula and lessons.

## BACKWARD MAPPING

Rather than just inserting a rubric into an established lesson plan, library media specialists can use a **"backward mapping" technique** to strengthen the assessment component of instruction. This means that they make an outcome-oriented investigation of current instruction.

Some of the steps in the reflective process involved include:

- Relating identified lessons to **state content and performance standards** to show that library instruction supports classroom goals.
- Indicating the selected lesson's **learning goal**, which specifies the learner(s) and exact skills or concepts to be learned.
- Behaviorally describing the lesson's **performance task**; i.e., what students must do to show they understand the learning goal, and at what level(s).

Copyright © Mometrix Media. You have been licensed one copy of this document for personal use only. Any other reproduction or redistribution is strictly prohibited. All rights reserved.
This content is provided for test preparation purposes only and does not imply an endorsement by Mometrix of any particular political, scientific, or religious point of view.

- Creating a strategy or tool for **assessing student performance quality**. This must be effective in letting both teacher and student indicate what is being learned, and how well. It can include rubrics, rating scales, checklists, graphic organizers, KWL charts, Venn diagrams, concept maps, etc.

## REFLECTING ON INSTRUCTION

Library media specialists can examine their existing instruction **reflectively** to identify evidence of learning outcomes. In addition to connecting lessons to state standards, identifying learning goals, behaviorally defining learning tasks, and making assessment techniques and tools, they can take these further steps:

- Compile **student assessment data** and analyze it. This can be done by inputting, aggregating, merging, and tabulating data in a spreadsheet program by course or grade level. Programs like MS Excel can also help by facilitating the production of charts and graphs of the data entered.
- Reflect on how to **enhance instructional techniques**, based on data collected. Media specialists can use data to consider what most students learned well, what presented problems for students, and how media specialists can change their teaching to make student learning better.
- Have students brainstorm how to **better their own learning skills**. An essential part of assessment is furthering student knowledge and confidence for reflecting on their personal progress accurately. Through self-assessment, students consider what they did well and what was difficult and why during a lesson, and what they might do differently next time.

## PORTFOLIO ASSESSMENTS

A library media specialist might assemble a **portfolio assessment** containing work collected over time to show the student's process and progress in learning. These are designed mainly so students can perform **self-assessment**, as well as sharing evidence of student learning and achievement through classroom instruction and independent study. **Evidence folders**, on the other hand, provide evidence that media specialists can share with other members and stakeholders in the learning community. This evidence shows how student learning and achievement has been affected through media center instruction. Evidence folders prove to school stakeholders that library media programs directly contribute to student performance. Their use for this purpose reinforces the concept that **assessment** is not an afterthought, but an essential component of media center instruction.

## RELATING LESSONS TO STANDARDS

The library media specialist should relate each lesson to **state content and performance standards**. For example, he or she can state that the lesson is connected to a language arts standard of finding age-appropriate resources for research projects.

- An example of a **clear learning goal**: "Fifth-graders will show their information access skills by using the Online Public Access Catalog (OPAC) to locate research project resources."
- An example of **describing a performance task**: "A student will individually use applicable subject headings to find at least two useful resources in an OPAC search for completing a research project."
- An example of how media specialists as instructors collaborating with classroom teachers can **reflect on their findings**: "Based on the data collected, the media specialist and classroom teacher agree to differentiated instruction."

Copyright © Mometrix Media. You have been licensed one copy of this document for personal use only. Any other reproduction or redistribution is strictly prohibited. All rights reserved.
This content is provided for test preparation purposes only and does not imply an endorsement by Mometrix of any particular political, scientific, or religious point of view.

Students meeting or exceeding criteria achieve progress by gathering information with teacher support. The media specialist consults with students who are not approaching or meeting criteria and assists them with locating techniques and keywords.

- An example of **students reflecting on the findings**: Students rate themselves on how they completed the assignment and write reflective comments on their own performance.

## COMMUNICATING VALUE TO STAKEHOLDERS

Stakeholders that influence school-level decisions—such as school advisory boards, teachers, and school administrators—may not realize the value library media specialists contribute to instruction, and ultimately to student achievement. So media specialists must provide evidence of this contribution. One way they can do this is with **evidence folders**. Because these will target stakeholder group audiences, they should avoid jargon and use language that is clearly understandable to non-educators and educators alike.

Evidence folder contents include:

- A summary of the **library mission** and how it aligns with the school mission
- A summary of the **primary learning goals** of the school for the school year
- A summary of how library media center instruction is **related** to the school's learning goals
- Student **work samples** for each of the lessons taught
- Graphic displays of **assessment data** showing what students have learned through media specialist instruction
- Samples of **student suggestions** for improving instruction
- Samples of **teacher suggestions** for improving instruction

Copyright © Mometrix Media. You have been licensed one copy of this document for personal use only. Any other reproduction or redistribution is strictly prohibited. All rights reserved.
This content is provided for test preparation purposes only and does not imply an endorsement by Mometrix of any particular political, scientific, or religious point of view.

# Library Management

## STAFFING AND SUPPORT

Effective library media programs require **professional and support staff** commensurate with their school's instructional program, facilities, services, size, and number of students and teachers. To help realize this requirement, media specialists can advocate for **suitable numbers of staff** to satisfy the learning needs of the whole learning community of the school. They can supervise and monitor clerical and technical staff to assure the program's smooth operations. Successful programs also require continuing administrative support.

To help in realizing this requirement, media specialists can:

- collaborate with principals and other administrators in developing the library media program's mission, goals, and objectives
- regularly tell principals and other administrators about the program's plans, accomplishments, and activities
- participate as members of the school administrative team in supplying information about the program's financial and other needs
- encourage school principals and other applicable administrators to support the program by communicating its contributions to student learning and achievement to all learning community members

## SUPERVISING LIBRARY WORKERS AND VOLUNTEERS

A public library director (Waterman, 2012) gives the following advice for **supervising** library staff and volunteers.

**Avoid** the following errors:

- Assuming nothing needs changing
- Wanting everyone to like you or assuming you are always right
- Ignoring problems and problematic behaviors
- Not asserting oneself, being indecisive, or delaying decisions
- Hiding in one's office
- Taking things personally
- Expecting others to read your mind

Take the following **actions**:

- Take responsibility for one's information-seeking behaviors
- Review the library staff manual
- Be honest, but without giving too much or inappropriate information
- Communicate clear expectations
- Share undesirable workdays and tasks
- Public service employees "should be working evenings and weekends"
- Do not request something you would not do from others
- Certain issues require immediate intervention
- Pursue opportunities for deserved, but not insincere, praise
- Admit when you are wrong
- Protect staff and volunteers from attacks by intermediate supervisors, co-workers, and the public by acting as a go-between

Copyright © Mometrix Media. You have been licensed one copy of this document for personal use only. Any other reproduction or redistribution is strictly prohibited. All rights reserved.
This content is provided for test preparation purposes only and does not imply an endorsement by Mometrix of any particular political, scientific, or religious point of view.

- Actions speak louder than words: Rather than telling them, model desired staff behaviors

## FUNDING

For any school library media program to be successful, it must have enough **funding**. This need is fundamental and crucial for the program. School library media specialists can help their library media program in securing sufficient funds. For example, they can work together with the other members of the school staff to ascertain their school's needs in terms of instruction and information. They should administer their **budget** for the library media program in accordance with valid procedures for accounting, and s/he should **report** all of the expenses incurred by the program in accordance with the requirements of local reporting policies. In addition, library media specialists should acquire, maintain, and regularly update information—in both traditional and electronic formats—about the **costs** associated with library media resources.

### CONSIDERATIONS FOR PUBLIC LIBRARY FUNDING

According to a 2008 study by the Online Computer Library Center (OCLC), funded by the Bill and Melinda Gates Foundation, most U.S. citizens have attended and used public libraries but do not know how they are funded. **Local taxes** fund over 80 percent of U.S. public library operations, whereas a much smaller 10 percent of operating costs are paid by **state and federal taxes**. This figure declined from 14 percent from 2000–2005. While U.S. taxpayers funded police and fire departments, public health, schools, and public parks with $800 billion in taxes in 2004, they paid over $9 billion in local taxes for public library operations. So public library funding equaled approximately **one percent** of total expenses for local community operations. Annual operations funding for libraries falls short of the resources and services necessary to fulfill their missions. Data from the National Center for Education Statistics show **decreasing budgets** in over one-third of American public libraries, and many others exceeded by inflation rates, forcing **reductions** in services, hours, and staff.

## RESOURCE MANAGEMENT

A strong school library media program must be supported by effective human, physical, and financial **resource management**. Some ways in which the school library media specialist can practice sound management include:

- developing and updating expertise with techniques and strategies in all areas of management, including supervision, scheduling, etc.
- regularly collaborating with members of the school staff and serving on the school's management team(s)
- regularly reporting to administrators about the status, plans, activities, needs, and accomplishments of the library media program
- assuming ongoing responsibility to assign and schedule staff and volunteer workers
- actively participating in the hiring, training, and evaluation of all staff in the program
- administering the budget for the program
- overseeing the acquisition and usage of library resources, equipment, furnishings, and space
- overseeing all parts of the program's daily operations

## BUDGET CUTS

Despite knowing that economic realities are causing universal cuts to library budgets, librarians still cannot help but take it personally when **budget cuts** affect their own libraries. They must consider whether cuts are **fair** (in proportion to cuts in other areas) or **unfair** (disproportionately applied to libraries singled out as easy targets). Librarians may ascertain that reductions are

79

Copyright © Mometrix Media. You have been licensed one copy of this document for personal use only. Any other reproduction or redistribution is strictly prohibited. All rights reserved. This content is provided for test preparation purposes only and does not imply an endorsement by Mometrix of any particular political, scientific, or religious point of view.

equitably distributed among the library and other departments and programs of their school, district, town, city, or county. If so, American Association of School Librarians experts advise that librarians view reductions as opportunities for showing decision-makers that **library leadership** is valuable to learning and wider communities, in easy and hard times alike. Since economic downturns began, the library has likely seen increased use. Librarians can collaborate with other department administrators to balance **losses** in some areas with **support** in others, like recreation centers or other facilities that might serve students during some evening hours that libraries may lose. **Alternative locations** for job-seekers and for other community computer access should be considered for additional library closure days. **Staff availability** for greeting seniors who read in library reference areas should also be considered.

## CONSIDERATIONS WHEN ENCOUNTERING BUDGET CUTS

Economic shortfalls necessitate budgetary cutbacks across school and municipality departments. However, sometimes these are **unfairly disproportionate** to library budgets. If so, librarians should consider **current impacts** to school and community materials and services, as well as **potential impacts** if the trend continues.

Librarians should consider:

- how school and community members value the library
- whether it has encountered successive budget reductions, and their cumulative effects
- whether other departments have similarly seen cuts and how these compare in size
- what kinds of supporters they have and how ready they are for dialogues with decision-makers
- whether they can collaborate overtly with supporters or must avoid publicity to protect their own jobs
- whether they and their school or community have the preparation to initiate an advocacy campaign for preventing or minimizing unfair budget reductions

Advocacy can convince decision-makers that libraries can both reflect and influence public well-being by affecting, among other issues:

- equal information access
- child and adult literacy
- employment
- crime
- truancy
- lifelong learning
- cultural enrichment

## BUDGET RESPONSE TEAM PLANNING

Librarians facing impending budget cuts should form **budget response teams** so they need not tackle these challenges alone. Members not only contribute networking, strategies, and insights, but they also gain greater understanding and support of their library. As **public advocacy representatives**, teams also protect public employee librarians from politically jeopardizing their jobs and from feeling they have defected from being team players in overtly opposing budget

Copyright © Mometrix Media. You have been licensed one copy of this document for personal use only. Any other reproduction or redistribution is strictly prohibited. All rights reserved.
This content is provided for test preparation purposes only and does not imply an endorsement by Mometrix of any particular political, scientific, or religious point of view.

reductions. **Team scenario planning** is critical because often library directors know of impending budget cuts, but not their amounts. They can consider impacts on:

- library hours
- staffing
- technology
- materials
- programming
- circulation
- after-school student and job-seeker access
- priorities for retaining versus sacrificing resources and services.

**Team members** may be senior management, Friends of Library members, certain library board members or trustees, and others with motivations and abilities for effective planning and advocacy. Member **roles** to consider include:

- advocacy organizers
- slogan or message-writers
- public speakers
- City Council or other meeting attendants
- media influencers
- elected official influencers
- famous or well-known individuals to speak on TV and/or radio and write op-ed articles

## RAISING TAXES TO INCREASE FUNDING TO PUBLIC LIBRARIES

The following findings were cited in a study by the Online Computer Library Center (OCLC, 2008):

- Most citizens surveyed claimed they would vote to support public libraries, but fewer are strongly committed to this.
- Much information about public libraries is unknown to most Americans.
- Library visitation and support are only slightly related. Therefore, aiming support advocacy efforts at library users is misdirected.
- Librarians perceived as passionate and involved in their communities have strong impacts on public library support.
- Public perceptions of libraries are that they provide practical information and answers. In the Information Age, this is an extremely competitive role, and thus libraries need market repositioning for continued relevance.
- People's funding support levels correlate directly with their belief that libraries are transformational in their lives.
- To increase library support, trade-offs of funding for other public services may not be necessary.
- Libraries have support, but not full commitment to increased funding, from elected officials. Therefore, library fundraising efforts must also recruit their highest and most likely supporters.

Copyright © Mometrix Media. You have been licensed one copy of this document for personal use only. Any other reproduction or redistribution is strictly prohibited. All rights reserved. This content is provided for test preparation purposes only and does not imply an endorsement by Mometrix of any particular political, scientific, or religious point of view.

# Promoting Libraries and Resources

## EVERYDAY ADVOCATES

According to the American Library Association's (ALA) Association for Library Service to Children, every child's librarian is an **advocate** for libraries. Children's librarians should advocate because they find libraries necessary to children. Advocacy occurs anywhere, anytime, just as children read anywhere and anytime. Children's librarians should view advocacy not as an additional role to assume, but as **central** to their existing duties and services. Children's librarians should consider whether they need **supervisor approval** for contacting Library Board members, elected officials, Friends of the Library, or the media, and under which conditions they can speak on behalf of their library. Librarians should determine **policy or legal limits** on campaigning or lobbying in their jobs rather than as private citizens, and should research their organizations' internal policies on electioneering or formal lobbying. "Everyday advocates" generate positive attitudes about service to children, its goals, and details about upcoming activities and their expected impacts. They affirm everybody's importance in welcoming children and families to libraries. They also invite co-workers' participation, help, and input, and engage their whole staff to celebrate successes.

## MIDDLE SCHOOLS

Strong library media programs are sufficiently funded, stocked, and staffed, with at least one full-time library media specialist and one full-time aide. Research finds that reading scores increase as funding, staffing, and collections increase. Effective media specialists collaborate with other faculty on school curriculum and standards committees, regularly convene staff meetings, and have the support of their principals. Students succeed when they work with administrators and teachers on management decisions to promote higher student achievement and when library staff collaborates with classroom teachers.

Good media specialists:

- help classroom teachers find supportive and enriching materials for instructional units
- offer in-service training opportunities for teachers
- teach students necessary information literacy skills
- embrace information technology and its networking

**Technology networking** enables access not only to the Internet, but also to local databases, licensed databases, electronic forms of full text, the library catalog, and other information resources basic to learning and teaching. Today's library media program is integrally part of educational endeavors that reach out to students and teachers, rather than vice versa.

## HIGH SCHOOLS

Numerous research studies in various states (Delaware, Wisconsin, Texas, and Florida, among others) find clear associations between academic achievement by high school students and the knowledge and skills those students gain through school library media programs. Through high school media programs, students acquire skills and tools in **research** and **information technology** they can apply in all school subjects. These programs also help students develop **critical thinking skills** and become aware of a broad range of **available information and resources**. These programs heighten students' interest in reading and get them more excited about learning. Studies have found positive correlations between library media collections with high quality and ready access, combined with application of sound administrative and instructional principles, and Academic Performance Index scores in **vocabulary and reading comprehension**. Research into the correlation of student academic achievement with library media principles—intellectual

Copyright © Mometrix Media. You have been licensed one copy of this document for personal use only. Any other reproduction or redistribution is strictly prohibited. All rights reserved. This content is provided for test preparation purposes only and does not imply an endorsement by Mometrix of any particular political, scientific, or religious point of view.

freedom, legal practices, curriculum-supportive collection, and program assessment—has found 14.6 percent of principle variance due to compliance-related activities.

## LIBRARY ADVOCACY

The American Association of School Librarians (AASL)'s Advocacy Committee has defined **advocacy** as a continuing process in which school library media specialists, other media center staff members, and other school staff members construct **partnerships** with others. This process of building collaborative relationships changes passive support for the school library program into **informed, active efforts** on its behalf by enabling and encouraging others to act with and for library staff. Advocacy starts with a **vision** for the school library program and a specific **plan** for accomplishing that vision. The program's vision and plan are coordinated with stakeholder priorities and agendas. Essential components of advocacy include Public Relations (PR) and Marketing. **PR** is a unilateral communication method conveying who the members of media programs are, as well as what they do, where and when they do it, and for whom.

**Marketing** is a process planned and maintained to evaluate:

- who users are
- user needs
- when and where to meet user needs
- what users can afford
- what services and materials meet those needs

### CORRELATIONS BETWEEN STUDENT SUCCESS AND LIBRARY ESTABLISHMENT

According to the ALA, at least 22 studies in the U.S. and Canada verify that school librarians **contribute to student achievement**. Research (Achterman, 2008) finds that students in schools with certified, full-time school librarians and support staff tend to attain "significantly higher" test scores. Positive correlations are found between spending on school libraries and student reading scores. Bill Cullifer, Executive Director of the WhyITnow.org initiative and WebProfessionals.org (2013) stated, "Information retrieval and evaluation is a lifelong skill that all workforce students need. School librarians provide that instruction." Global Director of Oracle Education Foundation Bernie Trilling (2010) commented, "School libraries are essential learning resources and librarians are the essential 'guides inside' our schools, leading everyday teaching and learning toward methods and outcomes that best prepare our students for the challenges of the 21st century." Pew research (2012) found 37 percent of Americans have no high-speed Internet access at home, but the ALA points out that good school libraries address that need.

### AMERICAN LIBRARY ASSOCIATION'S RESOLUTION IN ADVOCATING FOR SCHOOL LIBRARIES AND LIBRARIANS

The ALA 2012 Resolution directed its Presidential Task Force on School Librarians to lead ALA's ongoing mission to meet the urgent necessity of **advocacy** for school libraries and librarians. The task force also addressed effects on students and their achievement of curtailing and de-professionalizing school library instruction programs. It resolved that **school libraries** are necessary to the success and survival of all libraries, so the task force should continue engaging all kinds of librarians throughout the ALA to advocate for school libraries. It urged state associations and affiliates to influence **legislation** mandating sufficient school library staffing and funding at all school levels. It emphasized the priority of ensuring subsequent legislation in the **Elementary and Secondary Education Act (ESEA)**, which would acknowledge and specifically support the need for certified school librarians and successful school library programs. It indicated ALA efforts to support **federal lobbying** to include school libraries, digital literacy, and similar areas in

83

Copyright © Mometrix Media. You have been licensed one copy of this document for personal use only. Any other reproduction or redistribution is strictly prohibited. All rights reserved. This content is provided for test preparation purposes only and does not imply an endorsement by Mometrix of any particular political, scientific, or religious point of view.

legislation. It stated the ALA's active pursuit to partner with national organizations in meeting shared goals to support school libraries.

## PROMOTING BOOKS, ONLINE, AND DIGITAL RESOURCES

Although many teachers and other adults—and especially students—are comfortable and experienced with Internet use, when it comes to doing research, their habits are often limited simply to Google, Bing, Yahoo, or YouTube searches rather than accessing **authoritative online resources**. They are also often unlikely to view libraries as gateways to such trustworthy information sources. Moreover, online resources are initially invisible to users until accessed. Some library experts (cf. Johnson, 2013) point out that just as in the past, books did not "jump off the shelves" telling people to use them, today, online resources do not call user attention to themselves, so they must be both **displayed** and **promoted**. With 500 years of experience, librarians have mastered book promotion using many creative strategies including posters, author visits, contests, book talks, displays, and more. But online resources frequently go unused or underused after libraries have invested considerable money in them. Therefore, librarians need to learn new methods for promoting their newer digital resources.

### DESIGNING LIBRARY ORIENTATION PROGRAMS

When library media specialists design and deliver library orientation programs, they need to demonstrate **physical books** and **online resources** in their collections equally. When teachers have assigned research units to their classes, media specialists should take advantage of this to introduce students to **digital resources**. Doing this when students actually need the information will get their attention more and make the introduction more **relevant** to them. When librarians prepare bibliographies and/or WebQuests for instructional units, they should reference both **print and electronic resources**. When they conduct in-service trainings, attend faculty meetings, and publish school newsletters, they must inform the teachers about the media center's **digital resources** and train them in their access and use. They should also use their library websites by clearly marking links—either on their home page or a separate page linked on the home page—to their digital resources, and include notes with any special accessing instructions needed.

### DIGITAL RESOURCES

Library media specialists can insert links to **digital resources** on library websites, using clear, visible markings. This identifies available online materials to students researching class projects or to teachers doing curriculum research and researching sources to supply to students. They can also append notes with these links, giving any needed instructions to **access** the resources. These instructions not only assist library users, but they also reduce questions. Another strategy is to configure all media center computers to set the library's webpage, with links to electronic resources, as the **default home page** whenever a user launches a browser. Media specialists can also place **posters** near library media center workstations. These will visually remind students and teachers of available online resources. Because books are also still used, they can offer **bookmarks** with digital resource information printed on them. They can also start scavenger hunts and other **contests** to heighten online resource visibility: Similar to "Battles of the Books," they can offer "Battles of the Bases" (Johnson, 2013).

## USING BLOGS TO PROMOTE LIBRARY RESOURCES

Historically, many people have experienced difficulty creating web pages with HTML editors, using FTP programs to upload files to web servers, creating links, etc. In the last 10–15 years, blogging software has enabled people without technical expertise to **publish web content** easily. Today people can register accounts for their own blogs in mere minutes. Consequently, blogs have become extremely popular. The ease of establishing and publishing blogs also applies to librarians, who

Copyright © Mometrix Media. You have been licensed one copy of this document for personal use only. Any other reproduction or redistribution is strictly prohibited. All rights reserved.
This content is provided for test preparation purposes only and does not imply an endorsement by Mometrix of any particular political, scientific, or religious point of view.

found it too time-consuming in the past to maintain and update early websites. Such tedious work is erased by blogging programs. This software makes it easy not only to publish new content, but also to **archive** old blog posts and refresh and update home or main page information. The linking facility of blogging software has led to an explosion of bloggers linking their blogs to others. This has created a **blogging community**. Most people like knowing others recognize and read their writing, and bloggers get nearly instantaneous feedback from fellow bloggers and visitors sharing posts and ideas.

## CHOOSING THE RIGHT BLOGGING PROGRAM

Fortunately, many blogging programs today are free of charge or have modest costs. Librarians can open **free accounts** at several websites to learn and experiment with different blogging tools. This way they can get an idea of what program features they like and dislike. Soon they can select the software and site they prefer. Then they need to consider what kind of blog they want to create. Their initial task will be to plan their **marketing strategy** for promoting their library resources. This includes choosing **target audiences** and the most important **messages** they want to communicate.

When considering target audiences, librarians need to define several **reader characteristics and preferences**, such as:

- whether they like more fully developed articles or very brief posts
- which topics among library resources are of most interest
- whether the majority of the audience will be adults, children, or teens

## BLOGGING ARCHIVES

When choosing software, librarians may want to consider whether it can automatically create **archives**, and if it can do so daily, monthly, or annually based on blog content amounts. They may want **category divisions** for topics of interest (fitness, health, cooking, sports, etc). They might want a **search function** for users to find past posts in site archives. If a librarian wants to invite others to post content on the library's blog site, establish a place for readers to post comments, or even enable readers to enter information for personal profiles, then s/he can choose software with **community tools** for these purposes. Librarians can also consider whether readers would rather visit the blog site daily on their own, or receive daily, weekly, or monthly highlight e-mails. **RSS feeds** enable librarians to syndicate their blog content and headlines to share with websites of municipalities, library, and other organizations and associations. Corporate librarians can have RSS feeds to various department, task-based, and companywide events-and-news pages.

## USING SCHOOL BLOGS TO INFORM STUDENTS AND TEACHERS

With today's software, librarians can easily set up and write blogs. They can use these to share news of books, DVDs, other videos, and CDs they have newly acquired. They may want to establish different **blog topic areas** for each reading and viewing genre, such as nonfiction, history, novels, romance, horror, mystery, and so on. Academic librarians can inform various university departments of **new resources and websites** relevant to their subject areas. Public and academic librarians alike can involve their local communities by posting **reviews** of new books and **lists** of new book awards, and establishing areas on their blogs for **online book discussions** and **reader book recommendations** via posts and chats. Librarians can reach new community members by publishing blogs in **foreign languages** and offering new resources and upcoming programs. They can promote specific resources to schools and teachers for research, seasonal interests, book lists, and more. They may even publish newsletter blogs specifically for teachers.

Copyright © Mometrix Media. You have been licensed one copy of this document for personal use only. Any other reproduction or redistribution is strictly prohibited. All rights reserved.
This content is provided for test preparation purposes only and does not imply an endorsement by Mometrix of any particular political, scientific, or religious point of view.

## MISSION STATEMENT OF THE AMERICAN LIBRARY ASSOCIATION (ALA)

The American Library Association (ALA) states its mission: "to provide leadership for the development, promotion, and improvement of library and information services and the profession of librarianship in order to enhance learning and ensure access to information for all." The main significance of this is that all American citizens should have **access** to any available information they need and want for the following purposes:

- personal interests
- professional requirements
- academic requirements
- legal needs
- intellectual progress

The ALA states of its vision: "ALA is the leading advocate for: -The value of libraries and librarians in connecting people to recorded knowledge in all forms. -The public's right to a free and open information society (See "Policy Reference File": ALA Ahead to 2010: 2004–2005 ALA CD#31.2 - PDF, 2 pgs)." The ALA's vision of all members of American society having free access to recorded information, and of the role of libraries and librarians in helping them to attain that access, informs its mission.

## CORE ORGANIZATIONAL VALUES

The American Library Association (ALA) states its commitment to **enlarging library services**, both in the United States and worldwide. It is committed to public libraries, school libraries, academic libraries, and special libraries. It is also dedicated to librarians, other library personnel, trustees, and all other people endeavoring to **enhance the services of libraries**. It commits to providing service to its members and to creating and sustaining a setting that is inclusive, open, and invites people to work together. It is devoted to professional behaviors and attitudes, the integrity of libraries and library personnel, and ethical values and actions. The ALA is also dedicated to standards of excellence in libraries and librarians, as well as innovative ideas and initiatives. It values intellectual freedom as a constitutional right and principle. The ALA additionally values responsibility to society and to the good of the American public. The "Policy Reference File" (ALA Strategic Plan 2011–2015, ALA CD#36.2 - PDF, 8 pgs) provides more information on ALA plans for implementing these core values.

## KEY ACTION AREAS

The American Library Association (ALA) identifies "Key Action Areas" as principles to inform how it uses its resources and energy:

1. **Advocacy for Libraries and the Profession**: ALA strives to raise public knowledge about librarians' and libraries' critical importance; to further national and state laws benefiting library patrons and libraries; and to provide training, resources, and support networks to local advocates endeavoring to improve library support.
2. **Diversity**: ALA identifies diversity as one of its basic values, manifested in its dedication to recruiting people with disabilities and people of color to the library profession and to developing and promoting library services and collections for all persons.
3. **Education and Lifelong Learning**: ALA gives all library trustees and staff educational and professional development opportunities. Through a wealth of information and library services, it furthers lifetime learning for all persons.

Copyright © Mometrix Media. You have been licensed one copy of this document for personal use only. Any other reproduction or redistribution is strictly prohibited. All rights reserved.
This content is provided for test preparation purposes only and does not imply an endorsement by Mometrix of any particular political, scientific, or religious point of view.

4. **Equitable Access to Information and Library Services**: ALA promotes policies and funds supporting libraries as exemplary democratic institutions that serve all income levels, locations, ages, physical abilities, and ethnicities. It believes in supplying the complete variety of information resources people need to learn, govern, work, and live.

5. **Intellectual Freedom**: ALA identifies this as a fundamental right of all citizens in a democracy, as well as a core value in the library profession. ALA works actively to defend the rights of all people who use libraries to look for information, read information, and exercise their constitutional First Amendment right to freedom of speech.

6. **Literacy**: The ALA promotes literacy—the ability to read, write, find, understand, and communicate all sorts of recorded information—by assisting adults and children in developing the skills required for literacy, including how to read and to operate computers, because in our global information society, being able to look for information and use it effectively is required.

7. **Organizational Excellence**: ALA defines itself as inclusive as to its membership, responsive to its members' needs, and effective for them.

8. **Transforming Libraries**: ALA leads libraries and their services to transform accordingly with the globalizing, dynamic environment of digital information.

## VISIBILITY

Researchers who evaluate library media programs find the **visibility** of library media specialists to be a central factor in a program's **efficacy**. In effective school library programs, they are highly visible in their schools, districts, and communities. Members of school boards and parent groups are familiar with them. Successful media specialists **participate** in curriculum planning and development teams, in staff meetings, and as members of multiple district and school committees. Some are also members of their city councils' **broadband telecommunications committees**. Their committee memberships enable them to be known and visible to all district and school teachers, which also allows them to contribute significant **curricular and technological input**. Higher visibility also enhances **collaboration** with teachers and instructional partnership. In addition, effective media specialists have wide knowledge of their schools' **curricula** across subject content areas and grade levels, enabling them to better assist the classroom teachers.

## PROMOTING LIBRARY MEDIA CENTER PROGRAMS

In addition to being individually visible to students, faculty, and district and community members and making their library media programs equally visible, effective library media specialists indefatigably **promote** their programs. By giving **joint presentations with teachers** to explain their programs and how they contribute to both teaching and student achievement, they promote their programs to their school boards. They promote their programs to their school principals by **supplying information** about the operations and successes of their programs on a continual basis, and regularly inviting them to walk through their media centers. They collaborate with teachers to integrate electronic and print resources into established teaching units and to develop new units, and reach out to teachers less likely to request assistance from them. They take advantage of school open houses and PTA or PTO meetings to make presentations, and of local TV reports and local newspaper articles to publicize their programs.

### PROMOTING THE VALUE OF LIBRARIES AND LIBRARIANS

In 2003, the American Library Association (ALA) and American Association of School Librarians (AASL) jointly sponsored the Campaign for America's Libraries to promote the value of librarians and libraries in the 21st century to the public over a period of years, with school library media specialists and programs spotlighted during 2003–2004. The national AASL conference in 2003 was the occasion for launching the **School Library Campaign**.

Copyright © Mometrix Media. You have been licensed one copy of this document for personal use only. Any other reproduction or redistribution is strictly prohibited. All rights reserved.
This content is provided for test preparation purposes only and does not imply an endorsement by Mometrix of any particular political, scientific, or religious point of view.

The goal of this collaborative campaign was:

- to raise public recognition of the important contributions that school library media specialists make to advance student academic achievement and lifetime learning via school library media programs
- to reinforce the belief that media specialists and programs are valuable
- to position the profession of the media specialist among attractive career opportunities

The main audiences identified for this campaign included students, parents, school administrators, teachers, and boards of education. The community and legislators were identified as secondary audiences.

## STRONG BRANDING

The American Library Association (ALA) cites strong commercial **brands** like McDonald's, Starbucks, and Target as being instantly recognizable by their names and logos. In an effort to establish a similarly strong brand for American libraries, the ALA Campaign for America's Libraries created a **registered trademark** to be used by many libraries nationwide: "@ your library." ALA provides graphics for school library media programs to download and print, including templates and artwork to use in brochures, flyers, advertisements, and bookmarks on its website, www.ala.org/@yourlibrary. This site also offers sample slogans for school library media programs, such as: "Get more out of class @ your library," "Got questions, get answers @ your library," "Every student succeeds @ your library," "Get the score @ your library",' "Make the grade @ your library," "Get connected @ your library," and "Open a book, open your mind @ your library."

## INVITING PARTICIPATION FROM THE STUDENTS

The American Library Association suggests that librarians and teachers with K–6 students create **serial multicultural programming and displays**, using the slogan "It's a small world @ your library." Children can write what they think their pets' favorite books would be and why, making artwork and photos to illustrate. Librarians and teachers display these in the library and on the school or library website, and they can award essay and illustration prizes with the slogan "Read to your pet @ your library." Another elementary-level idea is "Get caught reading @ your library": Librarians and teachers take candid photos of children reading, displaying these on library walls and the website. Children could enter a prize drawing whenever they read a book. With the slogan "Join the All-Stars @ your library," librarians and teachers can form All-Star Reading Teams required to read specified numbers of books. They can enlist local athletic teams and businesses to donate free or discounted sports events tickets as prizes and invite local athletes to visit the library to meet the Reading All-Stars. Colorful bookmarks with suggested reading lists can be given to students. Students can write short book reviews to be displayed in school newsletters, websites, and in fronts of books with the theme, "Reading is fun @ your library."

## ALA SLOGANS

The American Library Association (ALA) suggests the slogan "@ your library? @ your library!" for sponsoring a student **slogan-writing contest**, enlisting school staff to judge, and then using the winning slogans. Slogans include:

- **Get the score @ your library**—librarians and teachers can:
  - sponsor information literacy skills clinics to coach students in database use, test preparation, bibliographic citation, etc.
  - wear whistles and sports caps during sessions

Copyright © Mometrix Media. You have been licensed one copy of this document for personal use only. Any other reproduction or redistribution is strictly prohibited. All rights reserved. This content is provided for test preparation purposes only and does not imply an endorsement by Mometrix of any particular political, scientific, or religious point of view.

- use sports-themed promotional materials they make with printable graphics (such as "Get the Score") from ALA's campaign website

- **Slammin' @ your library**—they can plan poetry-centered programs, including daily student PA readings of favorite poems by poets, friends, or themselves. ALA Graphics provides a manual and accompanying posters for holding a poetry slam.

- **Express yourself @ your library**—librarians and teachers can invite artists, musicians, poets, authors, and other creative figures to lead workshops on different modes of self-expression. They can display student self-expressions through talent shows, art exhibits, concerts, and special websites or publications.

- **Come together @ your library**—librarians can promote libraries as meeting places for students and classes for homework, research, and class projects. They can assist teachers in attaining classroom goals.

## GETTING STARTED WITH SLOGAN PROMOTION

As a part of the American Library Association's (ALA) Campaign for America's Libraries and AASL's associated School Library Campaign, these organizations offered ideas to help library media specialists start **promoting** their media centers to teachers and school administrators, incorporating the "@ your library" brand in slogans identifying activity themes:

- **We're here for you @ your library**—they can send personalized welcome or invitation letters to school faculty to tour the library and inform them of special resources and services they and their students can access, following up with phone calls

- **Beyond the Web @ your library**—they can offer school staff training in designing assignments that challenge students to use databases, surf the "invisible Web," and use other 21st-century research methods

- **Meet me @ your library**—they pick a day (perhaps an in-service day) inviting teachers to coffee and refreshments and consulting on lesson plans or other academic needs

- **New! @ your library**—they send short bulletins about new books and dates of review availability

- **Happy reading @ your library**—they send flyers to school staff, including recommended reading lists, wishing them happy vacations

## INCORPORATING THE ALA BRANDING INTO LIBRARY SLOGANS

Incorporating the "@ your library" brand into slogans, American Library Association (ALA) and American Association of School Librarians (AASL) have suggested ideas for library media specialists to promote their libraries to parents:

- **One Book. One School @ your library**—choose a book for faculty and students to read or have read to them, send parents promotional materials inviting them to read and discuss the book with children, and invite book discussions or author visits at times enabling parent attendance

- **Parents connect @ your library**—design and promote a Parent's Page on the website including resources and tips for parents to help children read, learn, and use the Internet

- **Every student succeeds @ your library**—invite PTA, PTO, or other parent and community groups to meet at the library and present to them the media center's and media specialist's essential roles in student achievement (ALA provides a PowerPoint presentation template)

- **Book some time @ your library**—publish colorful, simple brochures or flyers with tips to parents on encouraging children in reading, library use, safe Internet practices, and avoiding exclusive Internet use for homework

Copyright © Mometrix Media. You have been licensed one copy of this document for personal use only. Any other reproduction or redistribution is strictly prohibited. All rights reserved. This content is provided for test preparation purposes only and does not imply an endorsement by Mometrix of any particular political, scientific, or religious point of view.

- **Rally 'round @ your library**—hold a special parents' meeting to communicate not only your services, but also needs, like how parents can help by volunteering, fundraising, and forming Friends of the Library groups.

## CENTRAL MESSAGES OF AMERICAN LIBRARY ASSOCIATION AND AMERICAN ASSOCIATION OF SCHOOL LIBRARIANS' SCHOOL LIBRARY CAMPAIGN

School library media programs are crucial to learning. Library media specialist collaboration with classroom teachers, as well as teaching and incorporating information literacy into curricula, positively influence student performance. Media specialists help classroom teachers **instruct** students in conducting research, utilizing diverse resources, and presenting results. The programs are essential to meeting **school missions**. The learning community supports these programs financially and programmatically. Programs are incorporated in school technology plans and all learning and teaching. Media specialists are necessary to teaching students **strategies and skills** they need for achievement, learning, and effectively using information and ideas. They are teachers' partners in curriculum development, resource integration, and instruction. They find, assess, and apply **electronic resources** and then show faculty and students how to use them. Media centers offer quality print and electronic collections that support curriculum and meet diverse learning needs. They are places where all students can develop love for literature and reading, and can seek and find success. They are places where students can do research, collaboratively or individually, and share knowledge. Here, media specialists help students use print and electronic media to explore the surrounding world.

Copyright © Mometrix Media. You have been licensed one copy of this document for personal use only. Any other reproduction or redistribution is strictly prohibited. All rights reserved.
This content is provided for test preparation purposes only and does not imply an endorsement by Mometrix of any particular political, scientific, or religious point of view.

# Role of the Library Media Specialist

## IMPORTANCE OF THE LIBRARY MEDIA SPECIALIST IN TODAY'S LEARNING COMMUNITIES

Today's library media specialists are important figures in **contemporary learning communities**, which now consist of administrators, teachers, and parents. They are also part of international, national, state, regional, and local communities. Such communities transcend the borders of disciplinary field, occupation, age, time, and place. They are connected by shared needs, interests, and rapidly increasing technologies in telecommunications. Media specialists and student-centered media programs aim to aid students in attaining and improving their **information literacy**. As such, media specialists and their programs aim to help every student to creatively and actively find, evaluate, and use information to fulfill their own curiosities and imaginations by **pursuing reading and research activities**. This pursuit of information also encourages students to exercise and develop their own **critical thinking abilities**. Media specialists are central to student-centered media programs. They collaborate with school administrators, teachers, and others to expedite **student participation** in today's Information Age and Communication Age.

## ROLES PLAYED IN LEARNING COMMUNITIES BY TODAY'S LIBRARY MEDIA SPECIALISTS

Library media specialists today function as program administrators, information specialists, instructional partners, and teachers within contemporary learning communities. In fulfilling the function of **information specialists**, they utilize their skills for finding and evaluating information in a variety of formats as resources for learners and educators. They bring an **awareness** of various information-related issues to the attention of students, teachers, administrators, and other involved parties. They also serve to **model** the strategies students can learn to find, access, and evaluate information inside and outside of the library media centers. The environment of the media center has been critically impacted by the development of **technology**. Accordingly, the media specialist not only attains mastery over current advanced electronic resources, but must also continually focus on how information—both in more traditional forms and the newest technological forms—is used **ethically**, as well as focusing on quality and character of information.

## PROGRAM ADMINISTRATOR

In the library media specialist's role as a program administrator, s/he is responsible for directing and guiding all **activities** associated with the library's media program. Media specialists realize how important it is for students to use information effectively in order to support their **own future success**, both economically and personally. Media specialists advocate for the media programs that they administer in their libraries. Accordingly, they also supply these programs with the leadership, the vision, and the knowledge necessary to provide active and creative guidance in our contemporary times. They should have expertise in managing library and media center facilities, equipment, budgets, and staff. They should also know how to plan, implement, and assess a library media program to make sure that it is **relevant** to the learning environment and that it is the highest **quality** possible.

## INSTRUCTIONAL PARTNERS

Library media specialists today help learners and educators find, assess, and utilize information by playing the roles of program administrators, information specialists, instructional partners, and teachers. When they fulfill the functions of **instructional partners**, they collaborate with teachers, administrators, and other educators.

Copyright © Mometrix Media. You have been licensed one copy of this document for personal use only. Any other reproduction or redistribution is strictly prohibited. All rights reserved. This content is provided for test preparation purposes only and does not imply an endorsement by Mometrix of any particular political, scientific, or religious point of view.

To do this, they identify:

- connections among the information resources available
- needs that students have related to information
- content of school curricula
- learning results that are expected of students
- learning results that students achieve

Media specialists also adopt **roles of leadership** by collaborating with all members of the learning community to develop curricula, practices, and policies that will support and direct students in developing the complete gamut of skills in information literacy. In addition, they participate in close cooperative work with individual teachers to design **authentic learning activities** and **authentic learning assessments**, which are crucial. They also collaborate with teachers to integrate the information and communication skills needed to satisfy **content area standards**.

## TEACHER IN CONTEMPORARY LEARNING COMMUNITIES

Library media specialists perform the functions of information specialists, instructional partners, program administrators, and teachers. They are familiar with current research on learning and teaching. They also know how to apply such research findings to different **circumstances**.

This is especially applicable to circumstances that require students to:

- find information from a number of different sources
- evaluate that information critically
- make use of that information to support their own thinking, learning, creating, and application of knowledge

They perform the functions of teachers by working **directly** with students and other participants in their learning communities. They help to:

- analyze information and learning needs
- find resources that satisfy those needs
- utilize those resources
- understand the information they obtain from the resources
- communicate that information

Media specialists fulfill national media program standards in teaching students how to solve problems, and otherwise think critically, by using information.

## GOAL FOR A SCHOOL LIBRARY MEDIA PROGRAM RELATIVE TO REQUIREMENTS FOR A SPECIALIST

To have an effective library media program at the building level, each school needs at least one certified or licensed full-time library media specialist and qualified support staff. Media specialists can help fulfill this goal by regularly interacting with supervisors at school, system, district, and other applicable levels, both inside and outside of library media services, to assure sufficient program staffing with professional and support staff.

Copyright © Mometrix Media. You have been licensed one copy of this document for personal use only. Any other reproduction or redistribution is strictly prohibited. All rights reserved.
This content is provided for test preparation purposes only and does not imply an endorsement by Mometrix of any particular political, scientific, or religious point of view.

They should also make sure they meet professional requirements by continually updating their **personal competencies** for:

- administration
- supervision
- information access and delivery
- teaching
- learning
- use of technology

To obtain feedback and support for the program, and to be informed of issues and endeavors outside the school building, media specialists should regularly **participate** in activities at district and other levels as indicated. They should participate, both as employees and as staff supervisors, in **performance appraisals** in the interest of ongoing professional development. They should also stay current with **trends** and contribute to their profession by being active in national, state, and local professional **organizations and activities**.

Copyright © Mometrix Media. You have been licensed one copy of this document for personal use only. Any other reproduction or redistribution is strictly prohibited. All rights reserved.
This content is provided for test preparation purposes only and does not imply an endorsement by Mometrix of any particular political, scientific, or religious point of view.

# Professional Development, Leadership, and Advocacy

## Code of Ethics

### THE ALA CODE OF ETHICS

The principles in the **American Library Association (ALA) Code of Ethics** are not intended to indicate what to do in specific circumstances. Rather, they are **general standards** to guide library media specialists in making decisions **ethically**.

- **Principle I** states that media specialists should:
    - give the highest quality service to all library users by organizing resources for utility and appropriateness
    - make information access fair
    - applying equal policies for service
    - responding to all requests courteously, accurately, and without bias.
- **Principle II** states that media specialists support **intellectual freedom precepts**. This principle also prohibits all attempts at censorship of library resources.
- **Principle III** states that they guard each patron's right to **confidentiality and privacy** regarding the information they seek and/or obtain and regarding the resources they acquire, consult, borrow, or convey.
- **Principle IV** states that they acknowledge **intellectual property rights**. They maintain a balance between the interests of people holding those rights and of people using information.
- **Principle V** states that media specialists are fair, respectful, and trusting in their treatment of **co-workers** and other fellow workers. They support working conditions that protect the welfare and rights of all workers in their facilities.
- **Principle VI** states that they do not sacrifice the interests of library users, co-workers, or employer organizations to further their own **personal agendas**.
- **Principle VII** states that they keep **professional** responsibilities separate from **individual** beliefs. They do not let personal convictions impede equitable representation of the library's goals or giving access to information resources.
- **Principle VIII** states that media specialists **maintain and improve** their skills and knowledge, support colleagues' professional development, and cultivate aspiring professionals' goals in their pursuit of professional excellence.

> **Review Video: Ethical and Professional Standards**
> Visit mometrix.com/academy and enter code: 391843

### INTERNATIONAL FEDERATION OF LIBRARY ASSOCIATIONS AND INSTITUTIONS (IFLA)
#### CLAUSE 1 OF THE IFLA

Clause 1, the first ethical principle of the International Federation of Library Associations (IFLA) and Institutions Code of Ethics, is entitled "**Access to Information**." This clause states that the

Copyright © Mometrix Media. You have been licensed one copy of this document for personal use only. Any other reproduction or redistribution is strictly prohibited. All rights reserved.
This content is provided for test preparation purposes only and does not imply an endorsement by Mometrix of any particular political, scientific, or religious point of view.

central mission of librarians and other information specialists is to make sure that all people have **access to library information** for the following purposes:

- Education
- Leisure
- Cultural enrichment
- Personal development
- Economic pursuits
- Participating in our democracy in an informed manner
- Activities to improve that democracy

In order to achieve this mission, librarians and other information specialists refuse any kind of **censorship**. They advocate furnishing their services to library users free of charge. They offer their services and collections to all who might use them. Finally, they pursue adherence to the highest **standards** for providing people with access to all library services, both physical and virtual.

## CLAUSE 2 OF THE IFLA

The International Federation of Library Associations and Institutions (IFLA) Code of Ethics has six clauses. Clause 2 is entitled "**Responsibilities Towards Individuals and Society**." This clause states that librarians and others working with information services aim to eliminate **discrimination** and further **inclusion**. To this end, they make sure that no one is denied the right to access information and that fair services are offered to all persons. This provision of services is regardless of a person's citizenship, physical ability, mental ability, age, sexual orientation, gender identity, education, income, heritage, immigration status, status of seeking asylum, race, religion, origin, or language. This clause also states that this universal information access is furthered by providing **support** to library users in searching for information. Librarians help them in developing reading skills and information, as well as supporting them in the ethical application of information, particularly with regard to the welfare of young persons.

## CLAUSES 3 AND 4 OF THE IFLA

Clause 3 of the International Federation of Library Associations and Institutions (IFLA) ethical code, entitled "**Privacy, Secrecy and Transparency**," states that library workers respect the **privacy** of individuals and protect the **personal data** they are required to share with institutions. At the same time, they preserve the greatest possible **transparency** of public and private sector information, and of information from all other bodies whose actions affect individuals and society. Clause 4, entitled "**Open Access and Intellectual Property**," states that librarians and other information workers provide the best possible **access** to ideas and information in all formats or media, while protecting their **partnership** with authors, publishers, and other producers of copyright-protected material. They work to **respect the rights** of both users and producers. They support open source, open license, and open access principles. They pursue required, appropriate exceptions and limitations for libraries, particularly in limiting how copyright terms are expanded.

## CLAUSES 5 AND 6 OF THE IFLA

Clause 5 of the IFLA Code of Ethics, entitled "**Neutrality, Personal Integrity and Professional Skills**," indicates the stringent commitment of librarians and other information specialists to **unbiased and neutral positions** on service, collection, and access. They create policies of equitable service, seek to acquire balanced collections, and do not allow their personal beliefs to interfere with their professional responsibilities. They fight corruption and pursue professional excellence according to the highest standards. Clause 6, entitled "**Colleague and Employer/Employee Relationship**," describes the **respectful and fair treatment** librarians and

Copyright © Mometrix Media. You have been licensed one copy of this document for personal use only. Any other reproduction or redistribution is strictly prohibited. All rights reserved.
This content is provided for test preparation purposes only and does not imply an endorsement by Mometrix of any particular political, scientific, or religious point of view.

other information specialists give one another. They reject **discrimination** in any part of employment with regard to race, religion, gender, sexual orientation, marital status, origin, age, citizenship, political belief, or physical or mental ability. They advocate equal pay for equal work regardless of gender, share their own professional experience, and contribute to the work of their professional associations.

Copyright © Mometrix Media. You have been licensed one copy of this document for personal use only. Any other reproduction or redistribution is strictly prohibited. All rights reserved.
This content is provided for test preparation purposes only and does not imply an endorsement by Mometrix of any particular political, scientific, or religious point of view.

# Professional Development

## RELATIONSHIP OF STAFF DEVELOPMENT TO THE SCHOOL LIBRARY MEDIA PROGRAM

Continuing staff development is a critically necessary part of any school library media program. Staff development has two purposes: it facilitates the library media specialist's provision of **instruction** to administrators, teachers, and other members of the school's learning community, and it also facilitates the maintenance of his or her own **professional skills and knowledge**. To realize the goal of continual staff development, media specialists should establish **in-depth knowledge** and regularly update it with the research findings and best practices in all facets of the discipline. They should also work with other school staff members to **identify student learning needs**. Additionally, they should offer a continuing program of staff development. This staff development program should involve application of information literacy and integration of information technology into the school's curriculum, instruction, and practices. Media specialists should also **promote** this staff development program to school staff.

## REQUIRED COMPETENCIES

The School Library Manpower Project (1975), administered by the American Association of School Librarians (AASL), was a very comprehensive early endeavor to identify what job functions and roles were fulfilled by library media specialists. Among this project's results was a *Behavioral Requirements Analysis Checklist* (Case, 1973) which listed roughly 700 **job tasks** that they needed to perform.

These tasks were organized into seven main areas:

- human behavior
- learning and learning environment
- planning and evaluation
- media
- management
- research
- professionalism

Higher education programs that prepare school librarians have used the job tasks and functions identified in this checklist to design their **curricula**. Requirements for school librarian certification, performance assessment models, and research projects to examine media specialist competencies have also been based on the checklist. Other researchers (Schon, Helmstadter, and Robinson, 1991) surveyed school principals and media specialists, finding they agreed significantly on competencies needed in human behavior, learning, library materials, management, planning and evaluation, and professional matters.

## ONLINE RESOURCES OFFERING PROFESSIONAL DEVELOPMENT OPPORTUNITIES

Today, with budget cuts abounding, library media specialists must pursue professional development not only to keep knowledge and skills current, but also to **increase salaries**. Some online courses are free or inexpensive, and many award graduate or continuing education credits.

21st Century Schools lists **online courses or workshops for university credit** in:

- differentiated instruction
- classroom web tools
- curriculum design

Copyright © Mometrix Media. You have been licensed one copy of this document for personal use only. Any other reproduction or redistribution is strictly prohibited. All rights reserved. This content is provided for test preparation purposes only and does not imply an endorsement by Mometrix of any particular political, scientific, or religious point of view.

- after-school programs
- service learning
- interdisciplinary teaching and program improvement
- environmental literacy

Education Week's website offers a **Professional Development Directory** of resources, including computer technology and links to library media specialist-related organizations, schools, and websites. Education Week also offers a **Teacher Professional Development Sourcebook**, including Leadership, Practice and Pedagogy, and Specific Populations areas and a listing of 730 companies. Colorado State University's Annenberg Learner website offers a number of video workshops for library media specialists with graduate-level credits.

Walden University's Canter website offers online professional development courses for **graduate credit** in:

- curriculum
- instruction
- assessment
- leadership
- reading and literacy
- classroom management
- motivation
- parent involvement
- special education
- principals
- technology

## SPECIAL INTEREST GROUP THAT OFFERS PROFESSIONAL DEVELOPMENT OPPORTUNITIES

The Special Interest Group for Librarians, or **SIGLIB**, is offered by the International Society for Technology in Education (ISTE), a nonprofit organization dedicated to serving educators and education leaders globally. The SIGLIB offers school library media specialists a community to assemble and learn how to **enhance** school library media center programs and operations, **increase** information access, and create more **efficient and effective** environments for learning and teaching through the use of current technology. The SIGLIB provides a number of professional development opportunities for school library media specialists. SIGLIB members can become involved by helping to organize professional development activities that are offered by the group, including book discussions and webinars. SIGLIB's resources include **free professional learning content**, which its members can access on its website (www.iste.org/connect/special-interest-groups/siglib).

## CONTINUING EDUCATION COMMITTEE

The Association for Library Collections and Technical Services (ALCTS), a division of the ALA, formed a **Continuing Education Committee** in 2009. Its main purpose was to develop and help to deliver continuing education offerings. In its first year, it offered 11 **e-forums** with approximately 1,600 subscribers, 14 **web course sessions** with 207 registrants, and 16 **webinars** with 1,842 attendees. That year it had $23,000 budgeted and took in $29,800 from presenting webinars, achieving gross revenues of $51,500. It had $4,000 in continuing education sponsorships from four sponsors, including the HF Group and the Berkeley Electronic Press.

Copyright © Mometrix Media. You have been licensed one copy of this document for personal use only. Any other reproduction or redistribution is strictly prohibited. All rights reserved.
This content is provided for test preparation purposes only and does not imply an endorsement by Mometrix of any particular political, scientific, or religious point of view.

In the 2010–2011 period, the committee offered at least 20 **webinars** on diverse topics including:

- Sears Subject Headings
- Collection Weeding
- Data Sets
- Institutional Repositories
- Writing for Publication
- Functional Requirements for Bibliographic Records (FRBR)
- Resource Description and Access (RDA)
- Disaster Preparedness
- Using Modern Applications in Technical Services
- Buying Library Materials on the Out-of-Print Book Market
- Maximizing Revenue from Selling Withdrawn Books and Unwanted Gifts
- Digital Preservation: A Basic Introduction

## LEADERSHIP DEVELOPMENT ACTIVITIES

In 2010, the Association of Library Collections and Technical Services (ALCTS), a division of the American Library Association (ALA), collaborated at its annual conference with the Membership Committee and the ALCTS New Member Interest Group (ANMIG) in holding an ALCTS 101 event devoted to **leadership development**. They also presented a separate conference program entitled "Membership in the Division: What's in It for Me?" Presenters were surprised to learn that considerable numbers attending were not members of ALCTS or even of ALA. They felt their presentations met the goal of facilitating **involvement in ALCTS**. This group had recently completed a YouTube video project for ALCTS Emerging Leaders, which included both personal ALCTS leader testimonials and leader tips. They planned another Educational Leadership for the next year, potentially regarding **social media use**.

They planned a possible webinar and other efforts toward:

- online complete orientation and technology orientation for new ALCTS leaders
- departing leader content, real-time networking online
- website FAQs
- working with ALA Connect
- overall increased website content

## ORGANIZATIONS AFFILIATED WITH THE AMERICAN LIBRARY ASSOCIATION (ALA)

According to the American Association of School Librarians (AASL) and Association of College and Research Laboratories' (ACRL) Joint Task Force, the AASL Presidential Task Force for Coordinating the Implementation of the New National Guidelines and Standards can promote **collaboration** between K–12 and post-secondary librarians for information literacy by:

- developing a coordinated, coherent model for staff of the AASL and Association for Educational Communications and Technology (AECT) to define **pertinent actions and opportunities** in professional development
- planning for integrating and implementing **national standards and guidelines** in a comprehensive advocacy initiative
- **introducing** these new guidelines to school library media professionals and the wider learning community
- consulting with the AASL Affiliate Assembly to develop a plan for a **school library media specialist national advocacy campaign**

Copyright © Mometrix Media. You have been licensed one copy of this document for personal use only. Any other reproduction or redistribution is strictly prohibited. All rights reserved.
This content is provided for test preparation purposes only and does not imply an endorsement by Mometrix of any particular political, scientific, or religious point of view.

- producing a coordinated, coherent model for **continuing education activities** by the AASL
- collaborating with AASL staff in defining professional development activities and opportunities required for enabling media professionals to **apply guidelines nationally**

## EDUCATION AND BEHAVIORAL SCIENCES SECTION

The ACRL Education and Behavioral Sciences Section is an organization recommended by the AASL and ACRL's Joint Task for furthering the interests of librarians working in education and behavioral science programs. This group is recommended for promoting the **inclusion of library instruction** in teacher education programs. It can also investigate problematic issues in the administration of **curriculum materials** and recommend actions for improvement. This section reviews issues with the **subject access systems** for behavioral science and education literature and offers advice on effective methods for improving these systems. This ACRL section is also recommended by the Joint Task Force for its exploration of the potential for developing guidelines and/or standards for education library services in the areas of educational research and teacher education. These actions of the ACRL Education and Behavioral Sciences Section are recommended by the AASL-ACRL Joint Task Force to increase collaboration between the K–12 and post-secondary library professions for improving information literacy.

## INSTRUCTION SECTION RESEARCH AND SCHOLARSHIP COMMITTEE

The ACRL Instruction Section (IS) Research and Scholarship Committee is recommended by the ACRL-AASL (American Association of School Librarians) Joint Task Force to further instructional scholarship and research opportunities for research and academic librarians. This organization can identify **instruction-related research and study topics** for academic and research librarians. It can endorse research studies and projects in library instruction, report on their progress, and distribute research results. This committee should offer opportunities for academic and research librarians to share scholarship and research about instruction. It can help library schools and other library education organizations to identify **library instruction areas** that could benefit from graduate-level scholarship and research. This committee can also work with the ACRL Instruction Section Teaching Methods Committee. It can identify and further teaching materials and methods that practicing bibliographic instruction librarians will find useful. It also affords a forum for librarians with interests in instructional theory and design and in teaching methods theory and practice.

## INSTRUCTION SECTION EDUCATION COMMITTEE

The American Association of School Librarians (AASL) and ACRL's Joint Task Force encourage the use of the ACRL Instruction Section (IS) Education Committee to identify and expedite opportunities for instruction librarians to **pursue continuing education** and to **develop library instruction courses** in graduate school programs. This committee maintains a website that can help library educators, students, and practitioners to identify educational opportunities. In addition, it cooperates with the ACRL Professional Committee in overseeing ALA Midwinter discussion forums and other activities in continuing education. The ACRL IS Education Committee works to cultivate **communication** between graduate school faculty members and practitioners working in the field of library instruction. This Committee is also involved in the monitoring of the **status of library instruction** in graduate school programs.

## ALA LIBRARY INSTRUCTION ROUND TABLE

The ALA Library Instruction Round Table (LIRT) advocates for library instruction to develop and apply library and information access skills in the pursuit of **lifetime learning**. This organization raises **public and professional awareness** of the need for library instruction and encourages ALA policy development to promote library instruction. It also helps library practitioners to develop,

Copyright © Mometrix Media. You have been licensed one copy of this document for personal use only. Any other reproduction or redistribution is strictly prohibited. All rights reserved.
This content is provided for test preparation purposes only and does not imply an endorsement by Mometrix of any particular political, scientific, or religious point of view.

improve, and promote library instruction. This group furnishes opportunities for librarians working in all kinds of libraries to **share** their ideas on library instruction. It encourages **networking** among professional library instruction groups at the regional and state levels. It encourages library schools to include library instruction in their **curricula of bibliographic instruction education**. This round table organization additionally sparks conversations among ALA groups about issues pertinent to library instruction.

## PROFESSIONAL ORGANIZATION NOT ASSOCIATED WITH THE AMERICAN LIBRARY ASSOCIATION

The International Federation of Library Associations Round Table on User Education is a professional organization separate from the ALA. The American Association of School Librarians (AASL) and Association of College and Research Libraries' (ACRL) Joint Task Force recommend it as a group that can collaborate usefully with the ALA and other professional organizations to **promote information literacy** in library users, as well as the **education of library professionals**. This organization cultivates international cooperation to develop all facets of user education in all kinds of libraries, including librarian training. It works on developing projects that circulate information on programs and experts in user education and that further the development of **user education programs** in libraries. This international federation supports developing and spreading information about suitable instructional materials and methods of user education through its newsletter, its mailing list, and sponsorship of its programs at regional library conferences. It also monitors and nurtures the development of training and instruction in user education for librarians, such as projects, workshops, and various programs.

Copyright © Mometrix Media. You have been licensed one copy of this document for personal use only. Any other reproduction or redistribution is strictly prohibited. All rights reserved.
This content is provided for test preparation purposes only and does not imply an endorsement by Mometrix of any particular political, scientific, or religious point of view.

# Information Access and Delivery

## Bibliographic Citation

### BIBLIOGRAPHY, FOOTNOTES, AND ENDNOTES

To avoid plagiarism, one must always **cite** sources for a paper, article, book, or other written work. Research papers require bibliographies. A **bibliography** is a list of all sources used in the research and reported in the paper. A bibliography entry should generally include the author's name(s), title, publisher name and location, publication date, and page numbers (for sources such as articles within journals or chapters within books or other parts of volumes containing multiple sources). An **annotated bibliography** includes these elements but follows them with short descriptions of source content, quality, and utility. **Footnotes** are located at the bottoms of pages, referenced in the text by superscript numbers[1]. They are used to add interesting but not directly related comments, or sources relevant to something in the text. **Endnotes** are located at the end of a paper instead of the bottoms of pages. They serve the same purpose but do not interrupt text flow.

### WORKS CITED PAGES

**Footnotes** appear within the text of a paper or book at page bottoms, referenced by superscript numbers[2] in the text; **endnotes** appear at the end of the paper or book. Some professors or editors may require students or other writers to include a **Works Cited page**, listing all materials cited in the paper. This is particularly necessary when the writer has cited sources parenthetically in the text, so readers do not have to sift through comments and other information within text to find out the writer's sources. A Works Consulted page is complementary to Works Cited; it lists all sources the writer used, whether quoted or used in some other way. A **Works Consulted page** is essentially the equivalent of a bibliography. However, a **bibliography** may name relevant sources in addition to footnotes or endnotes. Writers may choose to title the bibliography "Selected Bibliography" or "Works Consulted" to indicate source relevance.

### MLA BIBLIOGRAPHIC CITATION

MLA Style bibliographic citation, used primarily in the humanities, lists works cited in alphabetical order by author surname. Works without authors are listed alphabetically by title. The first line of each work cited starts at the left margin, and following lines are indented five spaces. Some sources on MLA style specify double-spacing; others require single-spacing. Students should ask instructors which they prefer. Additional information can be found in *MLA Handbook for Writers of Research Papers* and *Using MLA Format*.

MLA format for **books** is:

> Author's name. <u>Book title.</u> Publication location: Publisher name, Publication year.

For **encyclopedias and reference books**, MLA format is:

> Article author. "Article title." Book title. Publication location: Publisher, Publication year.

For **website sources**:

> Author's name. "Article Title." Website name. Posting/revision date. Affiliated organization name. Access date. <URL>.

Copyright © Mometrix Media. You have been licensed one copy of this document for personal use only. Any other reproduction or redistribution is strictly prohibited. All rights reserved.
This content is provided for test preparation purposes only and does not imply an endorsement by Mometrix of any particular political, scientific, or religious point of view.

For **magazines and newspapers**:

Article author. "Article title." Magazine/newspaper name. Publication date: article page number(s).

For **pamphlets**:

Information source. Title. Publication location: Publisher, Date.

For **interviews**:

Interviewee name. Personal interview. Interview date.

## APA REFERENCE PAGES

APA-Style reference pages start on a separate page from the paper's text. "**References**" is centered at the page top and double-spaced, like the rest of the paper. After the first line, all following lines should use **hanging indentation**, meaning a half inch from the left margin. Author names are **directory-style** (last name first), with last names and first initials up to and including seven authors of the same work. Above seven, the first six author names are listed, followed by ellipses (...) and then the last author's name. Entries are **alphabetized** by the last name of each work's first author. Multiple works by the same author are listed **chronologically** from oldest to newest. Complete **journal titles** are listed, reproducing original capitalization and punctuation. References to books, chapters, articles, or web pages capitalize only the first letter of the title and subtitle's first word, the first word following a dash or colon in the title, and proper nouns. In hyphenated compound words, the second word is not capitalized. Longer **book and journal titles** are italicized. Shorter **essays or journal article titles** do not have italics, underlines, or quotation marks.

### APA BIBLIOGRAPHIES

In an APA-style bibliography, publisher locations are city and state, using unpunctuated postal state abbreviations, like New York, NY.

To cite **books**, the basic format is:

Author surname, A. A. (Publication year). *Book Title: Subtitle also capitalized.* Publisher location: Publisher name.

For **edited books with no single author**, APA format is:

Name, A. A., & Name, B. (Eds.). (Year). *Title.* City, State: Publisher.

For **edited books with an author or authors**, the format is:

Name, A. (Year). *Title.* C. D. Name (Ed.). City, State: Publisher.

For **translations**, both the translation republication year and original publication year are included when citing the work in the paper's text; for example, Name (1840/1960). The format is:

Name, D. D. (Year). *Title.* (E. Name & F. Name, Trans.). City, State: Publisher. (Original work published Year).

Copyright © Mometrix Media. You have been licensed one copy of this document for personal use only. Any other reproduction or redistribution is strictly prohibited. All rights reserved. This content is provided for test preparation purposes only and does not imply an endorsement by Mometrix of any particular political, scientific, or religious point of view.

For **chapters or articles in edited books**:

Name, G. G. & Name, H. H. (Publication year). Chapter title. In J. J. Editor and K. K. Editor
    (Eds.), *Book Title* (chapter/article page numbers). Publisher location: Publisher name.

## CITING JOURNAL ARTICLES

Basic format for citing **journal articles** in APA Style, including URLs for periodical articles accessed online, is:

Author, A. A., Author, B. B., & Author, C. C. (Year). Article title. *Journal/Periodical Title, volume*
    *number* (issue number), page numbers. http://dx.doi.org/xx.xxx/yyyy.

With journals **paginated by volume** (i.e., the first issue starts with page one and the second issue picks up where the first issue's page numbers left off), the format is:

Name, A. B. (Year). Article title. *Journal Name, volume number,* page numbers.

For journals **paginated by issue** (i.e., each new issue starts with page #1), issue numbers are parenthesized following volume numbers without italics or underlines:

Name. (Year). Article title. *Journal name, 10* (8), 2–17.

For **magazine articles**:

Name, A. B. (Year, Month Date). Article title. *Magazine name, issue number,* page numbers.

For **newspaper articles**, p./pp. are used for page numbers, unlike for other periodicals:

Name, A. (Year, Month Date). Title. *Newspaper name,* pp. 1A, 2A.

For **letters to the editor**:

Name, A. (Year, Month). Title [Letter to the editor]. *Newspaper/Magazine Title, Volume number*
    (issue number), page number.

For **reviews**:

Name, A. B. (Year). Title [Review of the book *Title,* by Author Name]. *Journal/Magazine Title, Volume*
    *number,* page numbers.

## FORMATTING RESEARCH PAPERS IN APA (AMERICAN PSYCHOLOGICAL ASSOCIATION) STYLE

APA format is used for bibliographic citation in the **social sciences**. Users can refer to the *Publication Manual of the American Psychological Association.* APA recommends 12-point Times New Roman font, double spacing, and one-inch margins on all sides.

- **Running heads**, no more than 50 characters including punctuation and spaces, are used at all page tops, flush with the left margin in all capitals. Page numbers are flush with the right margin.
- **Paper sections** are the Title Page, Abstract, Main Body, and References.
- **Title pages** include the title, centered in the upper half of the page in upper/lowercase, author's name without degrees or titles, and institution.
- **Titles** should be no longer than 12 words and one or two lines.

Copyright © Mometrix Media. You have been licensed one copy of this document for personal use only. Any other reproduction or redistribution is strictly prohibited. All rights reserved.
This content is provided for test preparation purposes only and does not imply an endorsement by Mometrix of any particular political, scientific, or religious point of view.

- **Abstracts** start a new page with "Abstract" header centered. The abstract concisely summarizes in 150–250 words the main research points; text is not indented. It includes theresearch topic, questions, participants, methods, results, data analysis, and conclusions. If desired, the abstract may also include implications and future research needs.

Copyright © Mometrix Media. You have been licensed one copy of this document for personal use only. Any other reproduction or redistribution is strictly prohibited. All rights reserved.
This content is provided for test preparation purposes only and does not imply an endorsement by Mometrix of any particular political, scientific, or religious point of view.

# Information Retrieval Processes

## SEARCHING A LIBRARY CATALOG

Most libraries today have **electronic database catalogs**. Users may search by keywords or all fields, subject, title, or author. Searching by **keyword or all fields** will yield the most results by finding everything in the whole catalog containing the word(s) specified. To narrow a search, a **subject search** can be used, which finds the specified word(s) in a particular field. **Title and author searches** are used when one knows the title and wants to find a specific book or article, or knows the name of a certain author. To develop a search strategy, first one must understand **call numbers**. For example, in Library of Congress (LC) classification, the first letters identify the subject class and subclass, so H is Social Sciences, and HF is Commerce. Next is the classification number, such as 5827 for Advertising. Third, a letter and number show the author, or title keywords; e.g., .G46 is Gender. Fourth is the publication year. So Luigi and Alessandra Mance's book *Gender & Utopia in Advertising* has the LC call number HF5827 .G46 1994 in the catalog. On the book's spine, there may also be a letter combination above the other items to identify the library where the book belongs.

## KEYWORD SEARCHES

Keyword searches are more comprehensive and less specific, finding all references to keyword(s) throughout the bibliographic record. **Keywords** help when:

- author name and/or title is lacking or incomplete
- researching multiple topics
- one does not know which subject headings to enter
- linking terms from different portions of a record (such as a word from a book title plus author name)

**Quotation marks** trigger searches for the exact phrase within the quotes. To find **multiple word variations**—such as any or all words containing advertise, advertising, advertisement, advertisements, and advertisers—simply truncate and add "\*" (in this case, "advertis\*"). **Boolean operators**, named after mathematician George Boole, broaden or narrow searches. **Connectors** AND, OR, and NOT are logical and helpful. For example, "female AND advertis\*" or "media influence" AND "body image" finds records including both terms. For broader searching, "United States" OR "America," or "image OR identity" will find either or both terms or variant spellings. To **narrow** searches, "advertisements NOT commercials" or "adolescents NOT male" finds the first term without the second. A single search statement can include multiple connectors. To **prioritize** searches or include **synonyms**, parentheses denote which term to find first, like (image or identity) AND "media influence."

## SEARCHING BY SUBJECT HEADINGS

When one wants to find multiple information sources about the same topic, title or author searches are inappropriate. **Subject headings** identify the subject matter contained in books and other media. Most U.S. university libraries use the **Library of Congress (LC) classification system**. When the user knows the LC subject heading or the National Library of Medicine subject heading for health sciences libraries, s/he can use a **subject search**. For example, to find information about the national Organization for Women (NOW), one types "national organization for women." To find information about Boston, Massachusetts, one types "boston mass." To find information about Susan B. Anthony, one types "anthony susan b." For some subject headings, **subdivisions** are included, such as "mass media—influence," "stereotypes (social psychology)—history," or "marketing—united states." Generally, words must not be omitted or abbreviated inside subject

Copyright © Mometrix Media. You have been licensed one copy of this document for personal use only. Any other reproduction or redistribution is strictly prohibited. All rights reserved. This content is provided for test preparation purposes only and does not imply an endorsement by Mometrix of any particular political, scientific, or religious point of view.

headings. One exception is that when searching for government departments, the abbreviation "dept" must be used. Quotation marks are required. Periods are not used with abbreviations (for example, "us dept of health and human services").

## SEARCHING BY AUTHOR NAME

Most university libraries use the LC system. If you know an author's name, just select the **Author (Last Name First) search option**. Then type the author's last name and the first initial. Capital letters, accent marks, and punctuation are omitted, though hyphens may be included or excluded: "weston-smith m" or "weston smith m" to find books by Miranda Weston-Smith, "dickens c" to find books by Charles Dickens, and "dos passos j" for books by John Dos Passos. With common surnames, type the whole first name instead of its initial, such as "smith stevie." When unsure of an author name, the **Author Keywords search option** can help. Author names can include **institution and organization names**, like the Institute of Electrical and Electronics Engineers (IEEE), typed as "institute of electrical and electronics engineers," or The International Society for Music Education, typed as "international society for music education." **Conference names** can be used in author searches to find their publications. Government departments, agencies, subcommittees, etc. are also searchable as authors.

## SEARCHING BY TITLE

Books, journals, plays, musical scores, government documents and other works can be found through **title searches**. When using the LC system as in most American university libraries, title searches should exclude title-initial articles like *the, a, an,* and foreign-language equivalents: for Johan Strauss II's German opera *Die Fledermaus*, type "fledermaus." For Antoine de Saint-Exupéry's French novel *Le Petit Prince*, type "petit prince." For Stephen King's novel *The Shining*, type "shining." Title search words are not abbreviated, but final words may be truncated, such as "american journal of educa" for The American Journal of Education. Capitalization is not used, and punctuation and accents may be included or excluded, such as "i'm ok, you're ok" or "im ok youre ok" for the book by Thomas Anthony Harris, M.D. Hyphenated title words may be searched with or without the hyphen, such as "cold-formed steel" or "cold formed steel." **Series titles** can be searched, like "lecture notes in mathematics" or "earthquake hazards reduction series." **Periodical title searches** should use the periodical title, not article title. Some databases name journal titles "Source."

## EVALUATING BOOKS FOUND IN A LIBRARY SEARCH

- **Authority**: Look on book title pages for their authors, author credentials, and publishers. Academic press publishers usually indicate scholarly resources.
- **Audience**: Look in book prefaces to discover if they were written for a general or specialized audience, and whether their focus suits your research topic.
- **Accuracy**: Look for footnotes and bibliographies to see if book information seems unsupported or adequately researched. Look for numerous errata versus few or none.
- **Objectivity**: Consider whether an author seems impartial or biased, or whether it was written objectively or attempts to affect reader opinion. When author views differ markedly from those of others in a discipline, closely inspect supporting evidence and data.
- **Currency**: Look at the back of book title pages for book publication dates and whether books are up-to-date for one's research topic, and whether books are new editions or revised. Sciences generally require more current research than humanities.

Copyright © Mometrix Media. You have been licensed one copy of this document for personal use only. Any other reproduction or redistribution is strictly prohibited. All rights reserved.
This content is provided for test preparation purposes only and does not imply an endorsement by Mometrix of any particular political, scientific, or religious point of view.

## EVALUATING JOURNAL ARTICLES IN THE RESULTS OF A LIBRARY DATABASE SEARCH

Although published journal articles listed in library databases have been reviewed and edited to be acceptable for publication, library users doing research should still **evaluate** them by six criteria:

- **Source**: Articles by subject experts, published in scholarly journals, are more reliable. They also contain references to more publications on the same topic. Some databases include searching by article type (reviews, clinical trials, editorials, research articles, etc.).
- **Length**: The citation states an article's number of pages, an indication of its research utility.
- **Authority**: Research sources should be authoritative, written by experts affiliated with academic institutions.
- **Date**: Many research fields are constantly changing, so research must be as current as possible. In areas with new research breakthroughs, some articles are not up-to-date.
- **Audience**: If an author has written an article for professional colleagues, it will include subject-specific language and terminology.
- **Usefulness**: Evaluate whether an article is relevant to one's own research topic.

## EVALUATING WEBSITES FOUND IN SEARCH RESULTS

Because people can publish anything on the Internet, students and researchers must critically evaluate websites in search engine results. Criteria for evaluating **website validity and applicability** include:

- **Authority**: Determine who produced a website or webpage. Search online databases, library catalogs, or sites like Google Scholar to find information about individual author credentials, affiliations, and qualifications. If an organization created a website, such as the American Library Association or American Medical Association, find background or qualification information on the site's own "About" page, or separately search the association or organization itself. Consider bias, viewpoint, and attempts to influence public opinion—for instance, different political parties have different websites.
- **Audience**: Consider if websites target particular age groups, sometimes making them inappropriate sources for research at other age levels. Also, discipline-specific sites can be inappropriate for general-audience research, and vice versa.
- **Content**: Determine if a website is a blog; contains articles, images, and other media; and has original or reproduced content. With reproduction, look for permissions to ensure correct, unaltered content. Domains (.org, .gov, .edu) can help inform site content.
- **Currency**: Check whether websites are updated recently (bottom of page).
- **Usefulness**: Consider website information levels regarding research needs and relevancy to research topics.

## MAJOR CLASSIFICATION SYSTEMS USED IN AMERICAN LIBRARIES

Most American public libraries use the **Dewey Decimal Classification (DDC) system**. Most American university, college, and research libraries use the **Library of Congress (LC) Classification system**. Most university and college health science libraries use the **National Library of Medicine (NLM) Classification**, developed by the National Library of Medicine of the National Institute of Health (NIH). Each of these systems uses numbers, alphabet letters, or combinations of the two to represent **subject areas**. For example, in the Dewey Decimal system, math and science books are classified in the 500s, while books on biology and human anatomy are in the 570s. In the Library of Congress system, math and science books are classified in the Qs, and books on biology and human anatomy are in the QM section. In the NLM system, math and science

Copyright © Mometrix Media. You have been licensed one copy of this document for personal use only. Any other reproduction or redistribution is strictly prohibited. All rights reserved.
This content is provided for test preparation purposes only and does not imply an endorsement by Mometrix of any particular political, scientific, or religious point of view.

books are also classified within the Q section, but books on biology and human anatomy are in the QS section.

## TRADITIONAL AND CONTEMPORARY FORMATS OF LIBRARY CATALOGS

Traditionally, library catalogs were file cabinets with drawers full of paper cards organized according to whichever classification system the library used. Today, **electronic catalogs**—online public access catalogs (OPACs)—are increasingly common, accessed via library computers. Many libraries still provide both card and electronic catalogs. New library users may often go straight to the stacks (bookshelves) and browse within a certain subject area, like art or science, to see what they can find. However, this method is arbitrary and may yield only a few useful books, if any. Professional researchers, scholars, and students must learn to access information more efficiently to save time and find more suitable and abundant resources. Every book in a library has an **entry, record, or listing**. This entry or record supplies the book's call number, author, title, publisher, publication city, and publication or copyright date. These are basic components of the book's citation and description. **Citations** are used both for finding books in the library and citing them as sources in research paper bibliographies or reference notes. Two common standardized academic citation styles are **American Psychological Association (APA)** and **Modern Language Association (MLA)** styles.

## PERIODICAL INDEXES

While library catalogs represent only the individual library's collection, **periodical indexes** are typically produced by outside publishers and sold to libraries. Libraries usually cannot directly influence which periodicals the publishers include in their indexes. Hence, a library will subscribe to certain indexes (such as the *General Science* index) but will not necessarily have every periodical listed in each index. Users can find which periodical issues have articles on specific topics they seek. Indexes use **subject headings** to list topics to facilitate these subject searches. An index typically includes the following basic **citation components**: an article's title, author name(s), periodical title, date, volume number, issue number, and page numbers of the article. Correct citations of periodicals allow users to determine if the individual library has the periodical and specific issue they want in print and/or electronic format and to find the article within the issue. In addition to citations, some indexes include **abstracts** (summaries of each article), which further help researchers locate useful articles.

## ELECTRONIC TOOLS USED TO SEARCH FOR AND ACCESS ELECTRONIC LIBRARY RESOURCES

Early digital resources included CD-ROMs ("Compact Discs, Read-Only Memory") containing periodical indexes. With Internet progress, periodical indexes are now found in **online databases**. Library users use **browsers** like Google Chrome, Mozilla Firefox, or Microsoft Internet Explorer to access not only text documents, but also audio files, videos, images, and graphics. **Search engines** like Google, Yahoo, Bing, and WebCrawler enable users to find hypertext documents on specific topics, including links for users to load and open other related documents. Advantages of links include speedy access and often numerous and varied additional websites available, affording a wealth of materials. However, a corresponding disadvantage is that web searches can sometimes result in **irrelevant results** and **inefficient searching**, as useful information is lost in the large number of results. Another is that due to the web's publishing freedom and lack of policing, **author credentials** are often not verifiable. Users must apply critical judgment and evaluation of pages and sites they find.

Copyright © Mometrix Media. You have been licensed one copy of this document for personal use only. Any other reproduction or redistribution is strictly prohibited. All rights reserved.
This content is provided for test preparation purposes only and does not imply an endorsement by Mometrix of any particular political, scientific, or religious point of view.

## GOALS RELATED TO THE INSTRUCTIONAL USE OF TECHNOLOGY

An example of a goal for a school library media program is for the program to integrate the application and use of technology for teaching and learning. Three examples of **objectives** for the library media specialist, associated with this goal, are:

- The library media specialist should develop and maintain knowledge and expertise for the **evaluation** of different technology processes and products.
- He or she should also **help and guide** students and members of the school staff in their knowledge and use of new technologies and media.
- The library media specialist should **model** for students and staff the most effective uses of technology for learning and teaching, and should also work to promote such effective uses of technology for these purposes.

Copyright © Mometrix Media. You have been licensed one copy of this document for personal use only. Any other reproduction or redistribution is strictly prohibited. All rights reserved.
This content is provided for test preparation purposes only and does not imply an endorsement by Mometrix of any particular political, scientific, or religious point of view.

# Interlibrary Loan

## INTERLIBRARY LOAN AND GOOD CUSTOMER SERVICE

Interlibrary loan experiences are more pleasant and easy when the librarian has a strong **customer service philosophy**. When patrons have a good experience, they are likely to return to the library. Good customer service policies benefit the librarian and library staff equally by making the interlibrary loan process easier and smoother for them as well, making it more cost-efficient and time-efficient.

**Best librarian practices** include:

- utilizing technology to save money and time
- providing library customers with quick turnaround times
- transferring requests through fewer individuals
- notifying library patrons promptly when materials they requested have arrived
- making sure the library's policies and procedures for ILL are easy for patrons to locate, access, and comprehend
- keeping an open mind to receiving library users' comments about what does and does not work
- focusing on the end user's needs and preferences
- conducting regular evaluations of library customer satisfaction

## BEST PRACTICES FOR INTERLIBRARY LOAN

Alternatively called benchmarking, program evaluation, or quality measurement, **assessment** in libraries is for the purpose of making decisions about **library services**. Librarians decide which services need improving, which need elimination, and which new services to develop. They can also use assessment to determine whether or not their library delivers services with the same quantity, quality, speed, and price as other libraries of the same size and kind.

Best practices among **frequently assessed interlibrary loan (ILL) activities** include:

- how often the library fills requests to borrow from other libraries (**fill rate**)
- how long it takes the library to respond to ILL requests and how long item delivery takes (**turnaround time**)
- what it costs the library to lend a photocopy or a returnable item (**cost studies**)
- **who** uses the library's ILL department, such as undergraduate students, graduate students, faculty, or academic groups and departments
- whether usage is **increasing**
- whether users are pleased with the services (**user studies**)
- what **material types and titles** are being requested and most frequently borrowed and lent
- **borrowing statistics** from library consortia

## RUSA RECOMMENDATIONS

RUSA recommends the following **resources for ILL assessment information**:

- the Association of Research Libraries (ARL) website – www.arl.org , including its Assessment Blog
- the National Center for Education Statistics
- the Leon/Kress Resource Sharing Cost Study Database

Copyright © Mometrix Media. You have been licensed one copy of this document for personal use only. Any other reproduction or redistribution is strictly prohibited. All rights reserved. This content is provided for test preparation purposes only and does not imply an endorsement by Mometrix of any particular political, scientific, or religious point of view.

Recommended **journals** include:

- the International Federation of Library Associations and Institutions (IFLA) Journal
- the Journal of Interlibrary Loan, Document Delivery and Electronic Reserve
- Interlending and Document Supply

**Market research studies** pertaining to ILL assessment include the Primary Research Group's 2009 study of academic libraries, "Higher Education Interlibrary Loan Management Benchmarks," which can be downloaded in PDF format for $89.50. It covers nearly 90 American and Canadian academic libraries. Librarians can use its results for comparison with their own libraries' ILL departments. A **checklist** featuring progressive, aggressive questions to help resource-sharing librarians consider the quality of their current and/or future practices is RUSA's STARS Rethinking Resource Sharing Initiative's STAR Checklist. A leaflet of **best-practice general, lending, and borrowing guidelines** is IFLA's "Guidelines for Best Practice in Interlibrary Loan and Document Delivery" (2007).

## PURPOSE AND SCOPE OF INTERLIBRARY LOANS

According to the U.S. Interlibrary Loan Code published by ALA, ILL's purpose is not to **replace** a local library's collection but rather to **complement** it, as the collection should be good enough to meet patrons' usual needs. The tradition of sharing resources among different sizes and kinds of libraries is the basis of ILL. ILL is also founded on the premise that regardless of how well-supported or large any library is, in today's environment no library is completely self-sufficient. ALA realizes some libraries lend more than borrow—they are "**net lenders**"—and others are "**net borrowers**," borrowing more than they lend. However, the ILL system is based on the idea that all libraries should be willing both to lend and borrow **reciprocally**. Regarding scope, the rules of the International Federation of Library Associations (IFLA) document, "**International Lending: Principles and Guidelines for Procedure**," regulate how international library loan is conducted. For example, Canada and Mexico border the U.S. but have their own ILL codes and infrastructures. ALA enjoins American librarians to familiarize themselves with international customs requirements for shipping materials, which supersede library agreements.

## ILL CONFIDENTIALITY

ILL transactions are **confidential library records**, like circulation transactions. ILL personnel should know state and local confidentiality laws and rules relative to ILL transactions. Although including user names on requests to suppliers does not violate the American Library Association's (ALA) U.S. ILL Code, **identification codes or numbers** should be used in lieu of names to preserve confidentiality whenever appropriate. Concerning **access** to ILL records and their **retention**, libraries should develop policies and procedures. Also, whenever ILL staff use the text from ILL requests as procedural examples, or post requests for assistance, they should be cognizant of **personal privacy considerations**. The ALA's Office for Intellectual Freedom has developed several policies on library records confidentiality. ILL personnel should conform to **principle III of ALA's Code of Ethics (1995)**, which reads: "We protect each library user's right to privacy and confidentiality with respect to information sought or received and resources consulted, borrowed, acquired, or transmitted."

## ENSURING ACCURATE LOANS

The best way to ensure that a library patron will receive the correct item is if the librarian provides a good **bibliographic description** of it. The ALA's U.S. ILL Code mandates that instead of giving details of descriptive aspects, the library requesting the ILL should include the information that best indicates the material being sought. This may be a long bibliographic citation, or a string of letters and numbers, depending on the individual case. The important thing is that the description

Copyright © Mometrix Media. You have been licensed one copy of this document for personal use only. Any other reproduction or redistribution is strictly prohibited. All rights reserved. This content is provided for test preparation purposes only and does not imply an endorsement by Mometrix of any particular political, scientific, or religious point of view.

is sufficiently **precise** to prevent the supplier from having to do extra work and to keep the user from becoming frustrated about the borrowing library's receiving the requested materials. For example, it would be sufficient for the borrowing library to request a journal article by verifying the title of the journal instead of the specific article.

## GUIDELINES FOR IDENTIFYING SUPPLIERS

Before making an ILL request of a possible supplier, borrowing libraries should employ all available resources to discover a specific title's **ownership**. Many libraries submit their collection information to major bibliographic utilities, such as Online Computer Library Center (OCLC) or DOCLINE, and freely supply their individual catalogs online. ILL-related lists, such as the ILL listserv, ill0l@webjunction.org, are also fine resources for borrowing libraries to find and/or verify items that are especially hard to locate. To find out **charges** and **lending policies**, they should use OCLC's Policies Directory and similar resources. The requests should clearly state an amount equal to or more than any supplier charges. Borrowing libraries are responsible to pay any lending library fees equal to or less than the amounts indicated on the requests. ALA advises libraries to use **electronic invoicing software**, like the Electronic Fund Transfer system that medical libraries use, or OCLC's Interlibrary Loan Fee Management (IFM) system.

## RESPONSIBILITIES OF LIBRARIES REQUESTING INTERLIBRARY LOANS

The ALA U.S. Interlibrary Loan Code states that whenever materials are shared among libraries, the borrowing library assumes some intrinsic **risk**. A small portion of materials sometimes becomes damaged or lost between being sent to requesting libraries and then returned. On the basis that materials would not have been exposed to such risk had they not been transported from supplying libraries, **borrowing libraries** are held responsible for any loss or damage to materials they borrow from other libraries. They are responsible for both **condition and location** from the time they leave lending library shelves to the time they are safely returned there. If a borrowing library requests ILL materials be delivered to a user's home or other location outside the library, it is also responsible for those materials during delivery and return. Whether the borrowing library must repair, replace, or pay for damaged or lost materials is the lending library's decision. The ALA ILL Code especially warns against attaching adhesive tape or labels to borrowed materials.

### RULES ABOUT PAYMENT FOR DAMAGED OR LOST MATERIALS

According to the ALA's U.S. ILL Code, libraries requesting loans of materials from other libraries are responsible for any **damage or loss of materials** during the sending and returning process, including payment for repair or replacement. This Code says requesting libraries are responsible for paying **bills** from supplying libraries, and/or notifying them of any **billing questions**, no more than six months after the date the supplying libraries bill them. Also, borrowing libraries are advised by the Code to make every effort to settle any billing questions within six months of informing lending libraries about apparent **billing errors**. The Code also states if a supplying library charges a requesting library for a damaged or lost item, the requesting library must pay these charges. However, the supplying library does not necessarily have to bill for an item that is lost. Borrowing and lending libraries may have to resolve such issues through **joint efforts**; for instance, the supplying library might have to ask the delivery firm to trace a lost item.

## RESPONSIBILITIES OF SUPPLYING LIBRARIES

Supplying libraries are responsible to **respond** to all ILL requests promptly. If unable to fulfill a request, suppliers should indicate this promptly via the same method used by the requesting library or other direct contact. Suppliers should respond before **automatic time-out or expiration intervals** on DOCLINE and OCLC. They should also provide specific **reasons** for unfulfilled ILL requests, like "in use" if requested items might be available later or "non-circulating" if only

Copyright © Mometrix Media. You have been licensed one copy of this document for personal use only. Any other reproduction or redistribution is strictly prohibited. All rights reserved. This content is provided for test preparation purposes only and does not imply an endorsement by Mometrix of any particular political, scientific, or religious point of view.

available for use within the library. ILL departments are responsible for **expediting material delivery** irrespective of other departments involved, such as mailrooms, copy services, and circulation departments. When charging for materials, supplying libraries should make all efforts to receive **various payment methods**, like credit cards, coupons, or vouchers. ALA Code encourages **electronic services**, like non-invoicing IFLA vouchers or OCLC's ILL Fee Management (IFM) system. Lending libraries are responsible to send final bills no more than six months past supply dates, final overdue notices no more than six months past final due dates, final billing for lost material replacement no more than one year past final due dates, and resolve billing questions no more than six months after billing error notification.

Copyright © Mometrix Media. You have been licensed one copy of this document for personal use only. Any other reproduction or redistribution is strictly prohibited. All rights reserved. This content is provided for test preparation purposes only and does not imply an endorsement by Mometrix of any particular political, scientific, or religious point of view.

# Legal Issues

## COPYRIGHT ISSUES

Suppose a school library media specialist finds a very appropriate, entertaining cartoon online and wants to share it with students' parents by including it in the library newsletter s/he sends out to them. Or a teacher recorded a TV program last year and wants to play back the recording in class. Or a school principal reads a very good chapter about reading across the curriculum in a book and wants to copy this chapter and distribute to the school. All three of these scenarios represent **copyright issues**. Most likely, none of the proposed actions is legal; however, in each situation, these educators could easily **acquire permissions**. Copyright protects the interests in the works of the creators. It also encourages individuals and groups to share information and take risks. The purpose of the copyright law is to **protect creators** from unauthorized copying, printing, publication, importation, or sale of multiple copies of their works by others.

## FAIR USE

The fair use law was created to offer guidelines for using **copyrighted materials**. Most property, including intellectual property, is owned by somebody. As a copyright expert has observed, **fair use** allows use of things that are owned by other people, but only within limits. This use includes asking the owners for their permission. This is reciprocal: an individual or group may be the owner, and sometimes asks other owners for permission to use what they own. The purpose of fair use is to strike a balance between the needs of **users** and the interests of **copyright owners**.

To satisfy the requirements of the fair use law, four pieces of **information** are required:

- the nature of the work to be used
- the portion or amount of the work to be used
- the purpose and nature of the use of the work
- the potential market for the use of the work

## CREATIVE COMMONS

A Creative Commons license gives permission to copy and distribute someone's work as long as they give **credit** to the creator and adhere to the **licensing conditions** specified. For example, someone might want to allow others to use and share his or her photographs, but does not wish companies to sell them. Someone else may want access to materials from university courses without enrolling in the courses. Bloggers might want to invite readers of their blogs to re-publish them, but make sure they receive credit for writing them. Musicians and music lovers might want to use and remix songs composed by others without paying royalties. **Creative Commons (CC)** is a nonprofit enabling people to use and share knowledge and creative products via free legal tools. CC provides **free copyright licenses** that are standardized, simple, and easy to use. These give the public permission to use people's creative works under the conditions the creators choose.

### COMMON COPYRIGHT LICENSES

CC licensing allows people to **change copyright terms** easily from the default "All Rights Reserved" to "Some Rights Reserved." CC licenses are not substitutes for copyrights; they function together with copyrights to modify the copyright terms so they apply best to the needs of the copyright and license owners. If an artist or creator of works wants to grant other people the right to use, share, and even add to a work s/he has created, s/he can publish the work under a Creative Commons license. CC licensing confers **flexibility**; for example, the creator might permit only noncommercial uses of the work. It also protects users from being liable for **copyright infringement**, providing they adhere to the conditions specified by the creator. Hundreds of millions of academic, scientific,

Copyright © Mometrix Media. You have been licensed one copy of this document for personal use only. Any other reproduction or redistribution is strictly prohibited. All rights reserved. This content is provided for test preparation purposes only and does not imply an endorsement by Mometrix of any particular political, scientific, or religious point of view.

and creative works like videos and songs are available for legal, free public use by the terms of CC copyright licenses.

## THE GOAL OF CREATIVE COMMONS

CC is a 501(c)(3) charitable, tax-exempt corporation, chartered in Massachusetts. CC is supported by contributions from donors and its users. CC and its supporters believe in a **global commons** and its potential. CC's vision is to realize the Internet's maximum potential of **universal access** to education and research and complete participation in culture, to fuel a "new era" of productivity, development, and growth. The mission of CC is to steward, support, and develop technical and legal infrastructures toward optimal digital innovation, creativity, and sharing. The Internet has enabled the concept of universal access, but social and legal systems often prohibit realization of that concept. **Copyright law** predated the Internet, causing difficulty with legally conducting many online processes most of us take for granted, such as copying, pasting, editing sources, and posting material to the World Wide Web. Advance, explicit **permissions** are required of all persons by copyright law's default setting. CC works to offer a standardized, public, free infrastructure that balances the realities of copyright laws and the Internet to fulfill the vision of universal access.

## CHARACTERISTICS OF THE CREATIVE COMMONS ORGANIZATION

Creative Commons (CC) provides an infrastructure through copyright tools and licenses within traditional existing copyright law. Through these tools, individuals (as well institutions and companies of all sizes) can find standardized, simplified means of preserving their copyrights while permitting others to make **specified uses** of their work. This changes the "All Rights Reserved" default to a "**Some Rights Reserved**" approach to copyrights, making educational, scientific, and creative content immediately more consistent with the Internet's full capability. A great, expanding **digital commons** is achieved through interaction of CC tools and users. This affords a content pool that users can distribute, edit, copy, remix, and build on while remaining within copyright law limits. CC licenses apply globally, respond to user needs, and are legally sound. CC has a **copyright reform policy**, based on the belief that even its revolutionary open licensing idea is insufficient for Internet inclusiveness and universal access. CC builds **infrastructure**, while its users build the **commons**. CC aims to increase its stewardship of interoperating commons infrastructure, its tools' adoption, and user support and responsiveness.

## PLAGIARISM

A popular way of viewing plagiarism is copying others' work or borrowing others' ideas. However, it is a serious **legal offense**: the Merriam-Webster Online Dictionary defines plagiarism as stealing others' ideas or words and misrepresenting them as one's own, using others' work without crediting sources, committing literary theft, or presenting products and ideas from extant sources and misrepresenting them as original or new. In other words, plagiarism is **fraud**. It includes both stealing others' work and lying about it. U.S. copyright law protects **intellectual property**—that is, it protects recorded expressions of original ideas.

Plagiarism includes:

- submitting others' work as one's own
- copying others' ideas or words without crediting them
- quoting without using quotation marks
- providing incorrect information about a quotation's source

Copyright © Mometrix Media. You have been licensed one copy of this document for personal use only. Any other reproduction or redistribution is strictly prohibited. All rights reserved.
This content is provided for test preparation purposes only and does not imply an endorsement by Mometrix of any particular political, scientific, or religious point of view.

- copying the sentence structure of others' writing while changing only the vocabulary words and not crediting the source
- copying sufficient ideas and/or words from a source to comprise the majority of one's presentation regardless of whether or not one credits the source

## ACCESS TO FEDERALLY FUNDED RESEARCH

The Fair Access to Science and Technology Research Act (FASTR) supports **open information access**. It would extend the 2008 National Institutes of Health (NIH) Public Access Policy to 11 more U.S. government departments and agencies to enhance access to taxpayer and federally funded research results. If the FASTR were passed, it would allow public, open access online to **research archives**, enabling librarians to help library users better obtain information and do research. The additional **agencies** covered include the Department of Agriculture, the Department of Commerce, the Department of Defense, the Department of Education, the Department of Energy, the Department of Health and Human Services, the Department of Homeland Security, the Department of Transportation, the Environmental Protection Agency, the National Aeronautics and Space Administration, and the National Science Foundation. Agencies would have to submit electronic copies of publications, preserve digital manuscripts long-term in publicly accessible repositories, make them available for free within six months of publication, and investigate whether open licensing would further useful analysis and application of research publications.

## PROVISIONS FOR SCHOOL LIBRARY MEDIA SPECIALISTS

Congress was scheduled to reauthorize the **ESEA** (formerly known as No Child Left Behind) in 2009, but did not. Congress held meetings and hearings during 2010 and 2011 about what reauthorization should include. While this law addresses requirements for state certification of classroom teachers and paraprofessionals, it does not include **school library media specialist qualifications**—even though their roles are critical in enabling states and school districts to meet ESEA student reading requirements. The American Library Association (ALA) has been lobbying to extend this law to media specialists. The Senate Committee on Health, Education, Labor and Pensions (HELP) proposed the **Strengthening America's Schools Act** (S. 1094) in June 2013 for ESEA reauthorization. This bill specifically provides for school libraries.

It applies the **Improving Literacy and College and Career Readiness through Effective School Library Program**, which requires:

- state-certified school librarians
- current materials, equipment, and technology
- regular school librarian-classroom teacher collaboration in developing and implementing curriculum

It also supports digital literacy skills development. As of early 2014, no Senate floor date was set for this bill.

## LIBRARY SERVICES AND TECHNOLOGY ACT (LSTA)

The LSTA is the only federal government program dedicated to libraries. The Institute of Museum and Library Services (IMLS) administers it. It funds **state libraries** for state initiatives and cooperative agreements and sub-grants to school, academic, research, public, and special libraries. It requires state-to-federal matching funds. The LSTA **expands** learning services and information resource access in all libraries for everybody and **consolidates** federal library programs. It supplies **electronic information access** to patrons through international, national, regional, and state

Copyright © Mometrix Media. You have been licensed one copy of this document for personal use only. Any other reproduction or redistribution is strictly prohibited. All rights reserved. This content is provided for test preparation purposes only and does not imply an endorsement by Mometrix of any particular political, scientific, or religious point of view.

networks. Many states include statewide information access, provided through state library networks' enriched-content databases.

Librarians across the U.S. use LSTA funds to assist users with searching, among other items:

- online job banks
- resume training
- career information workshops
- community and educational service links
- family literacy courses
- mentoring programs
- homework help
- assistive devices for people with disabilities
- access to government data
- providing a forum for improved civic involvement

State digital libraries have saved their taxpayers millions of dollars in some states.

## COPYRIGHT LEGISLATION RELATIVE TO WIRELESS PHONES AND OTHER DIGITAL DEVICES

H.R. 1123, the **Unlocking Consumer Choice and Wireless Competition Act**, was introduced March 13, 2013 to U.S. 113th (2013–2014) Congress in the House, passing the House (amended) on February 25, 2014. It concerns "unlocking" wireless phones to connect to wireless telecommunications networks, i.e., circumventing technological control of access to **copyrighted software used in wireless phones**. It repeals a prior Library of Congress (LOC) rule recommended by the Register of Copyrights regarding unlocking cell phones. As an exemption to the Digital Millennium Copyright Act (DMCA), which disallows unlocking, it restores an earlier LOC rule allowing owners of computer software and firmware programs to initiate unlocking for the sole purpose of connecting cell phones to **wireless networks**, provided the network operators authorize network access. It charges the Librarian of Congress, when recommended by the Copyright Register, with deciding whether to include this exemption to tablets and other wireless devices. The law permits network operator-authorized unlocking by device owners or their agents, or commercial service providers, for network connection purposes but not bulk resale purposes.

## CHILDREN'S INTERNET PROTECTION ACT AND THE NEIGHBORHOOD CHILDREN'S INTERNET PROTECTION ACT

The Children's Internet Protection Act (**CIPA**) and the Neighborhood Children's Internet Protection Act (**NCIPA**) both became effective April 20, 2001. These laws institute requirements for policies regarding Internet safety and for technology to filter and/or block Internet access to materials that are deemed **unsuitable for children**, such as pornography. These restrictions affect how libraries use **funding** they receive through Title III of the Elementary and Secondary Education Act (ESEA); grants from the Library Services and Technology Act (LSTA); and Public Law 106-554, which established the E-rate, a Universal Service discount program to libraries for computers and Internet access or internal network connections. A 2003 Supreme Court ruling upheld the CIPA. School libraries with ESEA Title III funding must certify compliance to the **Department of Education**. Libraries with LSTA state grants must submit certification to **Museum and Library Services**. Public libraries with E-rate discounts must certify compliance to the **Federal Communications Commission (FCC)**.

Copyright © Mometrix Media. You have been licensed one copy of this document for personal use only. Any other reproduction or redistribution is strictly prohibited. All rights reserved.
This content is provided for test preparation purposes only and does not imply an endorsement by Mometrix of any particular political, scientific, or religious point of view.

## CYBER INTELLIGENCE SHARING AND PROTECTION ACT (CISPA)

The CISPA charges the federal government with performing **security activities** to prevent, protect against, limit, address, and overcome incidents in cyberspace that threaten national security. It also charges the president with designating a body within the Department of Homeland Security (DHS) and within the Department of Justice as civilian federal entities for receiving information about **cyber threats** and **cyber security crimes**, respectively.

The DHS, Department of Defense (DOD), Director of National Intelligence (DNI), and Attorney General are jointly assigned policies and procedures to:

- mitigate cyber threat impacts on civil and private liberties
- protect cyber threat information from unauthorized acquisition and access
- protect this information's confidentiality related to specific individuals

These departments and officials must submit these procedures to Congress and create a program for overseeing and monitoring **federal agency compliance**. The law prohibits federal government use of personally identifiable information from library records and other sensitive personal documents.

Copyright © Mometrix Media. You have been licensed one copy of this document for personal use only. Any other reproduction or redistribution is strictly prohibited. All rights reserved.
This content is provided for test preparation purposes only and does not imply an endorsement by Mometrix of any particular political, scientific, or religious point of view.

# Library Policies and Decision Making

## FLEXIBLE SCHEDULING

As reported at an International Association of School Librarians (IASL) conference, specific educational needs have encouraged public school libraries to adopt **flexible scheduling** rather than regularly scheduled weekly class library visits. In many schools, flexible scheduling enables better **curriculum integration**. In others, various **reading initiatives and literacy support** inform flexible scheduling. Other schools have reported that strong reading initiatives and relevant curricular support help to motivate implementation of flexible scheduling. Flexible scheduling was found not to be an end in itself, but a **means** to other ends. It correlates with, initiates, contributes to, or extends program features rather than causing them. Flexible scheduling has been found to facilitate **consultation** between school library media specialists and teachers. Researchers also found that reading and educational culture, stakeholder acceptance of the concept of collaboration, and leadership by different persons enabled implementing flexible scheduling in individual schools. Schools where **strong reading initiatives** and **project-based learning** already exist seem to accept and implement flexible scheduling more easily.

## SUPPORT FROM ADMINISTRATION

Library media specialists have reported that **support from their principals** is crucial to implementing flexible library scheduling. Principals are often more supportive when they receive education from media specialists and district coordinators, and when they trust media specialists. Some principals attend meetings or read articles about flexible scheduling, while others visit different schools to observe it. While research studies found that most principals were unfamiliar with the concept of flexible scheduling before it was suggested, they were readily persuaded to use it once they realized its valuable **educational potential**. Initial **barriers to teacher acceptance** include losing planning time that librarians previously supplied via fixed schedules for class library visits. However, teachers joining schools after implementation of flexible scheduling accept it. Studies have found that even initially resistant teachers **adapt** over time to flexible scheduling. Principals who took ownership of the challenge to teacher planning time and addressed it in advance by offering equal time through various alternatives facilitated teacher acceptance of the shift.

## QUALITIES OF PERSONNEL SUPPORTING FLEXIBLE SCHEDULING

Principals and teachers report that **personal flexibility** is a key library media specialist characteristic facilitating implementation of flexible library scheduling. Principals also mention the following qualities that contribute to adoption of flexible scheduling:

- competence
- persistence
- knowledge of best practices and national trends
- energy
- enthusiasm
- capacities for interaction with diverse people
- senses of humor

When media specialists are **energetic** and **accommodating** as well as flexible, this eases adoption of flexible scheduling. They describe themselves as:

- enthusiastic
- organized

Copyright © Mometrix Media. You have been licensed one copy of this document for personal use only. Any other reproduction or redistribution is strictly prohibited. All rights reserved.
This content is provided for test preparation purposes only and does not imply an endorsement by Mometrix of any particular political, scientific, or religious point of view.

- accommodating
- willing to compromise with teachers and adjust to meet teacher needs
- energetic
- inquisitive
- willing to take risks and experiment
- hard-working
- not threatened by change
- reliable
- flexible

They attribute success in executing flexible library scheduling to these qualities. Principals, teachers, and media specialists name the following as **teacher qualities** promoting flexible library scheduling:

- flexibility
- creativity
- open-mindedness
- willingness to learn
- comfort with less structure
- cooperativeness
- openness to sharing
- trust in students to inquire and learn
- assertiveness
- risk-taking
- persistence
- being good communicators, team players, and planners
- willingness to share accountability and involvement
- concern with the "big picture"

Investigators have found that implementing flexible library scheduling in schools is largely enabled by the presence and efforts of **support staff**. The fact that many teachers did not recognize support staff positions, referring to plural "librarians" in schools with only one library media specialist, reflects how many things are accomplished when more adults work in the library, regardless of their job titles. Even in schools lacking support staff, researchers have found that libraries maintain flexible library schedules because teachers **collaborate** copiously with media specialists in planning and instruction, and student volunteers are employed extensively. In such schools, more support staff could enable far greater accomplishments, such as offering open and flexible library access throughout the day instead of limiting it to certain times. Schools vary in implementing flexible schedules, some by district mandate and others by media specialist or district coordinator suggestion. Some implement it schoolwide simultaneously, while others gradually phase it in, beginning with older students. Some principals embrace the concept immediately, but wait until strategic times to advocate for it to ensure greater success.

## DIFFERENCES IN PERSPECTIVES

Researchers have studied schools in which **curricular integration** was a goal and flexible library scheduling is a means to achieve that goal. However, they have noted that in these schools, media specialists tend to demonstrate more **integrated perceptions** of library programs and of the results of flexible scheduling than others. When discussing flexible scheduling, they have been found more likely to volunteer information and opinions about expanded collections of reading

Copyright © Mometrix Media. You have been licensed one copy of this document for personal use only. Any other reproduction or redistribution is strictly prohibited. All rights reserved. This content is provided for test preparation purposes only and does not imply an endorsement by Mometrix of any particular political, scientific, or religious point of view.

materials, unlimited student access to these, outcomes of resource-based learning, and other aspects of curriculum initiatives in general. In contrast, principals and teachers have more often been observed to **separate** the idea of flexible scheduling from curriculum and discuss it separately. Media specialists are most likely to perceive flexible scheduling as benefiting learning and curriculum integration because how library programs best support learning is a major motivator in their jobs but only a minor one in the others'.

## MITIGATING TEACHER CONCERNS

When public schools have shifted from fixed to flexible library schedules, teachers typically have not immediately accepted this change gladly. Some teachers were initially upset about losing **planning time** they had previously had during periods when their students were regularly assigned to receive library media specialist instruction and do work in library media centers. Once they were assured the same amounts of planning time via other alternatives, some teachers became excited about the potential for flexible library schedules. However, other teachers were still not sure how to handle flexible scheduling. Some resisted changes from past procedures they considered effective. Some media specialists reacted to such teacher resistance by considering dropping the initiative, although they ultimately did not. They tended to seek and build upon small successes while waiting out teacher resistance and apathy. **Patience** on the parts of media specialists, frequently for years rather than months, has ensured success with flexible scheduling and its teacher acceptance.

## CHALLENGES TO IMPLEMENTATION

When public schools have changed their traditional practice of fixed scheduling of class library times to implement flexible library scheduling, researchers have found that, although the new method may seem institutionalized when it continues and is routinely done that way, the process of change is actually more complex, so that it does not ever become **finalized**. Even after some schools have continued to use flexible library scheduling for many years, media specialists find they must **repeatedly convince** others of its worth—for example, when new district administrators, principals, and teachers are hired, they must be trained in it and/or persuaded all over again to accept it. Even when all parties involved have been very happy with how the media center supports learning and how flexible library scheduling contributes to this support, media specialists must still consider the possible necessity of addressing teacher planning time at some future point in the events of budget cuts, leaders with less vision, and/or added classes or enrollment.

## GOAL OF A SCHOOL LIBRARY MEDIA PROGRAM RELATIVE TO THE MISSION AND OBJECTIVES OF ITS SCHOOL

One goal for a school library media program is for it to support the mission, goals, objectives, and ongoing enhancement of its school. To further the program's ability to realize this goal, the library media specialist should first develop her or his own mission statement, goals, associated objectives, and policies and procedures that are **aligned** with and reflective of the school's mission, goals, and objectives. Second, he or she can serve on the school's **committee** or other body for making school-wide decisions. Third, he or she can make sure that all school personnel understand how **essential** the media program is to the school's instructional program, going through appropriate administrative channels.

## COMMUNICATING ABOUT THE LIBRARY MEDIA PROGRAM

Clear communication of the impact, functions, mission, and goals of a school library media program is a requisite for the program to be successful. This communication is one of the roles of the library media specialist, who must acquire and keep up to date a thorough knowledge of **research results** about the impacts that media programs have on student He or she must then communicate this

Copyright © Mometrix Media. You have been licensed one copy of this document for personal use only. Any other reproduction or redistribution is strictly prohibited. All rights reserved. This content is provided for test preparation purposes only and does not imply an endorsement by Mometrix of any particular political, scientific, or religious point of view.

information regularly to **administrators** and other school personnel and should regularly report the policies, plans, and accomplishments of the program to the **staff**. Moreover, the media specialist should develop and maintain an effective program of **advocacy** that can show the program's value to a wider audience. Finally, the he or she should develop a **public relations campaign** to promote the school library media program.

## JOINT DECISION-MAKING AND SHORT-TERM AND LONG-TERM PLANNING

In planning the library budget for the short and long terms, the school library media specialist needs to collaborate with a **committee**. Together they identify the **chief goal** of the library. They also need to identify the **bottom line** of the school and/or district, such as library expenses, services, student test scores, achievement, and so on. If they correlate library resources with academic content standards, and with how those resources help teachers by improving the curriculum, they can show how library goals support **students' academic success**. The collaborators should brainstorm to produce lists of **evidence** for "selling" to chief stakeholders. To disseminate their information to administrators, faculty, parents, and the community, they must create an **action plan**. This should engage stakeholders in evaluating the information as well as hearing or seeing it. The information should apply to both short-term and long-term planning.

### WORKING WITH A COMMITTEE TO ACHIEVE GOALS

The library media specialists should be working with a committee to demonstrate to key stakeholders how the resources and services of the library media center, and the expenditures necessary to provide these, **correlate** with improving the curriculum, helping teachers, and ultimately resulting in **increased academic achievement** by the students. They can also show stakeholders how such student performance will affirm the connection between the **library's goals** and the **school district's goals**. They should relate the library's collection development plan to the library's vision and mission. Making and articulating a plan to stakeholders will provide **measurable data**. It will also increase the stakeholders' comprehension of the relationships among access to library resources and services, financial support, and results. Ultimately, it will produce more **advocates** for the media center and its program.

### FACILITATING EFFECTIVE COLLABORATIVE PLANNING

The efficacy of school library media programs depends, among other things, upon strategic, comprehensive, and long-term **planning**, which should be done collaboratively. Library media specialists can facilitate this planning by establishing the priority of program planning and by allocating sufficient resources and time for the planning process on a continuing basis. They can contribute their participation to **school committees**, like site-based management teams, school improvement teams, curriculum development teams, and technology planning teams, which are tasked with the development and implementation of strategic, long-term plans for their school. They can regularly collaborate with students, teachers, administrators, and other members of their learning community in the development and implementation of strategic, long-term plans for the media program that will bring it into and keep it in alignment with **national curriculum standards**, and with the **school's goals and priorities**.

## LIBRARY USE AND LIBRARY USER BEHAVIOR

To assure full user access to library facilities and effective library service delivery, librarians and the governing entities of libraries need to address various user behavior challenges. The ALA states that the library's **regulation of user behavior** should be based on:

- U.S. principles of equal and fair treatment under the law
- the First and Fourteenth Amendments' constitutional standards

Copyright © Mometrix Media. You have been licensed one copy of this document for personal use only. Any other reproduction or redistribution is strictly prohibited. All rights reserved. This content is provided for test preparation purposes only and does not imply an endorsement by Mometrix of any particular political, scientific, or religious point of view.

- state and local statutes
- the Library Bill of Rights
- the ALA Code of Ethics

The First Amendment's right to freedom of speech allows **free expression**, which is the basis for publicly supported library service. American courts have acknowledged rights to obtain information in public libraries under the First Amendment. Publicly supported libraries have recognition as **public forums**, within limits, for information access. Hence library policies and procedures require higher review standards than other public facilities and services if they could interfere with these rights.

## GOVERNMENT SUPPORT OF PUBLIC LIBRARIES

The U.S. government has a substantial interest in maintaining environments in public libraries that enable all library users to exercise their constitutional right of **information access**. Because the Constitution grants this right and the government enforces it, it also authorizes libraries with public support to establish and sustain environments that are healthy and safe for users and staff, free of threats to well-being and safety, including intimidation or harassment. Therefore, libraries must establish and enforce policies and procedures that **protect** against any behaviors constituting such threats, and must **address** any such behaviors if and when they transpire. The ALA states that the governing body of a library can set "**reasonable restrictions**" on the places, times, and manners in which users access the library to protect user and staff safety, to protect library facilities and resources from damages, and to protect the rights of all users to access the library facility.

## CONSTITUTIONAL RIGHTS AND ALA POLICY

U.S. constitutional rights and principles are the basis for guidelines offered by the ALA's Intellectual Freedom Committee for developing **policies and procedures** to regulate how public library facilities are used. Law enforcement and legislation should be the first and main way to deal with criminal behavior, public safety, and other issues addressed by established federal, state, or local regulations. Many times this legal structure is enough to preserve or restore **order** in libraries. If a library's governing entity opts to write policies and procedures ("P&Ps") of its own about access to library facilities, resources, and services or user behavior, these P&Ps should cite the **ordinances or statues** that are the bases for their authority to create them. In addition, any P&Ps written to regulate how library facilities are used should be closely inspected to make sure they represent the principles of the *Library Bill of Rights*.

## POLICY AND PROCEDURES FOR LIBRARY FACILITIES

The ALA states that it is acceptable to establish "reasonable and narrowly drawn" policies and procedures, intended to prevent anyone from **interfering** with others' use of a library's services and facilities. Policies may also be established to prevent any actions that **contradict or deviate** from attaining the library's mission and objectives. ALA guidelines also state that any such policies and procedures must be frequently **reviewed and updated** as necessary by the library's legal counsel to ensure their **compliance** with:

- requirements of the federal and state constitutions
- federal and state civil rights laws
- all other federal and state legislation that applies
- all case law that applies

When library user behavior presents potential problems, the ALA guidelines dictate that library staff should make all efforts to **respond** openly, directly, and in a timely fashion. These guidelines

Copyright © Mometrix Media. You have been licensed one copy of this document for personal use only. Any other reproduction or redistribution is strictly prohibited. All rights reserved. This content is provided for test preparation purposes only and does not imply an endorsement by Mometrix of any particular political, scientific, or religious point of view.

also enjoin library personnel to **resolve** such problems positively, constructively, and without escalating them. They should use sensitivity, reason, and common sense.

## STAFF TRAINING AND POLICIES AND PROCEDURES

The American Library Association (ALA) advises that a public library's policy on user behavior should be the basis for developing a continuing **staff-training program**. The program should incorporate instruction to help library workers develop **understanding and empathy** for the economic and social problems that challenge some library users. Problematic library user behaviors result from a broad range of social and individual circumstances. Therefore, public libraries and their management should avail themselves of the knowledge and experience that mental health professionals, local social service agencies, law enforcement officials, advocacy groups, and other community resources can offer. By consulting with these resources, library managers and staff will be better able to develop **community strategies** with which they can consider and address user populations that include a diversity of backgrounds, characteristics, interests, and needs, and will be better able to meet such a variety of user needs.

## ESTABLISHING AND IMPLEMENTING POLICIES THAT LIMITING LIBRARY ACCESS

The ALA defines a number of conditions for policies or regulations that **restrict library access**. These policies should:

- only apply to activities that physically or significantly **impede the safety** of library users and staff, the protection of library facilities and resources, and the public right of access to library facilities.
- be written to **narrow prohibitions** such that they limit only as much as needed for serving their purposes.
- neither sacrifice individual rights in favor of the majority nor deny the rights of the majority of users in favor of individual user rights. Rather, they should endeavor to achieve a **balance** between such competitive interests.
- not **target** particular groups or users who might be expected or assumed to engage in disruptive behaviors. They should be based on **real behaviors**, not arbitrary class or individual distinctions.

### APPLICATION OF RESTRICTIVE POLICIES

According to ALA guidelines, whenever public libraries form any policies that restrict user access to the libraries, these policies should never be based on user behaviors or appearances that are simply **annoying, irritating, or angering** to other people. ALA standards for restrictive policies regarding users require that they be **objective and reasonable**, and related to actual behaviors, rather than to subjective negative reactions from others. The ALA guidelines require such policies to give **clear descriptions** of which behaviors are not allowed, and which **measures** are established for enforcement, to allow fair warning and due process to "reasonably intelligent" individuals. Libraries must clearly **communicate** these descriptions effectively and continuously to all library users. Such behavioral prohibitions should not deprive affected individuals of sufficient **alternate information access** in the library, as much as possible. These policies must be enforced equitably, not capriciously or arbitrarily to disadvantage or advantage any group or individual.

## PRIVACY POLICIES

- **Notice and openness**: Library policies should give users notice of their privacy and confidentiality rights and associated library regulations, including kinds of information collected and purposes and limitations in using it. To protect personal privacy and identifiable information, libraries must widely notify users via multiple methods.

Copyright © Mometrix Media. You have been licensed one copy of this document for personal use only. Any other reproduction or redistribution is strictly prohibited. All rights reserved. This content is provided for test preparation purposes only and does not imply an endorsement by Mometrix of any particular political, scientific, or religious point of view.

- **Choice and consent**: The library must offer users the choice to opt into or out of having their personally identifiable information (PII), necessarily acquired during library services, retained and used.
- **Access by users**: Users have the right to access their own PII, which should be stated in library privacy policy.
- **Data integrity and security**: When libraries collect PII, they must:
  o use only reputable data sources
  o afford consumer data access
  o regularly update information
  o destroy or render anonymous outdated data
  o remove PII from summary and aggregate data.
- Library personnel are responsible to destroy privacy-protected and confidential records to prevent unauthorized disclosure.
- **Enforcement and redress**: Libraries need effective mechanisms for enforcing privacy policies, assured via regular audits. Libraries must offer user redress in case of privacy or confidentiality violations.

## CONSTITUTIONAL RIGHT TO PRIVACY

U.S. constitutional rights to freedom of speech, thought, assembly, and inquiry require privacy. Library users have the right to privacy in making **open inquiries** without others' knowing the subjects of their interests. Libraries provide confidentiality by keeping users' **personally identifiable information (PII)** private. Advances in technology have been accompanied by increased occurrences of identity theft, increased surveillance by law enforcement, and passage of new laws. Thus librarians must revise and/or develop policies and procedures to **protect user privacy and confidential information** in all formats from abuse, as well as to protect libraries from **PR and liability issues**. While developing and revising policies, librarians must restrict the extent to which PII is disclosed, collected, monitored, and distributed. They must avoid producing unnecessary records. They must not keep records unnecessary for efficient library operation, including digital records, system backups, vendor-collected data, and data-related logs. They must also avoid library procedures and practices that make PII visible to the public.

## STUDENT ACCESS TO INTERNET RESOURCES

With Internet access so ubiquitous today, most public school systems deem it both a right and a privilege for all of their students. County or regional codes of school discipline govern school systems' **behavioral expectations** of students, which include safe and appropriate **Internet use**. School systems usually send publications of these expectations and rules to students' parents or guardians. With Internet access both common and increasingly required for school work, it is typical for schools to require parents or guardians to make **written requests** to their schools' principals if they want to prohibit their children from having Internet access. Most school systems today have established **telecommunications policies**, which typically define Internet use as being for educational purposes. These policies also outline their expectations for what constitutes acceptable and appropriate Internet use, their guidelines for online publishing in schools and offices, and their rules for complying with copyright laws.

Copyright © Mometrix Media. You have been licensed one copy of this document for personal use only. Any other reproduction or redistribution is strictly prohibited. All rights reserved.
This content is provided for test preparation purposes only and does not imply an endorsement by Mometrix of any particular political, scientific, or religious point of view.

# GACE Practice Test

Want to take this practice test in an online interactive format?
Check out the bonus page, which includes interactive practice questions and
much more: **mometrix.com/bonus948/gacemediasp**

**1. A librarian sees that a third-grade student's checked-out book is two months overdue. Several overdue notices have already been given to the student's teacher to give to him. Which of the following would be the best action for the librarian to take now?**

    a. The next time the class comes in for its library period, call that student's name and ask him in front of his classmates where the book is, why he has not returned it, and when he plans to do so

    b. Call the parents and ask them to help the student return the book

    c. Inform the principal that disciplinary action is called for because the student has ignored the overdue notices

    d. Give the student a "lost book" bill for the entire value of the book

**2. A librarian wants to have a fundraising book fair. Which of the following should be her first course of action?**

    a. Announce the book fair in the school newsletter

    b. Survey teachers for the types of books they would like to see at the book fair

    c. Check with the principal to be sure of the school calendar and any school or district guidelines for fundraising activities

    d. Ask students what kind of books they would like to buy at a book fair

**3. A new librarian discovers that her predecessor shelved all the "easy-to-read" books for younger children on the lowest shelves near the floor. What should she do about this, if anything?**

    a. Provide comfortable pillows on the floor for students to sit or kneel on as they search for books

    b. Remind primary students where these books are located so that they can easily access them

    c. Inventory these books to determine if they are age-appropriate

    d. Move the collection to higher shelves

**4. Which of the following is NOT a professional association for librarians?**

    a. Arizona Library Association

    b. American Library Association

    c. American Association of School Librarians

    d. American Union of Library Employees

Copyright © Mometrix Media. You have been licensed one copy of this document for personal use only. Any other reproduction or redistribution is strictly prohibited. All rights reserved.
This content is provided for test preparation purposes only and does not imply an endorsement by Mometrix of any particular political, scientific, or religious point of view.

**5. Which of the following criteria should be used when "weeding" books from a library's collection?**

    a.  The book contains material that is outdated or inaccurate

    b.  The book contains subject matter that is controversial

    c.  Students do not check out the book very often

    d.  Parent organizations have requested that the book be removed

**6. A new librarian in an elementary school wants to move the library schedule from fixed to flexible. Which of the following would not be helpful in order to obtain the greatest cooperation from staff members?**

    a.  Discuss with the principal the educational advantages and also the financial aspects of a flexible schedule. Flexible scheduling may require the hiring of a library assistant, for example. Offer to make the transition gradually so that the school budget for flexible library scheduling can be increased little by little

    b.  Involve teachers in planning for the change. Ask about their curricular and library needs. While the schedule is still fixed, ask teachers to stay when they bring their classes and help teach a coordinated lesson

    c.  Begin with a mixed schedule, where some classes, such as kindergartners, come for their weekly "story time," while classes from higher grades visit the library as needed

    d.  Bring the idea to the parents of students in all grade levels for discussion

**7. A librarian would use the MARC system when:**

    a.  When deciding what outdated or damaged books need to be weeded from the collection

    b.  When cataloging new books for the library collection

    c.  When deciding the best arrangement for books on the library shelves

    d.  When creating a library budget for the following year

**8. A librarian observes that a teacher has made 35 copies of the first page of a 7-page science article in a magazine, one copy for each of his students. He states that he has cleared this with the principal. Are the teacher's actions allowable under copyright law?**

    a.  Yes, under the Fair Usage provision of the copyright law.

    b.  No, because only a single copy may be made of copyrighted material.

    c.  Yes, because the teacher obtained permission from the principal to make these copies.

    d.  No, because by copying the article, the teacher denies the author financial gain from his or her work.

**9. Which of the following is the best way for a librarian to demonstrate respect for diversity in a school with a large population of Hispanic and Asian students?**

    a.  During library instruction, the librarian should repeatedly ask students if they understand her to make sure that students for whom English is a second language are receiving instruction that they understand

    b.  Create a display of books and other materials on ethnic topics and invite students and parents to visit one evening and browse the display. Then, have a discussion period during which parents and children are invited to share special aspects of their heritages and customs

    c.  Budget for books and media materials in Spanish, Chinese, Vietnamese, Korean, and Japanese at a variety of reading levels and on a variety of subjects

    d.  When classes come for their assigned library time, ask students of various heritages to identify themselves and tell the class (in English) about their customs and languages

Copyright © Mometrix Media. You have been licensed one copy of this document for personal use only. Any other reproduction or redistribution is strictly prohibited. All rights reserved.
This content is provided for test preparation purposes only and does not imply an endorsement by Mometrix of any particular political, scientific, or religious point of view.

**10. Which would be the most appropriate way for a librarian to instruct students in Internet research skills?**

a. Assign classes that come for their library period to choose a topic, locate information on the Internet and write down the website where they located it. When time is up, the librarian should call classes together to share

b. Prepare a slide show presentation that demonstrates the process of locating information on the Internet and present this program to all classes that come to the library

c. After conferring with each classroom teacher about his or her current curriculum, demonstrate separately to different classes how to use the Internet to find information on the topic each class is presently studying

d. Prepare a display of books about using the Internet and use class time to show these books to students, urging them to check out the books and read for themselves about ways to find information online

**11. A teacher asks the school librarian to find a specific book she needs for a lesson she is preparing. After consulting MARC records, the librarian determines that this particular book is not in her collection. What is the best choice she can make under these circumstances?**

a. Use her budget and immediately buy a copy of the book

b. Suggest an alternate resource to the teacher

c. Obtain the book through interlibrary loan

d. Apologize and suggest that the teacher consult the local public library

**12. All of the following are good ways that a librarian can raise funds for the library EXCEPT:**

a. Applying for a grant

b. Having a book fair

c. Asking for funds from the Parents Association

d. Soliciting paid advertising to run on the library's website

**13. Before creating a statement of standards for her media center, a librarian should first:**

a. Ask the principal what standards to use.

b. Ask librarians in other districts what standards they have used.

c. Research all applicable national, state, and district standards.

d. Call the superintendent's office and ask permission to create a library standards statement.

**14. What is the best way a librarian can assist a classroom teacher who has assigned a history research project to his class?**

a. Offer to visit the classroom and teach part of the lesson

b. Offer students a small reward for the best completed research project

c. Demonstrate to the class how to use the library's computers for research

d. Direct students to areas of the library that deal with history

**15. A librarian has just purchased new software for the library's computers that will make research easier and more effective. After the software is installed and she has become familiar with it, what should she do next?**

a. Hold a brief staff meeting to instruct teachers and library staff in using the new software

b. Circulate a memo explaining the changes and how to use the new software

c. Instruct each class that comes to the library about how to use the new software

d. As students enter the library to do research on the computer, instruct them individually about how to use the new software

Copyright © Mometrix Media. You have been licensed one copy of this document for personal use only. Any other reproduction or redistribution is strictly prohibited. All rights reserved.
This content is provided for test preparation purposes only and does not imply an endorsement by Mometrix of any particular political, scientific, or religious point of view.

**16. A librarian observes a student working at a computer who moves rapidly from on website to another, apparently having difficulty locating material. The best way for the librarian to help this student would be to:**

    a. Ask the student what she is looking for and then locate the proper information for her

    b. Wait for the student to become frustrated and ask for the librarian's help

    c. Ask the student if he or she would like some help and abide by the student's response

    d. Step forward and demonstrate to the student how to find an appropriate website

**17. In selecting new books for an elementary school library's collection, which of the following would be the librarian's best resource?**

    a. Journals such as "The Horn Book"

    b. Magazines such as "Atlantic Monthly", "Books & Critics"

    c. Newspapers such as "The New York Times Book Review"

    d. Online resources such as MAA Reviews

**18. Which of the following technological duties would NOT be part of the librarian's job description?**

    a. Housing and maintaining computer labs

    b. Producing the daily televised school announcements

    c. Monitoring student use of cell phones

    d. Maintaining the school's website

*Refer to the following for questions 19 - 21:*

> A school librarian is preparing her first monthly report to the principal. She is new to both this school and to her job.

**19. Before beginning her report, the librarian should do all of the following EXCEPT:**

    a. Review monthly library reports from the previous year.

    b. Check with her administrator to find out if there is a required format for monthly reports.

    c. Consider ways to make the report more meaningful and design a new format.

    d. Collect statistics on circulation, library classes, and computer and copier usage.

**20. What kind of statistics should not be included in the librarian's monthly report to the principal?**

    a. Circulation statistics

    b. The number of individual and class visits to the library

    c. Usage of technology, including computers, databases, printers, copiers

    d. Titles of individual books that have been checked out

**21. In a library media center that follows a flexible schedule, it is important for the librarian's monthly report to include what other kinds of information besides statistics?**

    a. Problems with staff and students

    b. Collaborative projects with teachers

    c. Future plans for library growth

    d. Budget requests

Copyright © Mometrix Media. You have been licensed one copy of this document for personal use only. Any other reproduction or redistribution is strictly prohibited. All rights reserved.
This content is provided for test preparation purposes only and does not imply an endorsement by Mometrix of any particular political, scientific, or religious point of view.

**22. The Online Public Access Catalog (OPAC) is a technological improvement of and a replacement for:**

   a. The MARC system
   b. The card catalog
   c. The Dewey Decimal system
   d. The Readers' Guide to Periodical Literature

**23. You have an opportunity to invite a published author of children's books to spend a day in your school library visiting with students. What is the best reason to give for this visit when discussing this idea with your principal?**

   a. The visit will be good PR for the school. The media can be advised of the visit
   b. The visit will contribute to literature appreciation for all students
   c. Opportunities will be provided to sell the author's books so that he can autograph them. This can be a fundraising activity for the library
   d. Students may check out some of his books, adding to the circulation statistics for the month

**24. A librarian is aware that students in one of her classes come from several different cultural backgrounds, and some do not speak or understand English well. She wants to have this group do some research on the Internet under her guidance. To be sure that the ESL students understand and are able to complete this assignment successfully, what is the librarian's best course of action?**

   a. Ask the teacher not to bring these students with the rest of the class. Arrange another time to instruct them individually or in small groups
   b. Have students work on the assignment in pairs or small groups. Assign students to groups in which each struggling ESL student will have a partner to help him or her understand and complete the assignment. Encourage groups or pairs to ask for help as needed
   c. Explain the assignment to the whole class in simple words, speaking slowly so that everyone can understand. Have students work independently
   d. Write the directions for the assignment and give them to students. Include diagrams that demonstrate what students are expected to do

**25. You observe a student at the computer cutting and pasting material from an online article into his own report. What is the best way to handle this situation?**

   a. Pretend you did not notice, but notify the teacher who assigned the report
   b. Quietly discuss with the student the rules about plagiarism, show him ways to put the information in his own words, and ask to see his report when he has rewritten it
   c. Send the student to the principal for a serious infraction of library and school rules
   d. Arrange a meeting between the student, the teacher who assigned the report, and the student's parents to discuss the student's plagiarism

**26. Which activities below would it be best for a beginning librarian NOT to engage in right after arriving at a new school?**

   a. Weeding and schedule changing
   b. Staff meetings on preventing plagiarism
   c. Fund raising activities such as book fairs
   d. Reorganizing the library furniture

Copyright © Mometrix Media. You have been licensed one copy of this document for personal use only. Any other reproduction or redistribution is strictly prohibited. All rights reserved. This content is provided for test preparation purposes only and does not imply an endorsement by Mometrix of any particular political, scientific, or religious point of view.

**27. Why is it a good educational idea for the librarian to have a "story time" for younger students in elementary school?**

    a. It frees the classroom teacher for a prep period
    b. The librarian can model proper library behavior
    c. During story time, the librarian can teach students word recognition skills
    d. Hearing stories read aloud contributes to students' interest in reading

**28. A school district is forming a committee of teachers to create a new curriculum guide for the teaching of middle school Language Arts. What is the strongest argument for including the school librarian on that committee?**

    a. Knowing about changes to the curriculum and participating in making those changes will enable the librarian to acquire materials that support the new curriculum
    b. As a professional educator, the librarian should be a member of all school committees
    c. The librarian may have more knowledge than teachers about state curriculum requirements in the area of Language Arts
    d. Librarians have a more global approach to curriculum than teachers

**29. A weekly block of library time is assigned to a seventh grade class in a middle school. The librarian could best use this time with students by:**

    a. Instructing them in effective ways to do research on the Internet and in efficient use of library reference materials and books on the library bookshelves
    b. Allowing this time to be a "free" period for students when they can return books, select others, and ask the librarian for help and guidance when they see a need for it
    c. Introducing them to new materials in the library's collection by reading short passages from new books and showing brief previews of new DVDs and audio books
    d. Asking them to be "library aides" during this period so that they can assist younger students who are looking for materials and also reshelf books

**30. Early in the school year, a school librarian sends a survey to classroom teachers asking for topics and tentative dates they plan to teach those topics in their curriculum this year. What should be the librarian's response to the information received in the survey?**

    a. In a school with a flexible schedule, the librarian will plan instruction in ways to research these topics on the appropriate dates when she meets with those classes
    b. In a school with fixed scheduling, the librarian will suggest that teachers sign up to bring classes to the library when they begin a new topic
    c. The librarian will pull material from the collection and loan the teacher a cart of appropriate research materials to use in the classroom at the time of each project
    d. This information wouldn't be useful to the librarian

**31. Before the first day of school, a librarian organizes her library. Which of these concepts of library design is most important?**

    a. Seating students apart from each other and facing a blank wall so that nothing around them is distracting
    b. Providing small chairs and tables for younger students and larger furniture for older students
    c. Organizing space into areas that can be flexibly arranged to accommodate different sizes of groups as well as community activities held after school
    d. Arranging groups of chairs and computer stations so that no one is out of the librarian's sight while she is checking out books

Copyright © Mometrix Media. You have been licensed one copy of this document for personal use only. Any other reproduction or redistribution is strictly prohibited. All rights reserved.
This content is provided for test preparation purposes only and does not imply an endorsement by Mometrix of any particular political, scientific, or religious point of view.

**32. According to state guidelines, the walls of the school library should display:**

a. Posters reminding students to be quiet
b. The school calendar for the year
c. Student-produced work
d. Materials created by the librarian

**33. Which of the following is a good way to ensure that library use extends beyond the school day and involves families and the community?**

a. Invite one or two classes for an hour-long after-school activity related to their area of study
b. Have an open house in the library once a month and invite families to browse the library's collection and get to know the librarian
c. Announce a plan to keep the library open one day a week for an hour after school so that students can do research
d. Email parents with a schedule that offers time in the library after school for certain families on certain dates

**34. The librarian is aware of students' different learning styles and addresses them by:**

a. Using a variety of instructional techniques that actively involve students in listening, working with various media and materials, reading, and writing
b. Dividing students into groups based on their learning styles and instructing each group separately
c. Devoting more time to those students who have trouble grasping ideas or reading different kinds of material while the rest of the group waits
d. Giving the struggling students books about different learning styles so they can learn to compensate

**35. A school librarian wants to keep families and the community informed about what is happening in the school media center. Which of the following would be the least efficient way to accomplish this:**

a. Creating a web page where students, families, and community members can find information about the library's current activities and upcoming events
b. Emailing parents periodically to keep them updated
c. Publishing a monthly newsletter that students can take home and that can also be sent electronically to local media outlets
d. Telling students to inform their families about what is happening in the library

**36. A teacher is having his class research the Civil Rights movement of the 1960s. He wants his students to perform an Internet search, but as librarian, you know that some of the sites that would help the students have been blocked by the school district's filter that prevents students from going to inappropriate sites. You arrange for the technology department to remove the block on the sites the history class will use, make a list of those sites, and give the list to the teacher. Which of the following reasons would you cite as justification for what you have done?**

a. The Patriot Act of 2001
b. The No Child Left Behind Act of 2002
c. An Acceptable Use Policy
d. MARC records

Copyright © Mometrix Media. You have been licensed one copy of this document for personal use only. Any other reproduction or redistribution is strictly prohibited. All rights reserved.
This content is provided for test preparation purposes only and does not imply an endorsement by Mometrix of any particular political, scientific, or religious point of view.

### 37. A Boolean library search involves

a. Mathematical input to narrow the search area
b. Using keywords with "or," "but," or "and"
c. Accessing a special information database
d. Using the Dewey Decimal System

### 38. Which of the following is NOT a responsibility of a school librarian?

a. Scheduling classes
b. Reporting statistics to administrators
c. Circulating library materials
d. Critiquing books

### 39. A teacher has brought his class to the library for instruction and book exchange. The teacher participates in the instructional session with the librarian, but when students are excused to look for books and disperse to different areas in the library, the teacher ignores their behavior. Two boys are chasing each other around a shelf of books. The teacher does not correct them. What should the librarian do?

a. Point out the behavior to the teacher
b. Ignore the behavior
c. Speak to the boys firmly about proper library behavior
d. Call for the principal to handle the problem

### 40. The library has been granted funding for a paid media clerk to assist the librarian. Hiring and supervising this clerk will be the librarian's responsibility. What is the first action the librarian should take?

a. Advertise the position in the local newspaper
b. Draw up a complete job description of the position
c. Call up friends who might want to take the job
d. Research how other librarians use media clerks

### 41. A librarian wants to weed the library's book collection. How should she go about doing this?

a. Cancel classes and spend a school day alone weeding the materials
b. After library hours are over, stay late and weed the materials
c. Form a committee of interested teachers to help weed the collection at a time that is convenient for everyone
d. Invite students to select the books they use and like the least and weed those first

### 42. Which of the following activities does not encourage students to read and enjoy reading?

a. A school book fair
b. Reading contests such as Battle of the Books
c. School book clubs
d. Book reports assigned in class

Copyright © Mometrix Media. You have been licensed one copy of this document for personal use only. Any other reproduction or redistribution is strictly prohibited. All rights reserved.
This content is provided for test preparation purposes only and does not imply an endorsement by Mometrix of any particular political, scientific, or religious point of view.

*Refer to the following for questions 43 - 44:*

> A student comes to the library and you observe him wandering confusedly in the library's section of science books.

**43. What is the first thing you should do to help him?**

 a. Ask the student what his assignment is and what kind of books he is looking for
 b. Tell the student that books are shelved by the author's last name and let him have the opportunity to use this information to find the books he is looking for
 c. Find an opportunity later on to ask his teacher what the assignment is so that if he has difficulty locating materials the next time he comes to the library, you can help him
 d. Send another student from his class over to help him, as they both have the same assignment

**44. You interview the student and he tells you that he has been assigned to write a paper on the annual migration of Monarch butterflies from North America to Mexico. Which of the following would you suggest that the student do first?**

 a. Look for books in the Dewey Decimal System with the number 590, Zoology
 b. Put "butterflies" into an Internet search engine
 c. Use OPAC to find MARC entries about Monarch butterfly migration
 d. Consult the Readers' Guide to Periodical Literature for articles on the topic

**45. Which of the following is the LEAST effective way to involve parents in library programs?**

 a. Put a notice in the school newsletter asking for parent volunteers to help in the library
 b. Write about what is going on in the library in your school newsletter and invite parents to visit the library on both a drop-in basis and at a scheduled parents' night
 c. Send a note home with students inviting parents to a "parents' night" at the library
 d. Put a notice on the school website that parents are invited to "parents' night" at the library

**46. A new school librarian is having difficulty getting everything done on time. Which of the following would be the BEST first step for her to take to solve her problem?**

 a. Supervise the media clerk more closely and assign that person more tasks
 b. Ask the principal to hire more help in the library than the library has traditionally had
 c. Make comprehensive daily, weekly, and monthly plans listing what needs to be done, the deadline for completing each task, and the person responsible for handling the task
 d. Put in overtime hours as necessary to complete all tasks on time

Copyright © Mometrix Media. You have been licensed one copy of this document for personal use only. Any other reproduction or redistribution is strictly prohibited. All rights reserved.
This content is provided for test preparation purposes only and does not imply an endorsement by Mometrix of any particular political, scientific, or religious point of view.

**47. A new librarian discovers that her predecessor had a fixed-schedule program that allowed classes to visit the library at assigned times every week, leaving little time open for other activities. The library did not host specials events such as book fairs, Battle of the Books, student reading clubs, etc. The new librarian's vision for her media center includes all these activities, as well as flexible scheduling to allow students more individual library time. What is the FIRST step she should take to accomplish these goals?**

    a. Announce her plans for flexible scheduling at the next staff meeting and implement them immediately. Time should not be wasted on outdated kinds of schedules

    b. Discuss her plans for change with the principal and get his/her input about the concept and affordability of flexible scheduling, as well as potential costs to the library in hosting special events

    c. Do nothing at the present because the staff and principal seem very content with the way the library functioned in the past and postpone the idea until next year

    d. Discuss with teachers, either at a staff meeting or individually, the advantages of flexible scheduling and plan to begin a flexible program with a few classes from each grade

**48. Which of the following would not be an effective way for a librarian to share her goals for the media center with district officials and the school administration?**

    a. Draw up a comprehensive statement of goals and visions for the media center

    b. Speak at a meeting of the school board and explain the goals for the media center

    c. Schedule a meeting with the principal to discuss implementing those goals

    d. Bring her ideas to the parents of students for discussion to gain support

**49. Which of the following best explains the difference between hardware and software?**

    a. Hardware is a program like Adobe Acrobat installed on the computer using a CD or DVD. Software refers to programs already on the computer when it is purchased

    b. Hardware is a physical component of a computer, such as a monitor, RAM, CPU, hard drive, or motherboard. Software is a series of coded instructions that direct the computer to perform certain operations

    c. Hardware includes the basic operating system of a computer, such as Windows Vista. Software refers to components of that system such as RAM and ROM

    d. Hardware is the security system of a computer, such as a firewall or virus protection. Software consists of programs on the computer that are vulnerable to viruses

**50. Which of the following would NOT be an effective way to communicate information to parents?**

    a. A slide show presentation to the parents' association meeting

    b. A telephone call to each family

    c. A newsletter sent to each family

    d. Teleconferencing with groups of parents at a time

Copyright © Mometrix Media. You have been licensed one copy of this document for personal use only. Any other reproduction or redistribution is strictly prohibited. All rights reserved.
This content is provided for test preparation purposes only and does not imply an endorsement by Mometrix of any particular political, scientific, or religious point of view.

**51. The school librarian has been invited to address a luncheon meeting of the local Kiwanis Club, an organization of business people. In order to do this, she will need to get the principal's permission. She will also need to arrange for release time, since the luncheon lasts much longer than school lunch period. She will have to prepare her talk, and to design and make copies of a handout about the media center to give the Kiwanis members. Will the media center or the school benefit if the librarian accepts this invitation, or should she politely reject it?**

   a. The librarian should accept the invitation because business people can support the media center in several ways, including donating computers, giving money for library projects, and supporting the goals and visions of the librarian and her school. By attending the luncheon, the librarian will create good will for the school and the library.

   b. There is really no point in the librarian going to this much trouble to speak to a small group of business people. There is no way they can provide direct help to the library or to the school, and her time is precious. She should politely turn down the invitation or have her principal reject the invitation for her. This kind of activity is not within the job description of a school librarian.

   c. She should attend the meeting and speak out of a sense of community obligation but should not expect anything productive from giving a speech at a luncheon meeting of business people. They invite a speaker every month and probably do not pay careful attention to whatever the speaker discusses. They will most likely be focused more on the food than on the content of her speech.

   d. The librarian should not speak to this group because they may have a political agenda she is unaware of. For example, they may want to ban some books from the library or may feel that the library is over-funded. When these businesspeople were in school, the library had a card catalogue and no computers. They will be likely to think that what was good enough then should be good enough now. Their minds may be made up, and her speech is not likely to change their attitudes.

**52. What are the advantages of getting to know public librarians and academic librarians in your area?**

   a. You can send students to these libraries to check out books they need
   b. You may exchange information from each other's databases
   c. These librarians may have children in your school
   d. The public and academic libraries may have collections you want to own

**53. As books and supplies are received by the library, what is the first step the librarian should take?**

   a. Paste labels giving required information on the spines of the books
   b. Decide where on the library shelves the new materials should be placed
   c. Stamp them with the name of the library/media center
   d. Check the items received against the purchase orders

**54. Why should the librarian periodically review online databases?**

   a. To make sure students are not plagiarizing from them
   b. To verify that the subject matter is accurate and covers student needs
   c. To make sure nothing inappropriate for students is on the database
   d. To assess the difficulty of the reading levels on the database

Copyright © Mometrix Media. You have been licensed one copy of this document for personal use only. Any other reproduction or redistribution is strictly prohibited. All rights reserved. This content is provided for test preparation purposes only and does not imply an endorsement by Mometrix of any particular political, scientific, or religious point of view.

**55. A lesson given by the librarian to staff and/or students on creating a slide show presentations should include all of the following EXCEPT:**

    a. Design
    b. Content Delivery
    c. Audience
    d. Bibliography

**56. Inviting a writer into the library for a day or a week to work with children on their own writing and encourage them in their reading should have all the following direct outcomes EXCEPT:**

    a. Encourage student interest in reading and writing
    b. Raise money for library needs and projects.
    c. Increase the number of books checked out by students
    d. Demonstrate through a successful role model that being a reader/writer is desirable

**57. The librarian creates a computer "scavenger hunt." Students work at computers to find items on a list of computer resources. The first student to successfully find all the items and write down the websites where they are located is declared the winner, the "Champion Computer Researcher." This activity promotes which of the following state goals for library media centers?**

    a. The ethical use of information resources
    b. The appreciation of diversity within a student group
    c. Effective oral and written communication
    d. Integrating technology into the library program

**58. A school librarian has an opportunity to help promote a proposed state law which would increase funding for school libraries, specifically in the area of granting funds for more technology in those libraries. She would have to make phone calls to voters and appear on TV to promote the library's technological needs. What should she do?**

    a. She should turn down the opportunity because public school employees are not supposed to get involved in politics
    b. She should limit her support activities to handing out flyers to her students to take home to their families, urging them to vote for the measure
    c. She should accept the opportunity but make phone calls to voters and give television interviews on her own time
    d. She should campaign only to her own school staff, urging them to vote for the measure

**59. A school librarian is cooperating with other librarians in the district to write a Fair Use Policy for the district that will be applied to all schools. Which of the following should NOT be included in that policy?**

    a. The conditions under which copies may be made of published material
    b. The length of time any one student may be allowed to spend on the Internet
    c. Guidelines for student access to the Internet, including whether or not students may have email accounts
    d. Penalties for violations of the Fair Use Policy, especially as it pertains to plagiarism

Copyright © Mometrix Media. You have been licensed one copy of this document for personal use only. Any other reproduction or redistribution is strictly prohibited. All rights reserved.
This content is provided for test preparation purposes only and does not imply an endorsement by Mometrix of any particular political, scientific, or religious point of view.

**60. A teacher approaches the school librarian with a lesson plan in Language Arts that will involve student research use several types of sources, including encyclopedias, biographies, and the Internet. How can the librarian best help the teacher achieve the goals of the lesson plan?**

a. Ask the teacher to give students the assignment and then schedule a time to bring the class to the library. Directly teach students research techniques for print materials and for the Internet. Show them how to locate internet databases that will meet their needs and how to coordinate information from several sources
b. Give the teacher a list of appropriate databases, show her where biographies and encyclopedias are shelved in the library, and ask her to schedule a time for her class to come in and do their research under her supervision
c. Schedule a time to visit the teacher's classroom and answer any questions students may have about doing this type of research
d. Assemble a cart for the teacher to check out for her classroom with encyclopedias and select biographies

**61. A teacher is concerned that some students in his class who were researching a topic through databases found some biased, incorrect information and unknowingly included it in their reports. What is the first action the librarian should take to prevent this from happening again?**

a. Have a staff meeting to discuss the problem of unreliable resources that may be biased. Ask teachers to help solve this problem
b. Obtain a list of suspect databases from the concerned teacher and evaluate each one carefully to see if the information is accurate, reliable, and unbiased. Remove these sources from the library's collection
c. Ask the concerned teacher to visit the websites himself and report to the librarian his opinion of the information he finds there
d. In your next period with this class, explain how to examine information obtained from the Internet for accuracy

**62. A librarian is drawing up a plan for a lesson on creating a slide show presentation. The class she is going to instruct contains several students for whom English is a second language. What is the best way for the librarian to handle the potential difficulties these students may have in understanding her?**

a. She should inform these students that if they feel they will not understand what she is saying, they are excused from the lesson and may spend the time browsing the library's collection
b. Since a slide show is a visual medium, she should take advantage of that and show what to do rather than lecturing about it. She can invite students to try some of the techniques she is teaching and make the lesson as hands-on as possible so that its content will cross the language barrier
c. She should assign each ESL student a student partner who will sit with them and help explain what she is saying
d. When she gives her lecture, she should speak very slowly and clearly and periodically stop to ask for anyone who does not understand the lesson to raise his or her hand

Copyright © Mometrix Media. You have been licensed one copy of this document for personal use only. Any other reproduction or redistribution is strictly prohibited. All rights reserved. This content is provided for test preparation purposes only and does not imply an endorsement by Mometrix of any particular political, scientific, or religious point of view.

**63. Several parents have volunteered to work in the library. The librarian wants to talk to all of them to find out what hours and days they have free and what kind of volunteer work they want to do. What is the most efficient way to gather this information and cause the least disruption to the potential volunteers?**

    a. Call each volunteer individually on the phone
    b. Send each volunteer an email and ask for email response
    c. Use teleconferencing so that they all can exchange information at the same time
    d. Ask the volunteers to attend an after-school volunteers' meeting

**64. Which of the following is not an advantage of the OPAC system?**

    a. Patrons can find materials easily
    b. Libraries can track what materials are checked out
    c. OPAC is an aid to purchasing and cataloging material
    d. It provides libraries with additional revenue

**65. A teacher wants to display the maps and models her students created during a geography unit. She approaches the librarian and asks if it would be appropriate to display them in the library. How should the librarian respond?**

    a. The librarian should say that geography is not related to English, reading, or literature, which are the library's primary goals and therefore not appropriate for library display
    b. The librarian should say that she has decorated the walls the way she wants them to remain during the school year, and it would be too much trouble to take them down for the teacher's display
    c. The librarian should say that children in other classes might become jealous if one class's material is on display and their own work is not
    d. The librarian should say that she will be happy to help organize a display of students' geography projects. After all, they did their geography research in the library. Other students will be inspired when they see the results of classroom work and library research

**66. A librarian receives a letter from a group that objects to a particular book in the school library. The group asks to have the book removed from the library's shelves. The librarian discusses the problem with her principal, who asks her to inform the group that in accordance with the selection policy adopted by the school district, the book will remain on the library shelves. What is the best form for her response to the protesting group to take?**

    a. Oral, in the form of a phone call to the leader of the complaining group
    b. Written, in the form of a letter to the group
    c. Electronic, in the form of an e-mail
    d. Nonverbal, no reply is given to the letter but a copy of the selection policy is sent to the complaining group

**67. When a school librarian is deciding to add to the library's collection, what is the first step she should take?**

    a. Create a written five-year collection plan
    b. Study the catalogs of the library's usual providers
    c. Evaluate the current collection and note any areas that lack materials
    d. Discuss adding to the collection with the principal

Copyright © Mometrix Media. You have been licensed one copy of this document for personal use only. Any other reproduction or redistribution is strictly prohibited. All rights reserved.
This content is provided for test preparation purposes only and does not imply an endorsement by Mometrix of any particular political, scientific, or religious point of view.

**68. A school librarian gives every student in the elementary school a book to read over the summer. Which of the following is the least beneficial reason to do so?**

    a. Students will have the opportunity to better maintain their reading skills

    b. Students could develop further interest in and knowledge of age-appropriate literature

    c. Students will have the opportunity to engage in an additional productive activity during the summer months

    d. Students will have the opportunity to get ahead on their reading for the next school year

**69. Plagiarism of materials is a common unethical practice by students. To help prevent it, a school librarian should do all of the following EXCEPT:**

    a. Early in the school year, teach a lesson to students about the ethical use of materials, how to put information in their own words, and the possible penalties for plagiarism

    b. Give teachers a list of websites that sell research papers

    c. Purchase software such as Turnitin.com that checks for plagiarism

    d. Notify the principal and send a letter to the student's parents whenever a student is observed using a website that sells research papers or copying material from the Internet into a report

**70. Which of the following actions taken by a librarian will best contribute to a library free of barriers?**

    a. Make sure that library chairs are the appropriate size for age groups that use the library

    b. Arrange books on shelves so that they can easily be reached from a wheelchair and are neither too high nor too close to the floor

    c. Have an area with a couch set aside for students to sit comfortably and read

    d. Automate the checkout process so it proceeds smoothly and students do not have to wait

**71. What is the educational impact of creating a comfortable reading area in the library, perhaps one with a couch or large armchair?**

    a. This area makes the library seem more like home than an institution

    b. The noise level in the library is reduced if some students are quietly reading

    c. Students may be challenged to select more difficult, challenging books to read

    d. Students will be encouraged to read when given a comfortable area, and their reading skills may increase with practice

**72. A librarian accesses some research models to help students find information for a report. Next, she shows students how to find these research models and tells them why they are more helpful than Google. What reasons does she give?**

    a. The research models are not as commercial as Google is

    b. Students can gain more detailed information from specific research models

    c. Her school district recommends this research model

    d. These research models are easier to use than search engines

**73. What kind of support would a librarian not expect from the Parents Organization at his school?**

    a. The Parents Organization collecting and donating books to the school library

    b. The Parents Organization holding fundraising activities, such as a school carnival, to raise funds that are donated to the school library

    c. The Parents Organization finding volunteers to help in the school library

    d. Support in getting the librarian a pay raise

Copyright © Mometrix Media. You have been licensed one copy of this document for personal use only. Any other reproduction or redistribution is strictly prohibited. All rights reserved.
This content is provided for test preparation purposes only and does not imply an endorsement by Mometrix of any particular political, scientific, or religious point of view.

**74. Which of the competencies for a beginning librarian did the librarian fulfill in the following conversation?**

Librarian: Juan, how can I help you today?
Juan:    I need something about World War II.
Librarian: Are you going to write a report about World War II?
Juan:    Actually, no. We are going to have a debate.
Librarian: About the whole war?
Juan:    No, just about the U.S. dropping that bomb on Hiroshima.
Librarian: Which side will you take in the debate, Juan?
Juan:    I am on the side that will argue that the bombing was justified.
Librarian: I know just the materials you want. We have some books over here. One is the autobiography of a man who was on that bombing flight. Over there, we have some DVDs with films of the aftermath and also an interview with President Truman during which the president explains his reasoning for giving the order to drop the bomb. And I'll write a list of websites where you can find more information.

a. Effectively interviews patrons to determine information needs
b. Applies bibliographic and retrieval techniques for organizing and using information sources
c. Employs a variety of techniques to guide the development of independent readers
d. Understands the role of the school library program as a central element in the intellectual life of the school

**75. In a school with a fixed library schedule, a classroom teacher asks the librarian if she could bring her class for two consecutive periods next week instead of the usual one. She has assigned her students to work in teams on different aspects of the U.S. Revolutionary War and feels that they will need more than just one class period to complete this research. What realistic but helpful response may the librarian give?**

a. Regretfully tell the teacher she has no extra time in her schedule. The school is on a fixed schedule and there are no "free periods." Suggest that small groups come to library on their free time at recess and lunch period
b. Respond that the library will be overcrowded if everyone in the class is looking for materials simultaneously. Suggest that the students come in shifts to do their research, perhaps team by team
c. Juggle the schedule, trading one teacher's period for another if necessary, to allow for the one-time-only extra time period and offer to start the class off by teaching some Internet research techniques and showing students where relevant books are located in the library
d. Decline the double period request because of the fixed library schedule but offer to pull a cart of relevant books instead and deliver these to the classroom

**76. A librarian's school has just been granted funding to hire a media clerk. The principal has asked the librarian to draw up a job description for the new position. Which of these items is not part of an appropriate job description for a media clerk?**

a. Assists in the checking in and checking out of library materials
b. Shelves materials as they are returned to the library
c. Prepares monthly library reports
d. Assists students who need help with research

Copyright © Mometrix Media. You have been licensed one copy of this document for personal use only. Any other reproduction or redistribution is strictly prohibited. All rights reserved.
This content is provided for test preparation purposes only and does not imply an endorsement by Mometrix of any particular political, scientific, or religious point of view.

**77. A librarian is approached by a student who wants to do an Internet search for Thomas Jefferson but does not know how. The student has been assigned to read a biography of Jefferson and then write a report on his life, which is due in ten days. What is the librarian's best course of action in this situation?**

a. The librarian shows the student how to do an Internet search using Google
b. Since the assignment is to read a biography, the librarian directs the student to the biography section of the library rather than to the Internet. She helps the student select a biography at his reading level
c. The librarian directs the student to database that will quickly provide a list of resources and articles pertaining to Thomas Jefferson
d. The librarian searches her computerized records, decides that none of the biographies in her school library are appropriate for this student, and initiates an inter-library loan. The borrowed biography will take about two weeks to arrive

**78. Which of the following activities would not encourage students to become independent readers?**

a. A contest that awards a prize to students who read the most pages in a given time
b. A student book club that meets weekly after school to discuss books they read
c. A book fair at which students and parents can purchase books
d. Book reports assigned in class

**79. Which of the following would not be a suitable organization for a librarian to join as part of her commitment to the library profession?**

a. The International Reading Association
b. The Scott O'Dell Historical Fiction Organization
c. The National Association of Librarians
d. The Association for Technology in Education

**80. In her media center, a librarian includes some audio CDs of books that are often assigned to students to read for their Language Arts class. She offers the recording along with the printed book to certain students. Which students should be allowed to use these audio books?**

a. Students who have hearing difficulties
b. Any student who requests an audio version of a book
c. Students who are struggling with reading skills
d. Students who have an auditory learning style

**81. Now that automated cataloging systems like MARC are available, when would a librarian need to use the Dewey Decimal system?**

a. When shelving books in the library
b. When checking whether or not a book is checked out
c. When preparing the monthly report for the library
d. When helping a patron use the card catalogue

**82. What is a computer network?**

a. A method for going online with a computer
b. A group of interconnected computers
c. A type of email used among employees or workers
d. An advanced anti-viral safety device

Copyright © Mometrix Media. You have been licensed one copy of this document for personal use only. Any other reproduction or redistribution is strictly prohibited. All rights reserved. This content is provided for test preparation purposes only and does not imply an endorsement by Mometrix of any particular political, scientific, or religious point of view.

**83. When materials are carefully cataloged and processed, the most important result is that:**
a. The library looks neat and well organized
b. Students and staff can easily find books and other materials
c. The librarian can devote more time to helping students
d. The librarian will probably receive a good evaluation

**84. Which document should be signed by both parents and students before that student may use the school's library computers?**
a. Acceptable Use Policy
b. Right to Information Act
c. Federal Privacy Policy
d. Copyright Law for Students and Teachers

**85. A librarian asks teachers to inform her as far ahead of time as possible about research projects and other reading or literature-oriented activities they are planning. Which of the following would not be a reason for this request?**
a. To set aside books on the topic reserved for a particular class
b. To plan a research lesson keyed to the area of study
c. To pull a cart of materials to be delivered to the teacher's classroom
d. To coordinate curriculum across grade levels so that different grade levels learn similar topics at similar times

**86. The library has received a large number of new acquisitions. How can the librarian best inform the staff about these new materials so that they can begin to use them?**
a. Make an announcement during the regular morning announcements and read aloud all the new titles
b. Circulate a memo advising staff members that new materials have arrived and asking that they check with the librarian to find out what they are
c. Post a list of the new materials on the checkout desk in the library
d. Announce at the next regular staff meeting that new materials have arrived, give a brief summary of what they are, and give teachers a handout that lists all the materials

**87. A middle school librarian is drawing up a budget to present to the principal for future funding of the library. She wants to shift library use from fixed scheduling to flexible scheduling and realizes this will require additional funding. What is a reasonable length of time for the librarian to forecast the completion of the shift so that the additional expenses can be gradually phased in?**
a. Sometime during the next school year, a period of nine months
b. One year
c. Two to four years
d. Three to five years

**88. Which of the following activities would be best to have as part of a "family night at the library"?**
a. Story time for young children
b. Book reviews of favorite books given by students who have read these books
c. A talk by the librarian on how the library functions
d. A speech by the principal on future goals for the library

Copyright © Mometrix Media. You have been licensed one copy of this document for personal use only. Any other reproduction or redistribution is strictly prohibited. All rights reserved.
This content is provided for test preparation purposes only and does not imply an endorsement by Mometrix of any particular political, scientific, or religious point of view.

**89. A librarian has arranged for a well-known historian to speak at the library on the topics of why history excites him and the methods he uses for research, both on the Internet and in books. Which of the following would be the best way to make sure that the community is aware of this event and invited to attend it?**

a. The librarian arranges for an announcement of the date and time of this event to be made during the school's morning announcements

b. The librarian draws up a flyer and sends copies to each classroom for students to take home

c. The librarian informs the local television station and invites them to send a film crew. She asks that a mention of the event be made during the evening news a few days before

d. As she meets with her scheduled daily classes, the librarian tells each class about the event and asks them to invite their families

**90. A student is using a library computer to research information about World War II. Among the websites she locates is one that represents a neo-Nazi group. How can the librarian help the student determine whether information from this website is factual and unbiased?**

a. The librarian can tell the student that this website is biased and not to trust it

b. The librarian can assist the student in finding information on the same topic from a different viewpoint. This situation provides the librarian with an opportunity to teach the student how to assess the reliability of information found on the Internet

c. The librarian can make sure that the library's filter will block that website in the future

d. The librarian can suggest that the student find three or four more resources before making a decision about this one

**91. A good way for a school librarian to assess students' performance is to:**

a. Start each lesson with a pop quiz on the last lesson

b. Point out student errors during discussion so that they will not repeat them

c. Incorporate unacceptable behavior into the grades she gives

d. Enlist the help of students in creating an evaluation system so that they understand and have some ownership of it

**92. Which of the following is not a reason for a school librarian to be able to demonstrate that her media center helps students meet national and state standards?**

a. Education today is standards-based

b. Meeting standards will cause the principal to look favorably on budget requests

c. Standards help organize the content of instruction

d. To help save the school money

**93. When a librarian is arranging the media center, an important consideration in the placement of the computer lab should be:**

a. Indirect lighting so that computer screens will be easily visible to students

b. The arrangement of computers so that each one can be seen by the librarian

c. The age and possible malfunctions of the computers

d. The placement of computers in a quiet part of the library so that students will not be distracted

Copyright © Mometrix Media. You have been licensed one copy of this document for personal use only. Any other reproduction or redistribution is strictly prohibited. All rights reserved.
This content is provided for test preparation purposes only and does not imply an endorsement by Mometrix of any particular political, scientific, or religious point of view.

**94. The circulation policy of a school media center needs to be fair and somewhat flexible because:**

   a. Students cannot always pay fines for overdue books
   b. Automated circulation procedures are easier to misuse
   c. The circulation policy controls the ease of access to materials in the media center
   d. Different materials should have different checkout periods

**95. Last week, a librarian taught students how to access certain databases. This week, the students are given the assignment to locate one database and answer questions based on what they find there. As the librarian moves from computer to computer, she observes that only a few of the students are managing to access the assigned database and, once there, are having trouble obtaining the answers to the assigned questions. What is the librarian's best course of action?**

   a. Help students individually at their computers
   b. End this unsuccessful assignment and use the period for student reading time
   c. Have the students leave their computers and gather around the librarian so that she can provide them with oral instructions about what to do
   d. Have the students leave their computers and gather around one computer so that they can observe the librarian as she models what they should do

**96. A librarian is helping a student create a slide show presentation that he is going to give to his classmates and teachers. Which of the following concepts would not be helpful for the librarian to bring to the student's attention as he creates his slide show presentation?**

   a. Design
   b. Content
   c. Audience
   d. Graphics creation

**97. What is the most important reason for a librarian to spend all her library funds before the administration "sweeps" the school's accounts?**

   a. A sweep means that remaining library funds will become unavailable
   b. A sweep before funds are spent will reduce the next year's funding
   c. The school expects her to use her budget every year
   d. The administration will be unhappy if she is seen as postponing expenditures

**98. The main focus of the lessons a librarian presents to classes should be:**

   a. How to use the Dewey Decimal System
   b. Information literacy concepts
   c. Improving students' reading skills
   d. Exposing students to literature at the appropriate grade level

**99. When is using interlibrary loan a better idea than purchasing the book or material?**

   a. When the book is too expensive
   b. When the book is controversial
   c. When the book is about an obscure subject
   d. When the book has been out of print for over five years

Copyright © Mometrix Media. You have been licensed one copy of this document for personal use only. Any other reproduction or redistribution is strictly prohibited. All rights reserved.
This content is provided for test preparation purposes only and does not imply an endorsement by Mometrix of any particular political, scientific, or religious point of view.

**100. What is the primary advantage of networking with librarians in other schools?**

    a.  A librarian will acquire advocates who will support her when she proposes a new idea for her library

    b.  A librarian will receive information about other libraries that she can use to improve her own program

    c.  A librarian will have a group of friends who have their work in common

    d.  A librarian will educate other librarians on new methods and technologies

Copyright © Mometrix Media. You have been licensed one copy of this document for personal use only. Any other reproduction or redistribution is strictly prohibited. All rights reserved.
This content is provided for test preparation purposes only and does not imply an endorsement by Mometrix of any particular political, scientific, or religious point of view.

# Answer Key and Explanations

**1. B:** Call the parents and ask them to help the student return the book. Parents will often know where the book is, will remind the child to return it, or will know if the book is lost or destroyed. Answer A would violate student privacy rules and embarrass the student. Answer C is incorrect because the responsibility of dealing with an overdue book lies with the librarian, not the principal. Answer D is incorrect because the librarian does not yet know if the book has been lost or destroyed.

**2. C:** Check with the principal to be sure of the school calendar and any school or district guidelines for fundraising activities. The school or district may have guidelines for fundraising activities. Discussing the book fair first with the principal is a collegial action, should help gain his/her support for the project, and clears the school calendar for the book fair date(s). Answers A, B and D are all appropriate activities, but they should take place after discussing the proposed book fair and its date with the principal.

**3. D:** Move the collection to higher shelves. Lower shelves do not allow wheelchair or handicapped access. Answers A and B are good ideas for non-handicapped students, but librarians are required to maintain a "barrier free" library environment. Answer C is incorrect because it does not address the problem of the books' location.

**4. D:** American Union of Library Employees. There is no such organization as the American Union of Library Employees. The other three answer choices are well-known professional associations that librarians should be encouraged to join in order to take advantage of their resources and support.

**5. A:** The book contains material that is outdated or inaccurate. As time passes, new information may supplant older, less accurate information. Books that will give the reader inaccurate information should be removed from the collection. Answers B and D are incorrect because organizations or parents should not make decisions about what books belong in the library. In conjunction with school and district administrators, the librarian will follow the district selection policy to determine the appropriateness of books in the collection. Answer C is incorrect because frequency of use should not govern when a book should be discarded. That rarely-used book may be the exact one needed by a student doing special research.

**6. D:** Bringing the idea to the parents for discussion before going through proper channels, even if the idea would be widely supported, would not help a new librarian gain cooperation from staff members.

**7. B:** When cataloging new books for the library collection. The MARC system is an electronic program for cataloging books. It replaces old card catalogs with a more efficient and user-friendly form of storing information. A is incorrect because weeding involves subtracting books from the collection, not adding them. The MARC system would not know if a book is damaged or its content outdated. C is incorrect because arranging books on the shelves is a physical action that involves a number of factors not tracked by the MARC system. D is incorrect because the MARC system is not a spreadsheet and is not designed for budgetary use.

**8. A:** Yes, under the Fair Usage provision of the copyright law. The Fair Usage provision of the copyright law states that copying and using selected parts of copyrighted works for specific educational purposes is permitted, especially if the copies are made spontaneously and are used temporarily. B is incorrect because of the Fair Usage provisions stated above. C is incorrect because

Copyright © Mometrix Media. You have been licensed one copy of this document for personal use only. Any other reproduction or redistribution is strictly prohibited. All rights reserved.
This content is provided for test preparation purposes only and does not imply an endorsement by Mometrix of any particular political, scientific, or religious point of view.

the principal is not the person who can grant permission to use copyrighted materials. D is incorrect because copying just one page and using it temporarily does not cause any loss of income to the author.

**9. B:** Create a display of books and other materials on ethnic topics and invite students and parents to visit one evening and browse the display. Then, have a discussion period during which parents and children are invited to share special aspects of their heritages and customs. This is the best activity because it involves both the community students in celebrating diversity. A might embarrass some students. C might involve spending a large part of the budget on books that only a few students would use. D might embarrass students because they are asked to speak in a language they may be just learning without any prior preparation.

**10. C:** After conferring with each classroom teacher about his or her current curriculum, demonstrate separately to different classes how to use the Internet to find information on the topic each class is presently studying. Teaching different classes to find materials they can use best supports the specific projects of each class. Students are more likely to pay attention to a demonstration if it involves something they need to do. A is incorrect because it leaves students on their own to blunder around trying to use an unfamiliar process. B is a good idea, but it takes the "one size fits all" approach to instruction. D is not the best approach because it encourages students to figure out a process by themselves, without teacher instruction or help.

**11. C:** Obtain the book through interlibrary loan. By using interlibrary loan, a librarian can expand access to books without exceeding the school's library budget. Answer A is not the best choice; since the book is not already in the school collection, it is probably one that not many students or teachers would use. Because of interlibrary loan, the librarian does not have to spend funds that may be needed for something else. B is not a good choice because the alternate resource may not be exactly what the teacher needs. In many cases, the teacher has already done some research to determine that a particular book is the one that best meets her needs. Answer D hands the problem over to another library and requires the teacher to make a visit that may or may not be successful.

**12. D:** Soliciting paid advertising to run on the library's website. If the library's website runs advertising promoting community bookstores, restaurants, or other local businesses that pay for this advertising, a conflict of interest might result. A, B, and C are common practices and are generally successful ways to raise funds.

**13. C:** Research all applicable national, state, and district standards. The librarian should thoroughly read all applicable standards and write a statement that complies with them. Answer A is incorrect because the principal may not be familiar with all the standards that apply to school libraries. Answer B is incorrect because other districts may have different standards from the ones that apply to this particular school library. Answer D is incorrect because the librarian does not need the superintendent's permission to draw up a statement of library standards; oftentimes, the superintendent or principal has asked the librarian to do this.

**14. C:** Demonstrate to the class how to use the library's computers for research. Answer A might involve leaving the library unsupervised and also may be viewed by the teacher as intrusive. Answers B and D are good ideas, but students who do not know how to use the library's computers for research will benefit most from demonstration and instruction.

**15. A:** Hold a brief staff meeting to instruct teachers and library staff in using the new software. If the staff knows how to use the software, they can assist individual students right away, even before students receive instruction from the librarian during their next scheduled library visit. Also, staff

Copyright © Mometrix Media. You have been licensed one copy of this document for personal use only. Any other reproduction or redistribution is strictly prohibited. All rights reserved.
This content is provided for test preparation purposes only and does not imply an endorsement by Mometrix of any particular political, scientific, or religious point of view.

members should become familiar with all new technology. Choice B risks that not all teachers will read the memo and be able to help their students use the software. C is the second action the librarian should take, but since she cannot meet with every class in one day, informing the teachers first is more important. D would carry individualized instruction to an extreme. The librarian would be unable to perform other tasks if she attempted to show students one at a time how to use the software.

**16. C:** Ask the student if he or she would like some help and abide by the student's response.

Some students would prefer to discover things by themselves without adult intervention. Answer A would result in success this time, but the student would not learn how to locate information in the future. Answer B involves waiting too long; frustrated students are not good learners. D is a good idea, but it should only be done if the student consents. Step C should come before D.

**17. A:** *The Horn Book*. This journal specializes in reviewing books at the elementary level. Answers B and C are incorrect because these resources mainly review adult literature. Answer D is incorrect because only books in the field of mathematics are discussed in the *MAA Reviews*.

**18. C:** Monitoring student use of cell phones. Student cell phone use is not part of the librarian's technological skill areas. The responsibility for students who bring cell phones to school belongs to the school, if it has regulations regarding cell phones at school, and if not, to the classroom teacher. Responsibilities described in Answers A, B, and D are increasingly becoming part of the school librarian's job description.

**19. C:** Consider ways to make the report more meaningful and design a new format.

The beginning librarian is better off not making any radical changes early in the term, especially if there is a required format for the monthly report. In the beginning, the report should look similar to the one from last year. The principal will expect and understand this format. Changes in it can be made gradually throughout the school year. Answers A, B and D are all good ways to prepare for writing the monthly report.

**20. D:** Circulation statistics, the number of individual and class visits to the library, and the usage of technology, including computer, databases, printers, and copiers, all add to the significance of a librarian's monthly report.

**21. B:** Collaborative projects with teachers. The primary purpose of the monthly report is to inform the principal how productive the library has been. This productivity includes more than circulation statistics. It includes projects the librarian has worked on with classroom teachers. Answer A is not a good choice because interpersonal problems, or infractions of the rules, are best dealt with informally and verbally. If written down, they may start conflicts or inflate concerns. Answer C is something to include in an annual budget request. A report details past events, not future plans. The same reasoning applies in Answer D. The monthly library report is not the proper venue for budget requests, although it is possible to write the report in such a way that it hints at future needs.

**22. B:** The card catalog. OPAC is a computerized catalog that patrons can use to search for resources. Answer A, The MARC system is a data base that can be accessed through OPAC. Answer C, The Dewey Decimal system is a system for manually organizing library materials based on common subject matter, and is still used for shelving books in the library and locating books. The Reader's Guide to Periodical Literature is a printed guide to locating periodic materials. It is being replaced by similar online services.

Copyright © Mometrix Media. You have been licensed one copy of this document for personal use only. Any other reproduction or redistribution is strictly prohibited. All rights reserved. This content is provided for test preparation purposes only and does not imply an endorsement by Mometrix of any particular political, scientific, or religious point of view.

**23. B:** The visit will contribute to literature appreciation for all students. The exposure to a successful writer will encourage students in their own writing, as well as encourage them to read the writer's books. Answer A is incorrect because while media attention may be a positive result of the visit, it is not the main reason. Library-generated activities should be focused on what is best for students. Answer C is incorrect for the same reason. The library might increase its funds a little, but that would not be the main, student-centered reason for inviting the author. Answer D is also a good result, but adding to statistics would not be the purpose for the visit.

**24. B:** Have students work on the assignment in pairs or small groups. Assign students to groups in which each struggling ESL student will have a partner to help him or her understand and complete the assignment. Encourage groups or pairs to ask for help as needed. Peer-based instruction is more likely to be accepted by an ESL student and is less embarrassing than if the student were singled out by the librarian for individual help. Answer A singles out these students and, in fact, leaves them out. The librarian may not have time for individual instruction later on. Meanwhile, the class will have moved beyond these students in computer research skills. Answer C does not guarantee that the ESL students will understand the instructions, even if they are given slowly and in simple language. These students may not ask for help because of not wanting to be singled out for their language difficulties. Some may simply not attempt the assignment. Answer D also does not guarantee understanding. Students who do not have enough English vocabulary will probably not understand written instructions better than oral ones.

**25. B:** Quietly discuss with the student the rules about plagiarism, show him ways to put information in his own words, and ask to see his report when he has rewritten it. By handling the matter in a firm but low-key way, the librarian will avoid embarrassing the student or making him defensive. However, to make sure he understood her explanation of plagiarism, the librarian should ask to see his report after he writes it in his own words. Answer A, notifying the teacher, passes on the problem to someone else. The teacher has not observed what the librarian has observed; therefore, the problem is best handled by the librarian. Answer C also passes on the problem and inflates it as well. It is possible the student did not understand about plagiarism. He should be given a second chance. Answer D also assumes that the student should be treated as a habitual offender. It might be a good choice should he plagiarize a second time.

**26. A:** Weeding and schedule changing. Librarians need to know the library's content thoroughly before deciding what materials to weed and what to acquire. If a librarian discards a teacher's favorite materials, she will lose a supporter of the library. The librarian should wait awhile before weeding. Answer B should be done early in the year so that staff members understand that plagiarism is widespread, sometimes inadvertent, and what teachers can do about it. Answer C is always a good idea whenever the librarian can find time in the school and library schedule. Answer D, reorganizing the furniture, can be done right away. The arrangement of the librarian's space should reflect her personal philosophy and competency.

**27. D:** Hearing stories read aloud contributes to students' interest in reading. Answer A is one reason why story hours are sometimes scheduled, but it is not an educational, student-centered reason. Answer B may be a result of a story hour, but it is not the main reason for this activity. Answer C may happen incidentally, but reading instruction itself is the responsibility of the classroom teacher.

**28. A:** Knowing about changes to the curriculum and participating in making those changes will enable the librarian to acquire materials that support the new curriculum. Answer B is not correct because the planned curriculum committee is at the district level. Answer C is not likely. Librarians

Copyright © Mometrix Media. You have been licensed one copy of this document for personal use only. Any other reproduction or redistribution is strictly prohibited. All rights reserved. This content is provided for test preparation purposes only and does not imply an endorsement by Mometrix of any particular political, scientific, or religious point of view.

and teachers are all given documents explaining state curriculum requirements. Answer D is also unlikely.

**29. A:** Instructing them in effective ways to do research on the Internet and in efficient use of library reference materials and books on the library shelves. Answer A fulfills both the librarian's responsibilities and the students' needs. Instruction of this sort can be tailored to ongoing classroom projects and individualized to meet the needs of students who need support, as well as students who can work on their own. Answer B does not produce any educational results. Part of assigned library time should be set aside for exchanging books, but not all of it. Answer C is like a "story time" for older students, although making students aware of new materials should be part of the librarian's instructional plans from time to time. Although answer D is very helpful to the librarian, it is of little educational value to the students.

**30. C:** By determining teachers' needs in advance, the librarian can give maximum assistance at the proper time and integrate the teacher's curriculum into her own. The librarian can pull material from the collection and loan the teacher a cart of appropriate research materials to use in the classroom at the time of each project. In a school with a fixed schedule, the librarian will plan instruction in ways to research these topics on the appropriate dates when she meets with those classes. In a school with flexible scheduling, the librarian will suggest that teachers sign up to bring classes to the library when they begin a new topic.

**31. C:** Organizing space into areas that can be flexibly arranged to accommodate different sizes of groups as well as community activities held after school. Answer A is probably not feasible in a library where the walls are filled with student work and other materials. The furniture size is probably already fixed in this library, and although it should accommodate students of different sizes, this is not a factor of room arrangement. Answer D is probably not feasible either, given that most libraries have bookshelves and small corners that cannot all be observed from the desk. Even if D could be accomplished, it still would not be most important aspect of arranging the library.

**32. C:** Student-produced work.

**33. B:** Have an open house in the library once a month and invite families to browse the library's collection and get to know the librarian. Answer A is too restrictive, involving only some students. Answer C is also too limited, involving only the option of research and, again, only students. Answer D assumes that all parents can receive e-mail, which may not be true. Also, the scheduled hours might not work for certain families.

**34. A:** Using a variety of instructional techniques that actively involve students in listening, working with various media and materials, reading, and writing. Answer B is not really feasible in a library setting. It would involve the librarian rushing from group to group and being unable to supervise the groups. Answer C would have the same problem, besides possibly embarrassing slower learners. Answer D is incorrect because the librarian would be disengaged from their learning process, and the students could be embarrassed or struggle with the written content.

**35. D:** The librarian should use electronic and print media to inform families and communities. Informing students and hoping the message gets to the families is not the most effective way to communicate.

**36. C:** An Acceptable Use Policy. An acceptable use policy outlines allowable Internet access. In order to access school computers, parents and students usually must agree to this policy in writing. On occasion, filters on library computer block a whole category, parts of which may contain information useful to students. The librarian should be able to unblock some harmless sites for

Copyright © Mometrix Media. You have been licensed one copy of this document for personal use only. Any other reproduction or redistribution is strictly prohibited. All rights reserved. This content is provided for test preparation purposes only and does not imply an endorsement by Mometrix of any particular political, scientific, or religious point of view.

specific reasons. Answer A is incorrect because the Patriot Act affects libraries mainly by attempting to seek lists of materials borrowed by certain users. Answer B, the No Child Left Behind Act, refers to academic progress and school accountability, not to acceptable Internet use. MARC records are used to track library materials and their usage.

**37. B:** Using keywords with "or," "but," or "and." A Boolean search enables a researcher to define precise limits for searches. For example, a student might enter "temples *and* Greece *but* not Athens" if looking for Greek temples that are not in Athens. Answer A is incorrect because mathematics is not involved in a Boolean search, although a certain level of logic is required. Answer C is incorrect because a Boolean search does not require a special database. Answer D is incorrect because the Dewey Decimal System is a way of organizing information, not a way of searching the Internet.

**38. D:** Critiquing books. The librarian should remain neutral about books and other materials in the library's collection, recognizing that there are many points of view on an issue and many writing styles. The librarian is responsible for scheduling classes and library-related events, reporting on the functioning and collection of the library, and maintaining and facilitating circulation of the library's materials.

**39. C:** Speak to the boys firmly about proper library behavior. Since the students are in the library, they are on the librarian's territory, and she has as much responsibility as the teacher to see that they behave correctly. The teacher has had a chance to correct these boys but has not done it. Speaking to him about their behavior might embarrass the teacher or make him resentful. He might continue to ignore it. After it is clear that the teacher is aware of the behavior and is choosing not to intervene, the librarian should corral the unruly students and remind them how to behave in the library. Answer D is not necessary because the problem can be handled by the librarian without the need to hand it over to someone else.

**40. B:** Draw up a complete job description of the position. Before a media clerk can be hired, the librarian must have a clear plan for how best to use this person's skills. Also, the applicant needs to know exactly what the job entails. The librarian should draw up the job description and then search for someone to fill it. The job description can also serve as the basis for evaluating the media clerk later on. Answer A would be a good second step. Answer C is not a good idea because it limits the pool of applicants to those the librarian already knows. Answer D is not a very productive idea because each library is unique and has its own needs.

**41. C:** Form a committee of interested teachers to help weed the collection at a time that is convenient for everyone. If teachers are involved in the process of weeding, they will support the idea and be content with its results. The librarian should seek faculty help for this task. Answer A, canceling classes, would deprive some students of instruction and book selection opportunities and might be in violation of the librarian's contract. Answer B is feasible but puts the entire decision-making task on the shoulders of the librarian. Also, it calls for working extra hours. Answer D is not a good idea because students do not yet have a clear grasp of criteria for keeping or removing a book from the library collection.

**42. D:** Book reports assigned in class would not encourage enjoyment of reading. The librarian is responsible for encouraging students to become independent readers. There are several strategies that help accomplish this goal, including the options listed in answer choices A, B and C.

**43. A:** Ask the student what his assignment is and what kind of books he is looking for.

Before the librarian can effectively help the student, she must interview him about his needs. If his answer is vague, such as, "Well, I have to write this science paper," she should ask him a series of

Copyright © Mometrix Media. You have been licensed one copy of this document for personal use only. Any other reproduction or redistribution is strictly prohibited. All rights reserved.
This content is provided for test preparation purposes only and does not imply an endorsement by Mometrix of any particular political, scientific, or religious point of view.

questions until she understands his exact need. Then, she can assist him in finding appropriate materials. Answer B assumes that the student knows what book he wants and does not know how to find it. This may not be the case. He may not know what book will help him. Answer C puts the problem off until another time, and the student may have a deadline to complete his assignment. Answer D takes valuable library time away from the student assigned help, and that student will not know as much as the librarian does about available materials.

**44. C:** Use OPAC to find MARC entries about Monarch butterfly migration. The student clearly needs guidance in locating research materials. OPAC is a computerized catalog that will help narrow his search to appropriate materials. The Dewey Decimal System has been replaced in most libraries with computerized catalogs like OPAC. B might be a helpful suggestion, but the topic is so broad that too many responses would probably be generated. D, the *Readers' Guide to Periodical Literature*, is another outdated print resource now generally replaced by online data resources.

**45. C:** Send a note home with students inviting parents to a "parents' night" at the library.

Sending a note home with students is often an unreliable way to communicate. Not all students remember to take home a note, or if they do take it home, many forget to give it to parents. Using the school newsletter and/or school website will be more effective. In your message asking for volunteers, remember to make volunteering in the library sound as interesting as it really is. For parents' night, serve refreshments, display students' work, and consider having a few students talk to the group about how they use the library.

**46. C:** Make a comprehensive daily, weekly, and monthly plan listing what needs to be done, the deadline for completing each task, and the person responsible for handling the task.

Making a detailed plan of goals, needs, assigned times, etc. will clearly lay out for the librarian what her tasks are. She can estimate the time required for each and assign a date and time for completion of each item. Answer A would not be the best first step, because after making the plan, it may be evident that the media clerk is already performing all that he/she can handle. Answer B might be a good second step, but it is not a good first step. If the library has traditionally managed with the number of employees it presently has, then the problem is more likely to be time management than the need for more help. After the beginning librarian has made her plans, she can show the principal item by item what the problems are and ask for his help if it turns out that her workload is indeed excessive. Answer D, putting in overtime hours, may be necessary but that fact will not be clear until the planning takes place. An exhausted librarian will not be efficient, so that option is not the most desirable.

**47. B:** Discuss her plans for change with the principal and get his/her input about the concept and affordability of flexible scheduling, as well as the potential costs to the library of hosting special events. There is likely to be a financial component to making these changes. In some school settings, having a flexible schedule means that the school must hire someone to give the teachers the prep periods they formerly had during a fixed schedule. Hosting special events can require extended hours for a school's custodial staff, along with additional electrical and heating expenses. The librarian needs to find out from the principal if the school budget can handle these changes. Also, as a matter of diplomacy, obtaining the principal's support for a change in practice is a good management technique. Answer A could cause dissension among staff members and bring criticism from an uninformed principal. Answer C is the easy way out, but it will not result in achievement of the librarian's goals. Answer D is a good second step for the librarian to take after she has obtained the support of the principal.

Copyright © Mometrix Media. You have been licensed one copy of this document for personal use only. Any other reproduction or redistribution is strictly prohibited. All rights reserved. This content is provided for test preparation purposes only and does not imply an endorsement by Mometrix of any particular political, scientific, or religious point of view.

**48. D:** Bringing the idea to the parents for discussion before going through proper channels, even if the idea would be widely supported, would not help a librarian communicate better with district officials or school administration. The librarian's vision for her media center should be written in a goal statement, perhaps with a reasonable time frame included if expensive changes are foreseen. After drawing up the statement (A), the librarian should share it with the principal (B), and get that person's feedback and suggestions, which can be included in a new draft of the goal statement to be shared with school district administration or the school board (C). This way, the librarian will find out if all of her goals are considered feasible and important by the people who will fund most of them.

**49. B:** Hardware is a physical component of a computer, such as a monitor, RAM, CPU, hard drive, or motherboard. Software is a series of coded instructions that direct the computer to perform certain operations. Hardware includes the physical parts of a computer that a person can touch. Software consists of the programs that run the hardware, such as a browser, operating system, or word processing program. Answers A, C and D all refer to software items on a computer.

**50. B:** A telephone call to each family. A telephone call to each family would require too much time, when it is possible to speak with a number of families at the same time through teleconferencing. A slide show presentation to the parents club or school board or a community organization can be a very effective way to demonstrate the library in action during the school day. A newsletter will inform parents of what is going on in the media center and of future dates for upcoming events, such as a parents' night, after-school book club, or book fair.

**51. A:** The librarian should accept the invitation because business people can support the media center in several ways, including donating computers, giving money for library projects, and supporting the goals and visions of the librarian and her school. By attending the luncheon, she will create good will for the school and the library. Answer B is incorrect in stating that making connections with the business community is not part of the librarian's job. This responsibility is specifically mentioned in Domain II, Competency 004. Also, creating good will in the community is important in order to have community support of the school and the library. Answer C offers a negative view of this opportunity. Through her speech and her handout, the librarian can impact the business community present at the meeting and the wider business community consisting of the members' friends and associates. She can explain the rationale behind the operation of a modern media center. There is no reason to think that her audience will not pay attention. Answer D also offers a negative view of the reason for her invitation. After the librarian's speech, there will probably be a question and answer period during which she can clear up any misconceptions.

**52. B:** You may exchange information from each other's databases. Answer A is incorrect because interlibrary loan is an easier way to obtain books students need that are not in your library. Answer C may be true, but that fact does not help the librarian in her job. Answer D is incorrect because once a librarian discovers what is in the collections of these libraries, she can use interlibrary loan to obtain needed materials on a temporary basis without having to purchase the books.

**53. D:** Check the items received against the purchase orders. As items arrive, it is important to first make sure that everything ordered in each purchase order has been received in the library. Answer A is incorrect because books will probably be processed with spine labels before they are shipped. Answers B and C are necessary actions to take after checking off the arriving items.

**54. B:** To verify that the subject matter is accurate and covers student and teacher needs.

Copyright © Mometrix Media. You have been licensed one copy of this document for personal use only. Any other reproduction or redistribution is strictly prohibited. All rights reserved.
This content is provided for test preparation purposes only and does not imply an endorsement by Mometrix of any particular political, scientific, or religious point of view.

Through this review, the librarian may discover that some subjects are not properly covered in the database, and she may need to purchase others. Answer A is incorrect because a review of the database will not reveal student plagiarism. Answer C is incorrect because a filter prevents students from accessing inappropriate sites. This information is not found on a database. Answer D is incorrect because students with a variety of reading skills will access each database.

**55. D:** Bibliography. A bibliography is not usually a part of a visual presentation such as a slide show. The purpose of a slide show presentation is to engage the audience visually. Techniques for doing this would be the main points of a lesson in creating a slide show presentations. A bibliography might be in the form of a handout to the audience after the presentation.

**56. B:** Raise money for library needs and projects. A visit by a writer is not likely to bring in much, if any, money for the library. If copies of the writer's books are sold to students so that he can autograph them, he will probably supply those copies and receive the funds from the sales. The purpose of having a visiting writer is expressed in the other three choices. The visit will encourage student interest in reading and writing, which may be evidenced by an increase in circulation. Some students may develop an interest in reading or writing they did not previously have, with the possible goal of becoming a writer themselves.

**57. D:** Integrating technology into the library program. By creating an interesting activity that prompts students to discover the functions of various computer programs, the librarian is integrating computer technology into the library program. Answer A, ethical use, does not apply here, as nothing is copied or plagiarized during the search. Answer B also does not apply because diversity is not an issue. Everyone is equal when using a computer. Answer C does not apply because the students are not using oral or written communication.

**58. C:** She should accept the opportunity but make phone calls to voters and give television interviews on her own time. It is very likely that the librarian's school district will appreciate her involvement in promoting the measure. Public school employees are usually prohibited from political involvement in the classroom or during the school day but not necessarily on their own time. Answer B is exactly the opposite of what the librarian should do. She should not advocate a funding measure in the library or give students handouts about it. Answer D is something she can do casually, during conversations in the staff room, but she is also free to promote the legislation more than that on her own time. In fact, according to Domain III, she should do so.

**59. B:** The length of time any one student may be allowed to spend on the Internet.

Student needs for Internet access vary by school, by program, and by the number of computers available for student use. The time constraints for usage should be determined school by school rather than through a district-wide Fair Use Policy. Answers A, C, and D should all be included in a district-wide Fair Use Policy.

**60. A:** Ask the teacher to give students the assignment and then schedule a time to bring the class to the library. Directly teach students research techniques for print materials and for the Internet. Show them how to locate internet databases that will meet their needs and how to coordinate information from several sources. Answer A provides the best way for students to learn research techniques, especially since they will be interested because of the assignment. Answer B puts the entire burden on the teacher with no real assistance from the librarian. Answer C may not be possible unless the library has a media clerk who can be present if the librarian leaves the library. Also, it is really not necessary because the teacher can bring the class to the library. Answer D is also incorrect because another one of the answer choices is more appropriate.

Copyright © Mometrix Media. You have been licensed one copy of this document for personal use only. Any other reproduction or redistribution is strictly prohibited. All rights reserved.
This content is provided for test preparation purposes only and does not imply an endorsement by Mometrix of any particular political, scientific, or religious point of view.

**61. B:** Obtain a list of suspect databases from the concerned teacher and evaluate each one carefully to see if the information is accurate, reliable and unbiased. Remove these sources from the library's collection. The librarian is the person responsible for assessing information from databases for accuracy and/or bias. Answer A, asking busy teachers to help with the problem, is asking them to do something they may not know how to do or have time to do. Answer C also puts the burden on the teacher when the responsibility for determining accuracy is the librarian's. Answer D is a good follow-up after the librarian has assessed the databases, but it is not the first step to take.

**62. B:** Since a slide show is a visual medium, she should take advantage of that and show what to do rather than lecturing about it. She can invite students to try some of the techniques she is teaching and make the lesson as hands-on as possible so that its content will cross the language barrier. All students enjoy a hands-on lesson, and by giving one, the librarian is making sure that ESL students are not derided or embarrassed by their language difficulties. Answer A singles them out and excludes them from learning something they would benefit from knowing. Answer C is not feasible because the partner would not be understood any more than the librarian. Answer D is apt to embarrass ESL students, although speaking slowly and clearly is a good idea.

**63. C:** Use teleconferencing so that they all can exchange information at the same time.

Answer A, calling each volunteer, is a time-consuming way to meet with volunteers and also deprives them of the opportunity to interchange ideas. Answer B, composing an email response, may be a difficult task for some volunteers—not everyone is Internet savvy. Answer D requires volunteers to travel to school at a time that may not be convenient for them.

**64. D:** OPAC (Online Public Access Catalog) is an automated system that helps patrons search for library materials, tracks checked-out materials, and assists in purchasing and cataloging. It does not provide libraries with additional revenue.

**65. D:** The librarian should say that she will be happy to help organize a display of students' geography projects. After all, they did their geography research in the library. Other students will be inspired when they see the results of classroom work and library research.

School libraries should be decorated with student work. As for Answer A, the subject matter of the proposed display is not relevant. Libraries should contain material on all subjects. Answer B is a selfish response, actually indicating that the librarian finds changing the displays to be too much work. Answer C offers an unlikely possibility.

**66. B:** Written, in the form of a letter to the group. A written response is best because it is a record of the school's decision in the matter. It can be used as evidence if the situation escalates and there are more protests. A, a phone call, would not be the best choice because there is no written record of what is said by both parties during the phone call. An e-mail is a form of written response but does not constitute evidence. Answer D might be seen as insulting by the group because there is no actual response to their complaint.

**67. C:** Evaluate the current collection and note any areas that lack materials. Before the librarian can plan for the future, she must assess the present status of the school library's collection. If there are materials lacking that teachers have requested, these should have priority in the new collection. Answers A, B, and D are steps that need to be taken in the acquisition process, but evaluating what is on hand must be the first step.

**68. D:** Not all school librarians will have funds to do this, but giving students a book for the summer will give them the opportunity to keep up both their reading skills and their interest in reading, as

**157**

Copyright © Mometrix Media. You have been licensed one copy of this document for personal use only. Any other reproduction or redistribution is strictly prohibited. All rights reserved.
This content is provided for test preparation purposes only and does not imply an endorsement by Mometrix of any particular political, scientific, or religious point of view.

well as possibly engage them in an additional educational activity. Assigning reading as homework over the summer in elementary school is unlikely to be productive or well-received by students or parents. In addition, it is not a best practice to require students to read too far ahead of time as they are less likely to be engaged in or remember the material when the student returns to classes.

**69. D:** Notify the principal and send a letter to the parents whenever a student is observed using a website that sells research papers or copying material from the Internet directly into her report. Actions A, B and C will be helpful to teachers and students in the effort to prevent plagiarism. As for D, those actions should probably not be taken by the librarian. The librarian who observes a student in the library plagiarizing should speak to the student and perhaps to the teacher. Taking the matter farther, to the principal or the family, should be the teacher's responsibility. The teacher will know the student better than the librarian and will be aware if this attempt to plagiarize is a first effort or an ongoing problem.

**70. B:** Arrange books on shelves so that they can easily be reached from a wheelchair and are neither too high nor too close to the floor. Having a barrier-free library means that the facilities are accessible to people with disabilites. Answer A refers to having small chairs for young children and larger chairs for older children, a plan that is necessary but unrelated to having a barrier-free library. Answers C and D encourage all students to read but do not particularly accommodate students with disabilities.

**71. D:** Students will be encouraged to read when given a comfortable area, and their reading skills may increase with practice. A well-designed school library should include some space for private reading. If such space is available, students will be encouraged to read as a leisure-time activity and at the same time may increase their reading skills. Answer A is not an educational impact of a having reading area. Answer B does not refer to any benefits the student may derive.

**72. B:** Students can gain more detailed information from specific research models; if school districts recommend or require the use of a specific research model, teachers and students will have the same framework for evaluating student projects. Answer A is not relevant because the financial backing of a particular research model does not reflect its relevance or the significance of its information. Answer C does not restrict the librarian to district-recommended materials. Answer D may or may not be true, but the importance of the task lies in the results, what students can find out by using these research models.

**73. D:** The school librarian should seek a relationship with the parents' organization at the school, because this organization is a source of funding, book donations, and volunteers. However, a librarian pay raise is not part of supporting the work of the school library.

**74. A:** Effectively interviews patrons to determine information needs. Note that in the beginning of the conversation between Juan and the librarian, he is at first vague and general about his topic. The librarian asks a series of skillful questions to narrow down the subject area and is then able to help Juan. Answer B would apply to the librarian's knowledge of appropriate materials, but her primary action in the conversation is to determine Juan's information needs. Answer C is incorrect because Juan is not trying to improve his reading skills. He is looking for information. Answer D deals with the librarian's philosophy and not with her ability to discover a patron's needs.

**75. C:** Juggle the schedule, trading one teacher's period for another if necessary to allow for the one-time-only extra time period and offer to start the class off by teaching some Internet research techniques and showing students where relevant books are located in the library.

Copyright © Mometrix Media. You have been licensed one copy of this document for personal use only. Any other reproduction or redistribution is strictly prohibited. All rights reserved.
This content is provided for test preparation purposes only and does not imply an endorsement by Mometrix of any particular political, scientific, or religious point of view.

Even on a fixed schedule, there are a few free periods for students to come to the library and exchange books. The librarian could trade periods with another teacher (with that teacher's permission) who is normally scheduled for the period before or after one of those free periods. Prior to the scheduled time period, the librarian and teacher can discuss and plan relevant instruction in research skills for this class. Answer A is too inflexible and discounts the possibility of juggling schedules. Answer B is unlikely, because a whole class at a time is usually in the library, especially if the schedule is fixed. Answer D offers to provide some help to the teacher, but not as much as in answer C.

**76. C:** Prepares monthly library reports. The preparation of monthly reports is the responsibility of the librarian. Checking in materials and shelving them, as well as helping students locate what they need, are part of the media clerk's job description.

**77. B:** Since the assignment is to read a biography, the librarian directs the student to the biography section of the library rather than to the Internet. She helps the student select a biography at his reading level. In this particular case, the student will benefit more from using the library's own resources than from using the Internet. The school library will probably have a biography of Thomas Jefferson, and the arrival date for the interlibrary loan would be too late for the student's needs.

**78. D:** Book reports assigned in class would not encourage enjoyment of independent reading.

**79. B:** Scott O'Dell Historical Fiction Organization. The Scott O'Dell Organization awards an annual prize to an author of children's historical fiction. It is not a professional library organization. The other three are.

**80. C:** Students who are struggling with reading skills. Some students who are having difficulty learning to read will benefit from "reading along" with a recording. They view and hear the words at the same time, which helps increase their reading vocabulary. Answer A describes students who would not benefit from listening to a story because they are deaf or hard of hearing. Answer B is probably not a good idea because some students, even good readers, would be tempted to listen to the tape instead of reading the book. Answer D is incorrect because reading requires a visual mode, and learning style is irrelevant in this situation.

**81. A:** When shelving books in the library. Library books are organized on library shelves according to the Dewey Decimal system. Automated systems like MARC keep track of books that are checked out. The librarian's monthly report will contain statistics, and she will not need to refer to the Dewey Decimal system to complete it. Most libraries do not have card catalogs anymore, so when a librarian helps a patron locate a specific book, she looks in her computer.

**82. B:** A group of interconnected computers. Computers may be connected in a variety of ways, wired or wireless, for a variety of purposes. Answer A refers to an Internet server such as Yahoo. Answers C and D refer to software that can be used on a computer.

**83. B:** Students and staff can easily find books and other materials. Since the main purpose of having a school library is to benefit students, a well-organized catalog and shelving system accomplishes that goal. Answer A, a neat library, is a nice feature of a library, but it is not as important as answer B. Answer C may not be a result of careful processing of materials, but of other factors. Answer D, a good evaluation for the librarian, may or may not happen because a number of other factors enter into an evaluation.

Copyright © Mometrix Media. You have been licensed one copy of this document for personal use only. Any other reproduction or redistribution is strictly prohibited. All rights reserved. This content is provided for test preparation purposes only and does not imply an endorsement by Mometrix of any particular political, scientific, or religious point of view.

**84. A:** Acceptable Use Policy. The Acceptable Use Policy outlines ethical computer research needs, such as plagiarism and other kinds of copyright violation. By signing it, students and parents agree to abide by its regulations. Answers B, C and D are not valid documents.

**85. D:** If the librarian knows the topic a class will be studying in advance, there will be time to set aside books on the topic at the students' reading level, plan a lesson on how best to research this particular topic, and even deliver a set of support materials to the classroom.

**86. D:** Announce at the next regular staff meeting that new materials have arrived, give a brief summary of what they are, and give a teachers a handout that lists all of these materials. The librarian's report is backed up by the written materials list. Answer A, make an announcement and read aloud the titles, is not practical because it would take too long. Also, teachers might not be listening, as morning announcements are generally directed to students. Answer B does not give enough information for the teacher to decide which new materials are worth scrutinizing. Also, there is no guarantee the teachers will read the memo. Answer C, posting a list on the checkout desk, does not guarantee that very many teachers will see the list because most books are checked out by students.

**87. D:** Three to five years. In a middle school, a fixed library schedule is oftentimes used to provide a prep period for teachers. A flexible schedule would eliminate library time as prep time, and the school would need to hire additional staff to cover the prep periods. School board approval might be required, depending on district regulations. If the librarian can gradually phase in the flexible scheduling, perhaps one grade level per year, her plan is more likely to be approved.

**88. B:** Book reviews of favorite books given by students who have read these books. Family night is an opportunity for the librarian to celebrate what students have accomplished in the library. Student-produced materials, including book reviews, oral reports, and research-based art projects, should be part of every family gathering at the library. The other activities would probably not be very successful. If the librarian gathers young children and reads them a story, she is removing herself from the other people attending family night. If she gives a speech or if the principal gives a speech, the audience will not be as impressed with the library as they would be by seeing their own children's work on display.

**89. C:** The librarian informs the local television station and invites them to send a film crew. She asks that a mention of the event be made during the evening news a few days before.

Involving the local media is the most effective way to inform a whole community of a special event. Students cannot be depended on to remember an oral announcement, whether it comes over the classroom speaker or is told to a group by the librarian. Likewise, the librarian cannot be certain that flyers will be taken home.

**90. B:** The librarian can assist the student in finding information on the same topic from a different viewpoint. This situation provides the librarian with an opportunity to teach the student how to assess the reliability of information found on the Internet. Answer A is not wrong, but it is not the best course of action. The librarian can tell the student that this website is biased, and not to trust it, but it is not the best solution because the student may face the same problem again. Teaching someone how to recognize biased language or to recognize that a certain website is run by an organization with a strong viewpoint will give a student much-needed analysis skills for the future. Answer C is something to be done in the future, but it will not help this student in the present. Answer D leaves all the responsibility up to the student to find more websites and compare them. The student needs established criteria before comparing information from different sources.

Copyright © Mometrix Media. You have been licensed one copy of this document for personal use only. Any other reproduction or redistribution is strictly prohibited. All rights reserved.
This content is provided for test preparation purposes only and does not imply an endorsement by Mometrix of any particular political, scientific, or religious point of view.

**91. D:** Enlist the help of students in creating an evaluation system so that they understand and have some ownership of it. The best way to evaluate students is to let them know the criteria from the beginning so that they understand the librarian's expectations. If they have been involved in drawing up the criteria, they will be more accepting of the librarian's evaluation of their progress. Answer A, start each lesson with a pop quiz, would not be practical because some students might have missed the lesson. Also a quiz tests only knowledge, not performance. Answer B, point out student errors, requires the librarian to be careful not to alienate students by embarrassing them and does not foster change. Answer C, incorporate unacceptable behavior into grades, would make the grades too ambiguous. The librarian should evaluate growth in library skills. Generally, most reporting forms have a section where the evaluator can indicate a need for behavior improvement.

**92. D:** Every state has standards for student performance at each level and in each subject. The library educational program is included. If the librarian's report indicates which standards the library program has assisted students in meeting, the school principal will probably accept the need for materials to continue this success. Standards are a useful way for the librarian to check off the goals she is trying to meet through her instruction.

**93. B:** The arrangement of computers so that each one can be seen by the librarian. The librarian must be able to view computer screens easily so that she can quickly help any student who needs assistance. Lighting is not generally a factor in computer placement because the screens are bright enough to be visible in most lighting situations. The age of the computer is not relevant to where in the media center it is placed. Students at computers are no more easily distracted by noise than students elsewhere in the media center.

**94. C:** The circulation policy controls the ease of access to materials in the media center.

A circulation policy should make the continual use of library materials possible. If the policy is too strict, patrons will have difficulty accessing some materials. For example, a checkout period of three weeks means that no one else can access that book until it is returned. A shorter period would be better. Answer A, whether or not students should pay fines, may be part of a circulation policy, but it is not the most important reason for having one. Answer B refers specifically to automated check-in and does not refer to a circulation policy. Answer D is probably true, but again, it is not the main reason for having a workable circulation policy.

**95. D:** Have the students leave their computers and gather around one computer so that they can observe the librarian as she models what they should do. By modeling what students can do, the librarian can demonstrate to the whole group at the same time what the correct procedures are. If she tries to help students individually, others will continue with the problem while she is spending time with one student. Assuming that the skill is important, the librarian should not give up on students' ability to master it and end their assignment Oral directions will not work as well as an actual demonstration.

**96. D:** A slide show is for creating visual presentations, not graphic design. A slide show presentation needs to be organized with a specific design, a plan for content delivery, and a direction toward a certain audience. The librarian can guide the student to create this kind of organization for a presentation.

**97. A:** A sweep means that remaining library funds will become unavailable. Near the end of the year, the administration may "sweep" all remaining unspent funds into a surplus account. This makes them unavailable for use. The school librarian needs to have spent her funds before this happens. If she does not, a reduction in the next year's funding is also possible. If the library budget

Copyright © Mometrix Media. You have been licensed one copy of this document for personal use only. Any other reproduction or redistribution is strictly prohibited. All rights reserved.
This content is provided for test preparation purposes only and does not imply an endorsement by Mometrix of any particular political, scientific, or religious point of view.

has money left over, the administration may conclude that the library is overfunded and reduce the budget for the following year. Answer C, the school expects the funds to be spent is not relevant to a sweep. Answer D, the administration will be unhappy, is also not as important as spending the funds before that happens.

**98. B:** Information literacy concepts. Information literacy includes the ability to locate necessary information through whatever methods are appropriate, whether technological or written. Students who are information literate know how to find material for a report and also know how to find a good book to read for pleasure. Answer A, the Dewey Decimal System, is not as important to students as it used to be. They can use a computer to locate a book or magazine and at the same time discover the Dewey Decimal number that tells where the material is shelved. Answer C, improving reading skills, is a task for the classroom teacher. Answer D is an activity the school librarian should provide, but it is not the most important goal of the librarian's instruction.

**99. C:** When the book is about an obscure subject. All of the answers represent possible reasons for an interlibrary loan, but such loans are usually requested in a case when only one teacher or student is apt to use the book because it is about an obscure subject. In that case, the cost, the ability to buy the book, and whether it is controversial do not matter because there is no point in purchasing a book that only one or two people are likely to use.

**100. B:** A librarian will receive information about other libraries that she can use to improve her own program. By keeping in touch with professional colleagues, the librarian will have an opportunity to share her ideas and accomplishments and at the same time learn new ideas from her colleagues. Answer A is incorrect because librarians from other schools, districts, or communities are not likely to step forward in support of someone in a different library. If the librarian needs advocates for a new idea, her best sources will be the parents and staff at her own school. Answer C, making friends, is incorrect because it is a side effect of networking and not the main professional benefit. Answer D is unlikely because the librarian who networks probably receives as much new information as she shares and will find that other librarians are discovering the same new technologies that she is.

Copyright © Mometrix Media. You have been licensed one copy of this document for personal use only. Any other reproduction or redistribution is strictly prohibited. All rights reserved. This content is provided for test preparation purposes only and does not imply an endorsement by Mometrix of any particular political, scientific, or religious point of view.

# How to Overcome Test Anxiety

Just the thought of taking a test is enough to make most people a little nervous. A test is an important event that can have a long-term impact on your future, so it's important to take it seriously and it's natural to feel anxious about performing well. But just because anxiety is normal, that doesn't mean that it's helpful in test taking, or that you should simply accept it as part of your life. Anxiety can have a variety of effects. These effects can be mild, like making you feel slightly nervous, or severe, like blocking your ability to focus or remember even a simple detail.

If you experience test anxiety—whether severe or mild—it's important to know how to beat it. To discover this, first you need to understand what causes test anxiety.

## Causes of Test Anxiety

While we often think of anxiety as an uncontrollable emotional state, it can actually be caused by simple, practical things. One of the most common causes of test anxiety is that a person does not feel adequately prepared for their test. This feeling can be the result of many different issues such as poor study habits or lack of organization, but the most common culprit is time management. Starting to study too late, failing to organize your study time to cover all of the material, or being distracted while you study will mean that you're not well prepared for the test. This may lead to cramming the night before, which will cause you to be physically and mentally exhausted for the test. Poor time management also contributes to feelings of stress, fear, and hopelessness as you realize you are not well prepared but don't know what to do about it.

Other times, test anxiety is not related to your preparation for the test but comes from unresolved fear. This may be a past failure on a test, or poor performance on tests in general. It may come from comparing yourself to others who seem to be performing better or from the stress of living up to expectations. Anxiety may be driven by fears of the future—how failure on this test would affect your educational and career goals. These fears are often completely irrational, but they can still negatively impact your test performance.

## Elements of Test Anxiety

As mentioned earlier, test anxiety is considered to be an emotional state, but it has physical and mental components as well. Sometimes you may not even realize that you are suffering from test anxiety until you notice the physical symptoms. These can include trembling hands, rapid heartbeat, sweating, nausea, and tense muscles. Extreme anxiety may lead to fainting or vomiting. Obviously, any of these symptoms can have a negative impact on testing. It is important to recognize them as soon as they begin to occur so that you can address the problem before it damages your performance.

The mental components of test anxiety include trouble focusing and inability to remember learned information. During a test, your mind is on high alert, which can help you recall information and stay focused for an extended period of time. However, anxiety interferes with your mind's natural processes, causing you to blank out, even on the questions you know well. The strain of testing during anxiety makes it difficult to stay focused, especially on a test that may take several hours. Extreme anxiety can take a huge mental toll, making it difficult not only to recall test information but even to understand the test questions or pull your thoughts together.

Copyright © Mometrix Media. You have been licensed one copy of this document for personal use only. Any other reproduction or redistribution is strictly prohibited. All rights reserved.
This content is provided for test preparation purposes only and does not imply an endorsement by Mometrix of any particular political, scientific, or religious point of view.

# Effects of Test Anxiety

Test anxiety is like a disease—if left untreated, it will get progressively worse. Anxiety leads to poor performance, and this reinforces the feelings of fear and failure, which in turn lead to poor performances on subsequent tests. It can grow from a mild nervousness to a crippling condition. If allowed to progress, test anxiety can have a big impact on your schooling, and consequently on your future.

Test anxiety can spread to other parts of your life. Anxiety on tests can become anxiety in any stressful situation, and blanking on a test can turn into panicking in a job situation. But fortunately, you don't have to let anxiety rule your testing and determine your grades. There are a number of relatively simple steps you can take to move past anxiety and function normally on a test and in the rest of life.

# Physical Steps for Beating Test Anxiety

While test anxiety is a serious problem, the good news is that it can be overcome. It doesn't have to control your ability to think and remember information. While it may take time, you can begin taking steps today to beat anxiety.

Just as your first hint that you may be struggling with anxiety comes from the physical symptoms, the first step to treating it is also physical. Rest is crucial for having a clear, strong mind. If you are tired, it is much easier to give in to anxiety. But if you establish good sleep habits, your body and mind will be ready to perform optimally, without the strain of exhaustion. Additionally, sleeping well helps you to retain information better, so you're more likely to recall the answers when you see the test questions.

Getting good sleep means more than going to bed on time. It's important to allow your brain time to relax. Take study breaks from time to time so it doesn't get overworked, and don't study right before bed. Take time to rest your mind before trying to rest your body, or you may find it difficult to fall asleep.

Along with sleep, other aspects of physical health are important in preparing for a test. Good nutrition is vital for good brain function. Sugary foods and drinks may give a burst of energy but this burst is followed by a crash, both physically and emotionally. Instead, fuel your body with protein and vitamin-rich foods.

Also, drink plenty of water. Dehydration can lead to headaches and exhaustion, especially if your brain is already under stress from the rigors of the test. Particularly if your test is a long one, drink water during the breaks. And if possible, take an energy-boosting snack to eat between sections.

Along with sleep and diet, a third important part of physical health is exercise. Maintaining a steady workout schedule is helpful, but even taking 5-minute study breaks to walk can help get your blood pumping faster and clear your head. Exercise also releases endorphins, which contribute to a positive feeling and can help combat test anxiety.

When you nurture your physical health, you are also contributing to your mental health. If your body is healthy, your mind is much more likely to be healthy as well. So take time to rest, nourish your body with healthy food and water, and get moving as much as possible. Taking these physical steps will make you stronger and more able to take the mental steps necessary to overcome test anxiety.

Copyright © Mometrix Media. You have been licensed one copy of this document for personal use only. Any other reproduction or redistribution is strictly prohibited. All rights reserved.
This content is provided for test preparation purposes only and does not imply an endorsement by Mometrix of any particular political, scientific, or religious point of view.

# Mental Steps for Beating Test Anxiety

Working on the mental side of test anxiety can be more challenging, but as with the physical side, there are clear steps you can take to overcome it. As mentioned earlier, test anxiety often stems from lack of preparation, so the obvious solution is to prepare for the test. Effective studying may be the most important weapon you have for beating test anxiety, but you can and should employ several other mental tools to combat fear.

First, boost your confidence by reminding yourself of past success—tests or projects that you aced. If you're putting as much effort into preparing for this test as you did for those, there's no reason you should expect to fail here. Work hard to prepare; then trust your preparation.

Second, surround yourself with encouraging people. It can be helpful to find a study group, but be sure that the people you're around will encourage a positive attitude. If you spend time with others who are anxious or cynical, this will only contribute to your own anxiety. Look for others who are motivated to study hard from a desire to succeed, not from a fear of failure.

Third, reward yourself. A test is physically and mentally tiring, even without anxiety, and it can be helpful to have something to look forward to. Plan an activity following the test, regardless of the outcome, such as going to a movie or getting ice cream.

When you are taking the test, if you find yourself beginning to feel anxious, remind yourself that you know the material. Visualize successfully completing the test. Then take a few deep, relaxing breaths and return to it. Work through the questions carefully but with confidence, knowing that you are capable of succeeding.

Developing a healthy mental approach to test taking will also aid in other areas of life. Test anxiety affects more than just the actual test—it can be damaging to your mental health and even contribute to depression. It's important to beat test anxiety before it becomes a problem for more than testing.

# Study Strategy

Being prepared for the test is necessary to combat anxiety, but what does being prepared look like? You may study for hours on end and still not feel prepared. What you need is a strategy for test prep. The next few pages outline our recommended steps to help you plan out and conquer the challenge of preparation.

## STEP 1: SCOPE OUT THE TEST

Learn everything you can about the format (multiple choice, essay, etc.) and what will be on the test. Gather any study materials, course outlines, or sample exams that may be available. Not only will this help you to prepare, but knowing what to expect can help to alleviate test anxiety.

## STEP 2: MAP OUT THE MATERIAL

Look through the textbook or study guide and make note of how many chapters or sections it has. Then divide these over the time you have. For example, if a book has 15 chapters and you have five days to study, you need to cover three chapters each day. Even better, if you have the time, leave an extra day at the end for overall review after you have gone through the material in depth.

If time is limited, you may need to prioritize the material. Look through it and make note of which sections you think you already have a good grasp on, and which need review. While you are studying, skim quickly through the familiar sections and take more time on the challenging parts.

Copyright © Mometrix Media. You have been licensed one copy of this document for personal use only. Any other reproduction or redistribution is strictly prohibited. All rights reserved.
This content is provided for test preparation purposes only and does not imply an endorsement by Mometrix of any particular political, scientific, or religious point of view.

Write out your plan so you don't get lost as you go. Having a written plan also helps you feel more in control of the study, so anxiety is less likely to arise from feeling overwhelmed at the amount to cover.

## STEP 3: GATHER YOUR TOOLS

Decide what study method works best for you. Do you prefer to highlight in the book as you study and then go back over the highlighted portions? Or do you type out notes of the important information? Or is it helpful to make flashcards that you can carry with you? Assemble the pens, index cards, highlighters, post-it notes, and any other materials you may need so you won't be distracted by getting up to find things while you study.

If you're having a hard time retaining the information or organizing your notes, experiment with different methods. For example, try color-coding by subject with colored pens, highlighters, or post-it notes. If you learn better by hearing, try recording yourself reading your notes so you can listen while in the car, working out, or simply sitting at your desk. Ask a friend to quiz you from your flashcards, or try teaching someone the material to solidify it in your mind.

## STEP 4: CREATE YOUR ENVIRONMENT

It's important to avoid distractions while you study. This includes both the obvious distractions like visitors and the subtle distractions like an uncomfortable chair (or a too-comfortable couch that makes you want to fall asleep). Set up the best study environment possible: good lighting and a comfortable work area. If background music helps you focus, you may want to turn it on, but otherwise keep the room quiet. If you are using a computer to take notes, be sure you don't have any other windows open, especially applications like social media, games, or anything else that could distract you. Silence your phone and turn off notifications. Be sure to keep water close by so you stay hydrated while you study (but avoid unhealthy drinks and snacks).

Also, take into account the best time of day to study. Are you freshest first thing in the morning? Try to set aside some time then to work through the material. Is your mind clearer in the afternoon or evening? Schedule your study session then. Another method is to study at the same time of day that you will take the test, so that your brain gets used to working on the material at that time and will be ready to focus at test time.

## STEP 5: STUDY!

Once you have done all the study preparation, it's time to settle into the actual studying. Sit down, take a few moments to settle your mind so you can focus, and begin to follow your study plan. Don't give in to distractions or let yourself procrastinate. This is your time to prepare so you'll be ready to fearlessly approach the test. Make the most of the time and stay focused.

Of course, you don't want to burn out. If you study too long you may find that you're not retaining the information very well. Take regular study breaks. For example, taking five minutes out of every hour to walk briskly, breathing deeply and swinging your arms, can help your mind stay fresh.

As you get to the end of each chapter or section, it's a good idea to do a quick review. Remind yourself of what you learned and work on any difficult parts. When you feel that you've mastered the material, move on to the next part. At the end of your study session, briefly skim through your notes again.

But while review is helpful, cramming last minute is NOT. If at all possible, work ahead so that you won't need to fit all your study into the last day. Cramming overloads your brain with more information than it can process and retain, and your tired mind may struggle to recall even

Copyright © Mometrix Media. You have been licensed one copy of this document for personal use only. Any other reproduction or redistribution is strictly prohibited. All rights reserved.
This content is provided for test preparation purposes only and does not imply an endorsement by Mometrix of any particular political, scientific, or religious point of view.

previously learned information when it is overwhelmed with last-minute study. Also, the urgent nature of cramming and the stress placed on your brain contribute to anxiety. You'll be more likely to go to the test feeling unprepared and having trouble thinking clearly.

So don't cram, and don't stay up late before the test, even just to review your notes at a leisurely pace. Your brain needs rest more than it needs to go over the information again. In fact, plan to finish your studies by noon or early afternoon the day before the test. Give your brain the rest of the day to relax or focus on other things, and get a good night's sleep. Then you will be fresh for the test and better able to recall what you've studied.

## STEP 6: TAKE A PRACTICE TEST

Many courses offer sample tests, either online or in the study materials. This is an excellent resource to check whether you have mastered the material, as well as to prepare for the test format and environment.

Check the test format ahead of time: the number of questions, the type (multiple choice, free response, etc.), and the time limit. Then create a plan for working through them. For example, if you have 30 minutes to take a 60-question test, your limit is 30 seconds per question. Spend less time on the questions you know well so that you can take more time on the difficult ones.

If you have time to take several practice tests, take the first one open book, with no time limit. Work through the questions at your own pace and make sure you fully understand them. Gradually work up to taking a test under test conditions: sit at a desk with all study materials put away and set a timer. Pace yourself to make sure you finish the test with time to spare and go back to check your answers if you have time.

After each test, check your answers. On the questions you missed, be sure you understand why you missed them. Did you misread the question (tests can use tricky wording)? Did you forget the information? Or was it something you hadn't learned? Go back and study any shaky areas that the practice tests reveal.

Taking these tests not only helps with your grade, but also aids in combating test anxiety. If you're already used to the test conditions, you're less likely to worry about it, and working through tests until you're scoring well gives you a confidence boost. Go through the practice tests until you feel comfortable, and then you can go into the test knowing that you're ready for it.

# Test Tips

On test day, you should be confident, knowing that you've prepared well and are ready to answer the questions. But aside from preparation, there are several test day strategies you can employ to maximize your performance.

First, as stated before, get a good night's sleep the night before the test (and for several nights before that, if possible). Go into the test with a fresh, alert mind rather than staying up late to study.

Try not to change too much about your normal routine on the day of the test. It's important to eat a nutritious breakfast, but if you normally don't eat breakfast at all, consider eating just a protein bar. If you're a coffee drinker, go ahead and have your normal coffee. Just make sure you time it so that the caffeine doesn't wear off right in the middle of your test. Avoid sugary beverages, and drink enough water to stay hydrated but not so much that you need a restroom break 10 minutes into the

Copyright © Mometrix Media. You have been licensed one copy of this document for personal use only. Any other reproduction or redistribution is strictly prohibited. All rights reserved.
This content is provided for test preparation purposes only and does not imply an endorsement by Mometrix of any particular political, scientific, or religious point of view.

test. If your test isn't first thing in the morning, consider going for a walk or doing a light workout before the test to get your blood flowing.

Allow yourself enough time to get ready, and leave for the test with plenty of time to spare so you won't have the anxiety of scrambling to arrive in time. Another reason to be early is to select a good seat. It's helpful to sit away from doors and windows, which can be distracting. Find a good seat, get out your supplies, and settle your mind before the test begins.

When the test begins, start by going over the instructions carefully, even if you already know what to expect. Make sure you avoid any careless mistakes by following the directions.

Then begin working through the questions, pacing yourself as you've practiced. If you're not sure on an answer, don't spend too much time on it, and don't let it shake your confidence. Either skip it and come back later, or eliminate as many wrong answers as possible and guess among the remaining ones. Don't dwell on these questions as you continue—put them out of your mind and focus on what lies ahead.

Be sure to read all of the answer choices, even if you're sure the first one is the right answer. Sometimes you'll find a better one if you keep reading. But don't second-guess yourself if you do immediately know the answer. Your gut instinct is usually right. Don't let test anxiety rob you of the information you know.

If you have time at the end of the test (and if the test format allows), go back and review your answers. Be cautious about changing any, since your first instinct tends to be correct, but make sure you didn't misread any of the questions or accidentally mark the wrong answer choice. Look over any you skipped and make an educated guess.

At the end, leave the test feeling confident. You've done your best, so don't waste time worrying about your performance or wishing you could change anything. Instead, celebrate the successful completion of this test. And finally, use this test to learn how to deal with anxiety even better next time.

> **Review Video: Test Anxiety**
> Visit mometrix.com/academy and enter code: 100340

## Important Qualification

Not all anxiety is created equal. If your test anxiety is causing major issues in your life beyond the classroom or testing center, or if you are experiencing troubling physical symptoms related to your anxiety, it may be a sign of a serious physiological or psychological condition. If this sounds like your situation, we strongly encourage you to seek professional help.

Copyright © Mometrix Media. You have been licensed one copy of this document for personal use only. Any other reproduction or redistribution is strictly prohibited. All rights reserved.
This content is provided for test preparation purposes only and does not imply an endorsement by Mometrix of any particular political, scientific, or religious point of view.

# Thank You

We at Mometrix would like to extend our heartfelt thanks to you, our friend and patron, for allowing us to play a part in your journey. It is a privilege to serve people from all walks of life who are unified in their commitment to building the best future they can for themselves.

The preparation you devote to these important testing milestones may be the most valuable educational opportunity you have for making a real difference in your life. We encourage you to put your heart into it—that feeling of succeeding, overcoming, and yes, conquering will be well worth the hours you've invested.

We want to hear your story, your struggles and your successes, and if you see any opportunities for us to improve our materials so we can help others even more effectively in the future, please share that with us as well. **The team at Mometrix would be absolutely thrilled to hear from you!** So please, send us an email (support@mometrix.com) and let's stay in touch.

> **If you'd like some additional help, check out these other resources we offer for your exam:**
> **http://MometrixFlashcards.com/GACE**

Copyright © Mometrix Media. You have been licensed one copy of this document for personal use only. Any other reproduction or redistribution is strictly prohibited. All rights reserved. This content is provided for test preparation purposes only and does not imply an endorsement by Mometrix of any particular political, scientific, or religious point of view.

# Additional Bonus Material

Due to our efforts to try to keep this book to a manageable length, we've created a link that will give you access to all of your additional bonus material:

**mometrix.com/bonus948/gacemediasp**

Copyright © Mometrix Media. You have been licensed one copy of this document for personal use only. Any other reproduction or redistribution is strictly prohibited. All rights reserved. This content is provided for test preparation purposes only and does not imply an endorsement by Mometrix of any particular political, scientific, or religious point of view.